# Cash Flow Management

## with Framework

W. M Greenfield

Dennis P. Curtin



**Curtin & London, Inc.**
Marblehead, Massachusetts 01945

**Prentice-Hall**
Englewood Cliffs, New Jersey 07632

Printed in the United States of America

Published in 1986 by Curtin & London, Inc.;
Prentice-Hall
A Division of Simon & Schuster, Inc.
Englewood Cliffs, New Jersey 07632

Prentice-Hall International, Inc., *London*
Prentice-Hall of Australia Pty. Limited, *Sydney*
Editora Prentice-Hall do Brasil Ltda., *Rio de Janeiro*
Prentice-Hall Canada Inc., *Toronto*
Prentice-Hall Hispanoamericana, S.A., *Mexico*
Prentice-Hall of India Private Limited, *New Delhi*
Prentice-Hall of Japan, Inc., *Tokyo*
Prentice-Hall of Southeast Asia Pte. Ltd., *Singapore*
Whitehall Books Limited, *Wellington, New Zealand*

Concept development: Dennis P. Curtin
Editor: Katherine Carlone
Managing editor: Nancy Benjamin
Production editor: Mary Babic

Cover design: Kredlow & Gonzalez
Interior design: Geoffrey Mandel
Illustrations: Geoffrey Mandel

10 9 8 7 6 5 4 3 2 1

**Library of Congress Cataloging in Publication Data**

Greenfield, W. M
Cash flow management with Framework.

Includes index.
1. Cash flow—Data processing. 2. Cash management—Data processing. 3. Framework (Computer program) I. Curtin, Dennis, 1941–
II. Title.
HG4028.C45G715 1985 658.1′5244 85-20528
ISBN 0-13-120106-9

**Disclaimer**

**This book and accompanying magnetic disk are designed to help you improve your business judgment. However, the authors and publishers assume no responsibility whatsoever for the uses made of this material or for decisions based on its use, and make no warranties, either express or implied, regarding the contents of this book or any accompanying magnetic disks, its merchantability or fitness for any particular purpose.**

**Neither the publishers nor anyone else who has been involved in the creation, production, or delivery of this product shall be liable for any direct, incidental, or consequential damages, such as, but not limited to, loss of anticipated profits or benefits resulting from its use or from any breach of any warranty. Some states do not allow the exclusion or limitation of direct, incidental, or consequential damages so the above limitation may not apply to you.**

**Acknowledgments**

Framework and FRED are registered trademarks of Ashton-Tate, Inc. © 1984. The screen images used in this book are © 1984 by Ashton-Tate, Inc., and are reproduced here by permission.

# Contents

## Framework Tips

# Preface

This is a book about how you can let your computer help you make better use of your business cash. It deals with two fairly intimidating things—computers and money. It is our objective, however, to make both less frightening by showing you how to control them to your advantage.

As you know, companies cannot run without cash. While your customers are always trying to convince you to let them pay later, your suppliers are continually after you to pay earlier. Figuring out how to pay the bills when due (let alone early!) is a critical and difficult task for the owner or manager of any business—large or small.

This book presents an approach to planning for and maximizing the cash that your company has or can generate. It begins by discussing why cash is important to your business and how your cash flow differs from your accounting results. It also shows you how to monitor your business' cash to ensure that your plans for your company are on track. Finally, it considers some strategies for making money from the money you have. In short, the approach described in this book will help you to wring the most from every nickel that passes through your business' doors.

We also provide the tools that you will need to implement the approach we describe. These tools are in the form of spreadsheets that you will build using your computer and Framework software. Framework makes what used to be a complex and time-consuming task almost fun. It permits you to test your results and theories almost instantly—with virtually no number-crunching and minimal difficulty. In short, once we have walked through the basics, you will be able to play—to seek out and put in place the cash flow management strategies that will be most advantageous to you and your company.

Bankruptcies are caused by lack of cash, rather than lack of profit. This has been amply demonstrated by the enormous accounting losses recently racked up by companies that are still operating (auto makers and steel companies, for example). To the extent that business owners can manage their cash better, then, they become more resistant to potential disaster. It is our hope that, through using your computer and this book, you, too, will become better insulated and will, in fact, prosper.

# 1 Your Computer System and Framework

## Introduction

A personal computer and easy-to-use business software like the Framework program can make the management of your cash flow more efficient and effective. Don't be fooled, however, by the ads; the computer won't do all (or even any) of the work for you. Understanding the ideas behind your cash budget and collecting data still take time, although once the initial effort is made, you can compile your budget and explore "What Ifs" many times faster than traditional methods allow. Before we begin to explore how you can more effectively control and manage your cash, we'll describe some of the things you should know about the Framework program and your computer system.

Framework was introduced initially for the IBM PC and compatibles and is being adapted to run on a wide variety of computers. If you don't already have a computer, check with your dealer to find out which will support Framework. Here are some basic guidelines for choosing your system:

**The computer.** Framework was initially released for the IBM PC with a minimum memory of 320K (384K to use telecommunications). To make full use of the program, the more memory you have, the better. The program will address up to 640K. As a general guide, your computer can create documents up to the following sizes with the indicated amount of memory: 256K, 12 pages; 384K, 42 pages; 512K, 73 pages.

**Disk drives.** The Framework program requires either two double-sided 360K floppy disk drives or one double-sided 360K floppy disk drive and one hard disk drive. It also requires a copy of the PC- or MS-DOS 2.0 disk operating system, or later versions. The storage space on your disks is also measured in kilobytes, or K's; for instance, a double-sided floppy disk on an IBM PC can store 360K of data (the equivalent of 180 typed, double-spaced pages), and a hard disk can usually store about ten times as much as a floppy disk.

**Display monitor.** The Framework program can be displayed on either a monochrome (single-color) display or a color monitor.

**Printers and plotters.** Many kinds of printers and plotters can be used with the Framework program. *Letter-quality printers* work just like electronic typewriters and produce high-quality "typed" printouts; *dot matrix printers* "simulate" letters and numbers with clusters of tiny dots. *Plotters* can be used to produce high-quality graphs and color graphs. A dot matrix printer, or plotter, is needed to print Framework graphs, but all other data can be printed by either a dot matrix or a letter-quality printer.

When you buy a printer, make sure that it is wide enough for the kinds of things you'll be printing out. For instance, if you're going to be printing a lot of wide financial statements, it makes sense to buy a wide-carriage dot matrix printer rather than one that can only print on 8½ × 11-inch paper. Also, if you plan to use a letter-quality printer to print out long documents or reports, a *tractor feed* (with pegs that fit into the holes on that side-punched computer paper) or a *sheet feed* (which feeds in individual sheets of paper) is essential.

**The Framework program.** The Framework program consists of four disks — two system disks (System Disk #1 and System Disk #2), a Utility disk, and a Tutorial disk — and two accompanying manuals.

**Disks.** There are all kinds of floppy disks — single-sided, double-sided, soft-sectored, hard-sectored, single-density, double-density, 5¼-inch and 8-inch, so make sure you get the right kind of disks for your computer. If you have an IBM PC or COMPAQ, you'll probably want 5¼-inch double-sided double-density soft-sectored disks.

## The Computer System You Need

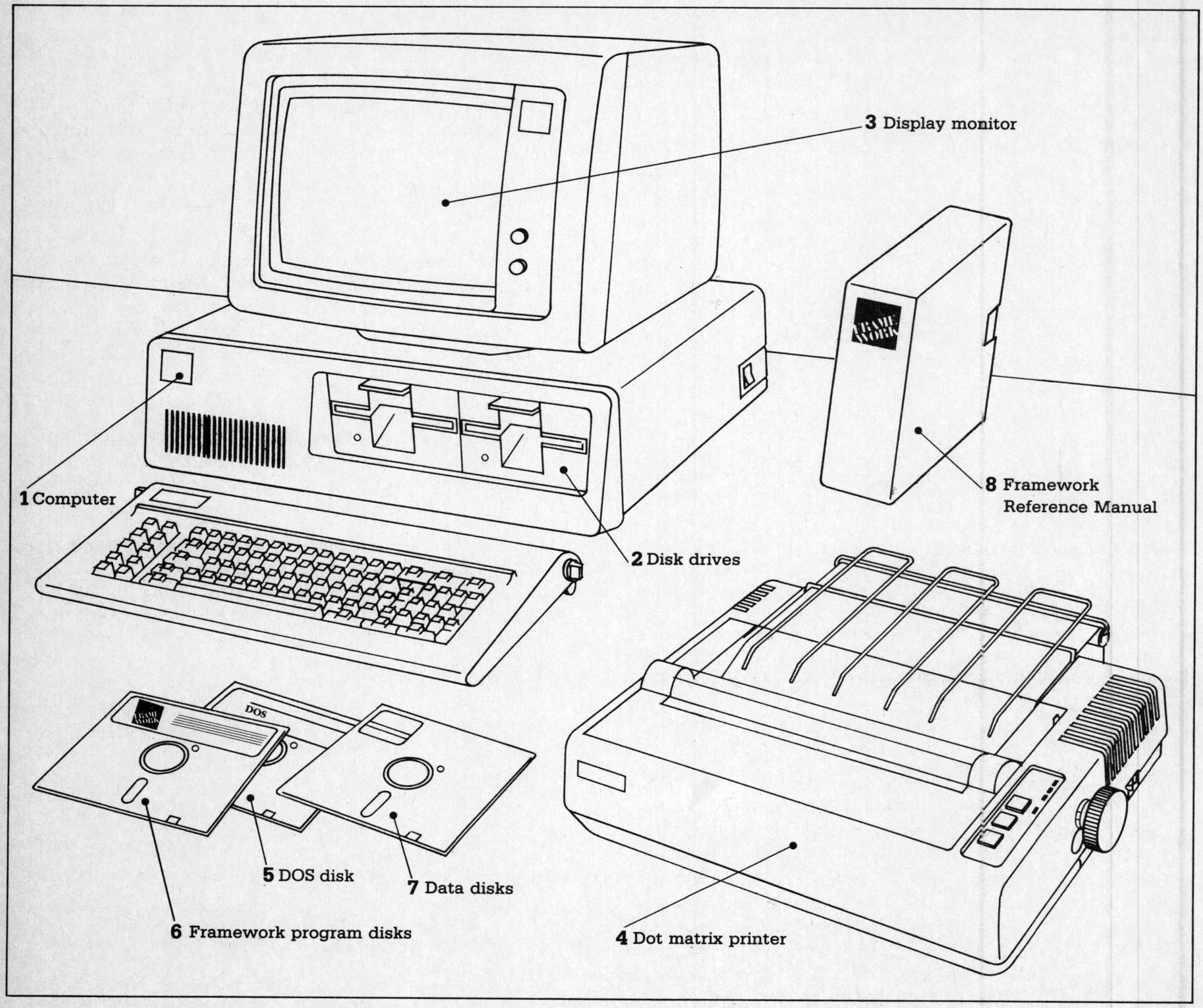


This illustration shows the complete computer system you will need to prepare and analyze your cash budgets with Framework. The various components are:

**1** A computer capable of running the Framework program.

**2** Two floppy disk drives or one floppy and one hard disk drive.

**3** A display monitor (or monitors) that can display both spreadsheets and graphs.

**4** A printer that can print out both spreadsheets and graphs.

**5** Your computer's operating system disk.

**6** The Framework program disks.

**7** Blank, formatted, floppy disks for saving the spreadsheets and graphs. (If you are using a hard disk drive you won't need these except as backups.)

**8** The Framework manual.

# Framework: An Integrated Planning Tool

The Framework program is an integrated system that has the ability to do spreadsheets, graphics, word processing, communications, and database management; it offers the ideal combination for financial planning and analysis. You will probably find that the spreadsheets and graphs are the most useful parts of the program for this purpose, as they allow you to enter, manipulate, and analyze numbers much faster than you ever could with pencil and paper. You never have to recalculate the total for a column or row of numbers; when you want to see the effects of a change to your spreadsheet, just type in the new numbers and Framework does the recalculation for you automatically — and instantly! With Framework, it's easy to try out new combinations of numbers and explore a wide range of alternatives for your business. Even better, with just a few keystrokes you can graph the results and view the numbers and your graphs on the screen at the same time.

Although not covered in detail in this book, you can also use Framework's outline, word processing, and database management features to keep notes, maintain customer lists, and gather other information that's important for your planning and your business.

## What Are Frames?

Frames are containers you create on the desktop for specific tasks. When frames are on the desktop, they can be sized, zoomed, and dragged around; they can be linked together so a change in one is reflected in others; and data can be easily copied or moved from one to another. There are six kinds of frames:

**1 Outline frames** are used to organize ideas. Behind each heading is another frame that can be used for text, spreadsheet analysis, graphs, or databases. When the ideas on the outline are reorganized, the frames containing the contents automatically follow the new arrangement.

**2 Word frames** are used for word processing so you can write memos, reports, or other documents without leaving Framework.

**3 Spreadsheet frames** are organized into rows and columns like a ledger pad; any changes you make can be automatically recalculated throughout the worksheet.

**4 Database frames** are divided into fields and records for organizing and storing data — for instance, inventory, mailing lists, or customers. Formulas can be used to automatically calculate data, and the database can be sorted or specific records extracted.

**5 Graph frames** display any of six kinds of graphs: bar, line, pie chart stacked bar, XY, or marked points.

**6 Empty word frames (containing frames)** contain other related frames, so they can be saved, retrieved, used, or printed together.

# Using Framework: A Reference Section

## The Framework Desktop

You'll find that it's very easy to learn and use the Framework program. When you load Framework, a display appears on the screen with a menu bar across the top and a message area across the bottom. In the middle, the majority of the screen is occupied by the *desktop*, on which you create *frames*, in which you work with outlines, words, numbers, graphs, or databases.

**1 The menu bar.** Most of the commands you will use with Framework are selected from menus that "pull down" from the nine menu names at the top of the screen. Over a hundred frequently used commands are available with the press of the **Ins** key so you don't have to memorize a long list of complicated and confusing commands. The **clock** shows the current time if you entered it when you loaded the program.

**2 The desktop work area.** This shaded (dotted) area of the screen is where frames appear. You can create frames for text, outlines, graphs, databases, or spreadsheets. Also appearing in the desktop area (upper-right corner) are frames representing your **disk drives** — they are marked <A:> and <B:> (and more if your system has additional floppy disk drives or a hard disk). The drives are where you save and retrieve your work.

**3 The status panel.** This bright area immediately below the desktop provides you with information about where you are in the program; it is divided into three sections. See Tips on "Understanding the Status Panel."

**4 The message area.** This area in the lower-left corner includes two lines: an **edit line** and a **message line**. When you type in text, numbers, or formulas, the entry is displayed on the edit line (and can still be changed) until you press (↵). You can also recall your work to this line for editing (with the **Space Bar**, for labels, and the **Edit Formula (F2)** key, for numbers and formulas). The message line describes highlighted menu choices, and prompts you with any choices you might have to make.

**5 The cursor.** The blinking rectangle (currently highlighting drive B) identifies your position on the desktop. You can move the cursor around with a number of keys, including **Scroll Lock, Down Level (Gray +)** and **Up Level (Gray −)** and **Home**.

## Using Function and Other Special Keys

Framework has assigned the most frequently used commands to your computer's function keys. These keys call up screens of help text, edit formulas, size and drag frames, recalculate spreadsheets, select frames or other data, copy and move frames and data, zoom and unzoom frames, or change the view of any frames from frames to outlines and back again.

The location of the keys to which these commands have been assigned varies from computer to computer. A plastic "template" designed specifically for your computer keyboard is included with the Framework package. When laid over your function keys on the keyboard, it acts as a guide to help you find the keys you need.

If you can't remember exactly what a key is used for, Framework has a quick way for you to find out. Press the **Help (F1)** key and highlight the choice Key Help at the bottom of the screen, and press ⏎. The prompt Press the key on which you want help will appear. Press the key you want to know more about and a frame of text describing it will appear on the screen. To clear the text from the screen and return to the desktop, press **Esc**.

In addition to the function keys, Framework has assigned other keys on your keyboard important tasks. There are only a few you have to know immediately.

The following tables briefly describe the function keys (the number following in parentheses corresponds to the IBM PC function key commands on the left side of the keyboard), as well as other important keys that you'll use.

## Function Keys

| | |
|---|---|
| **Help (F1)** | Calls up help screens (see the Tips on "Framework's Help Facility" on page 44). |
| **Edit Formula (F2)** | Enables you to enter formulas beginning with letters, enter formulas on frame borders, and return numbers or formulas to the edit line (the line below the status panel) for editing. (This key is abbreviated within the keystroke instructions by the symbol EDIT.) |
| **Drag (F3)** | Enables you to use the cursor keys to drag a highlighted frame around on the desktop. |
| **Size (F4)** | Enables you to use the cursor keys to change the size of highlighted frames. |
| **Recalc (F5)** | Recalculates all formulas in highlighted spreadsheets, graphs, or databases, or on frame borders. |
| **Extend Select (F6)** | Enables you to use the cursor movement keys to extend the highlight. You can then highlight any number of frame borders, spreadsheet cells, database fields and records, and text characters so one command can be used to affect the highlighted selection simultaneously. |
| **Move (F7)** | Enables you to move selected frames, words, numbers, formulas, or data from one place to another. |
| **Copy (F8)** | Enables you to copy selected frames, words, numbers, formulas, or data from one place to another. |
| **Zoom (F9)** | Zooms and unzooms a highlighted frame so it temporarily fills the desktop and then returns it to its original size. Zoomed frames can also be unzoomed with the **View (F10)** and **Up Level (Gray−)** keys. The **Zoom** key will also zoom long formulas appearing on the edit line so the entire formula is displayed on the screen. They are then unzoomed by pressing the **Recalc (F5)** key. |
| **View (F10)** | Toggles outline or containing frames (any frame that contains one or more other frames within it) so the entire frame or just the frame labels are displayed. |

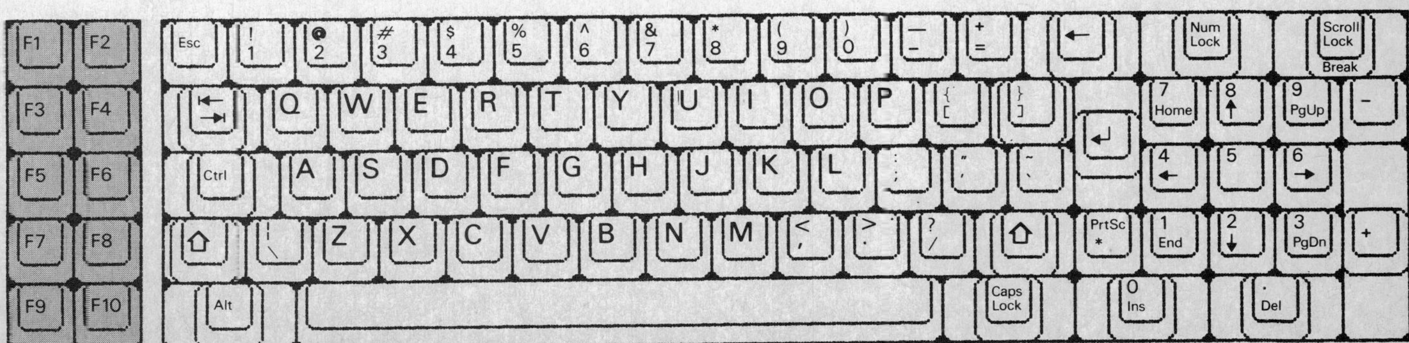

## The Cursor Movement Keys

**Scroll Lock** Moves the cursor back and forth between the most recently selected desktop frame and disk drives.

**Up Level (Gray −)** Moves the cursor up from inside a frame to the frame border.

**Down Level (Gray +)** Moves the cursor down from the frame border into a frame.

**↑** Moves the cursor up within a frame or between frames when the cursor is on a frame border or desktop tray.

**↓** Moves the cursor down within a frame or between frames when the cursor is on a frame border or desktop tray.

**→** Moves the cursor right within a frame or between frames when the cursor is on a frame border or desktop tray.

**←** Moves the cursor left within a frame or between frames when the cursor is on a frame border or desktop tray.

**PgUp** Moves the cursor up to the top of a frame and then up a complete frame at a time when the cursor is within a frame.

**PgDn** Moves the cursor down to the bottom of a frame and then down a complete frame at a time when the cursor is within a frame.

**Home** Moves the cursor in different ways depending on where the cursor is positioned when the key is pressed.

| Cursor position | Effect of **Home** key |
|---|---|
| On disk drives | To first drive |
| In an open disk drive frame | To first file |
| On a frame border or tray | To first frame in trays |
| In a spreadsheet | To far left cell on row |
| In a database | To far left field in record |
| In a word frame | To first character on line |
| On the edit line | To first character |

**End** Moves the cursor differently depending on where the cursor is positioned when the key is pressed.

| Cursor position | Effect of **End** key |
|---|---|
| On disk drives | To last drive |
| In an open disk drive frame | To last file |
| On a frame border or tray | To last frame in trays |
| In a spreadsheet | To far right cell on row |
| In a database | To far right field in record |
| In a word frame | To last character on line |
| On the edit line | To last character |

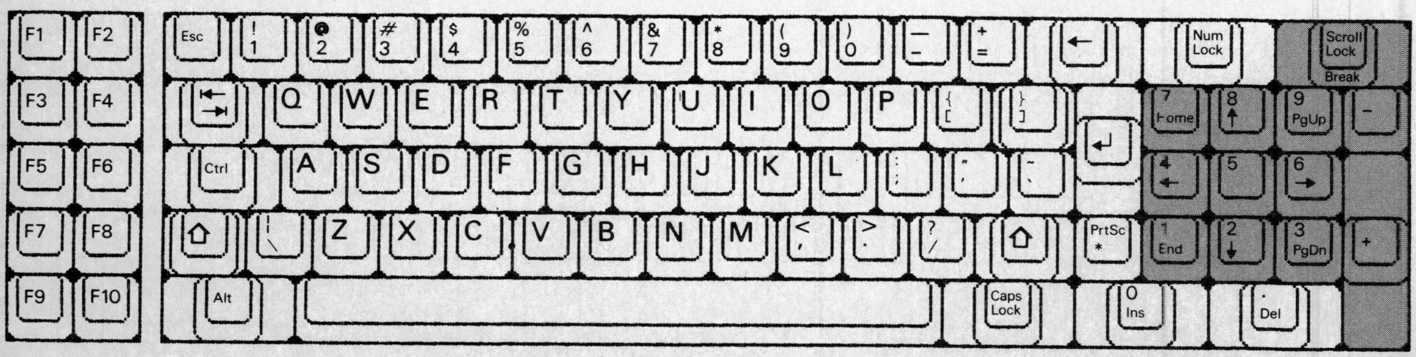

## Other Important Keys

↵ The Return or Enter key is located where the carriage return would be on an electric typewriter. Completes commands, closes or opens desktop frames and drives, and loads highlighted files onto desktop.

| Cursor position | Effect of **Return** key |
|---|---|
| When entering data | Completes the entry |
| On disk drives | Opens the drive |
| In an open disk drive frame border | Closes the drive |
| On a file in a drive frame | Puts file on desktop |
| On an open frame border | Closes the frame into tray |
| On a closed frame tray | Opens the frame onto desktop |
| In a spreadsheet | Moves cursor down a row |
| In a database | Moves cursor down record |
| In a word frame | Inserts Return and breaks line |
| In a zoomed formula | Inserts Return and breaks line |
| Using **Extend Select** | Completes selection |
| Pointing to Move destination | Moves selected data |
| Pointing to Copy destination | Copies selected data |

**Ins** Highlights most recently used pull-down menu command.

**Del** Deletes (erases) highlighted data or frame.

**Backspace** Moves the cursor left one space and erases any character in that position.

**Tab** ⇥ Moves the cursor to next tab stop in a word frame, to the next field in a database frame, and to the next column in a spreadsheet.

**Shift** Two shift keys (one on either side of the keyboard) look like ⇧ on an IBM PC or COMPAQ — they work just like the shift keys on a typewriter.

**Shift PrtSc** Sends text on the screen to the printer. If the DOS graphics program is loaded, you will be able to print graphics as well as text by using this combination of keys.

**Caps Lock** When engaged makes all letters typed capital letters.

**Num Lock** Toggles the cursor movement pad into a number pad and back again.

**Alt** The Alternate key executes macros.

**Esc** The Escape key cancels a command or procedure in progress.

**Ctrl** The Control key is used in combination with cursor movement keys to *extend* their movement. Can also be used to *repeat* a character a specified number of times (by holding down **Ctrl**, pressing a number from 0 to 255, releasing **Ctrl**, and then pressing desired character). Also used as a quick way to call up menus — **Ctrl-D**, for instance, pulls down the Disk menu.

# Using Menus

One of the best things about the Framework program is the menus and special keys you will use to execute most of the commands.

Unlike other programs that require you to memorize a series of commands, or make a selection from a menu that brings up other menus (called nested menus), Framework uses what are called *pull-down* menus. Nine menu names are listed along the menu bar at the top of the screen at all times. When you press the **Ins** key, these menus are "pulled down" and a highlight appears on the menu bar. As you use the arrow keys to move the highlight along the menu bar, menus "descend" from the highlighted area. You then select items listed on the pull-down menu by moving the highlight up and down with the arrow keys; when your choice is highlighted, you then press ⏎.

Although all the commands listed on the pull-down menus don't work in all the frames, the ones that do function in various frames work the same way in all so you don't have to learn a new series of commands when creating spreadsheets, databases, or text.

Framework always remembers what your previous command was, so the next time you press the **Ins** key the most recently used command will be highlighted on the pull-down menu.

Menus are very helpful when you are first learning a program, but after a while they get in your way — especially if you're a good typist. Framework gets around this problem by giving you a shortcut to using the menus: holding down the **Ctrl** key and pressing the first letter of one of the menu names immediately pulls down that menu. Typing the first letter of any of the commands listed in the pull down menu then executes the command.

## Selecting the Area to Be Affected

You can use most of the menu commands to affect an entire frame, a specific subframe, or a selected area within a frame. Before calling up the menu, you have to indicate the area you want to affect.

**Highlight** the frame border to affect everything in the frame

*or*

**Highlight** a subframe border to limit effects to that subframe

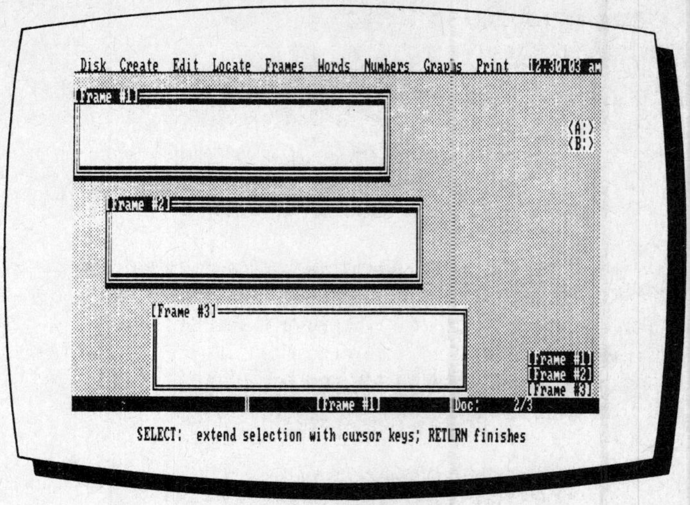


**Press** **Extend Select** (**F6**) and then use cursor movement keys to select a group of frames or subframes, or an area within a frame

## Pulling Down Menus from the Menu Bar

There are two ways to pull down a menu. When no menu is pulled down, using the **Ins** key moves the highlight to the menu and the command you used last.

*To call up the most recently used menu:*

**Press** **Ins**

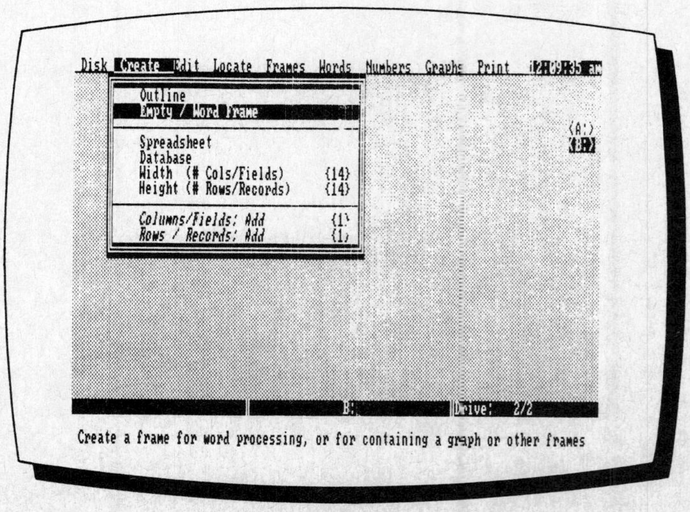


*To call up a specific menu:*

**Press** **Ctrl**

**Type** the first letter of desired menu name (e.g., **C** for Create)

**Release** **Ctrl**

## Moving Along the Menu Bar

As you move the highlight along the menu bar, pull-down menus descend from the highlighted menu names, and a description of the menu appears on the message line at the bottom of the screen. The highlight will "wrap around" the menu when moved past the selections at either end of the menu bar. Sometimes you'll find it faster to wrap around than to use the arrow keys. With the highlight on Graphs, for instance, you can get to Disk faster by using [→] to wrap around the menu bar than by using [←] to move back across the menu bar. If you decide not to make a selection from one of the menus, you can leave the menus and return to the desktop by pressing **Up Level (Gray –)** or **Esc**.

*To move the highlight along the menu bar:*

**Press** [←] and [→] to move the highlight along the menu bar
**Home** to move the highlight to the first menu on the menu bar
**End** to move the highlight to the last menu on the menu bar

## Making Selections from a Menu

When a menu is pulled down, you can select a command either by typing the first letter of the listed command, or by using the arrow keys to move the highlight over it and pressing [↵]. Commands displayed in normal (or boldface) type are available to you, but items in italicized (or dim) type are not.

You can wrap from the last menu command back to the first and vice versa, just like on the menu bar. Whenever the highlight is over a selection, its description is displayed on the message line at the bottom of the screen. Selections with a ▶ in front of them contain submenus with additional selections, which are discussed in the next section. You can also choose menu commands by typing the first letter of your selection. There are four kinds of menu selections you can make:

**Command execution selections** are immediately executed, for example, creating a frame, cleaning up the desktop, and so on.

**Toggle selections** turn a selection on or off. When the selection is on, the word on appears before the selection. When it is off, two dashes appear. You can have more than one selection on at a time.

**Either/or selections** are selections that are mutually exclusive; only one can be on at a time. For example, words can be aligned only in one place, numbers can be formatted only in one way.

**Fill-In selections** prompt you to enter data. These choices are identified by braces {}, into which you enter a setting. Examples include the width and height of a spreadsheet and graph titles.

*To move around in a menu and make a selection:*

**Press** [↑] and [↓] to move the highlight up and down the menu
**Home** to move the highlight to the first menu selection
**End** to move the highlight to the last menu selection
[↵] to select a highlighted choice on the menu

**Type** the first letter of your command and it will be selected

## Using Submenus

Items on the pull-down menus preceded with a ▶ are titles for submenus. The submenus can be opened by typing the first letter of their name or by highlighting them and pressing **Ins**, **Down Level (Gray +)**, or [↵].

*To call up a submenu from the main menu:*

**Type** the first letter of selection

*or*

**Highlight** selection desired

**Press** **Ins,** or **Down Level (Gray +)**, or [↵]

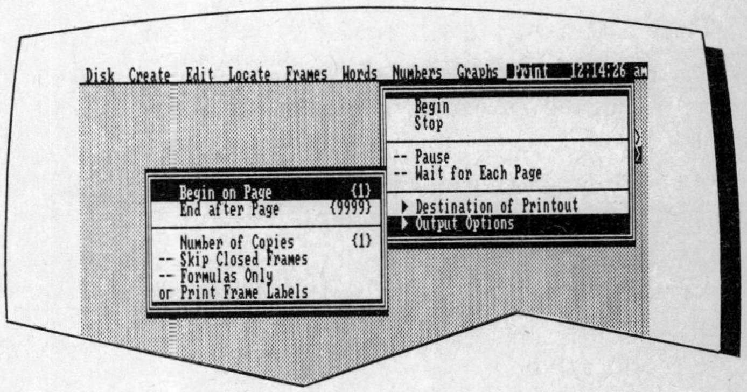


*To leave a submenu and return to the main menu:*

**Press** **Up Level (Gray –)** or [←] or [→]

*To leave a submenu and return to the desktop:*

**Press** **Esc**

# The Framework Spreadsheet

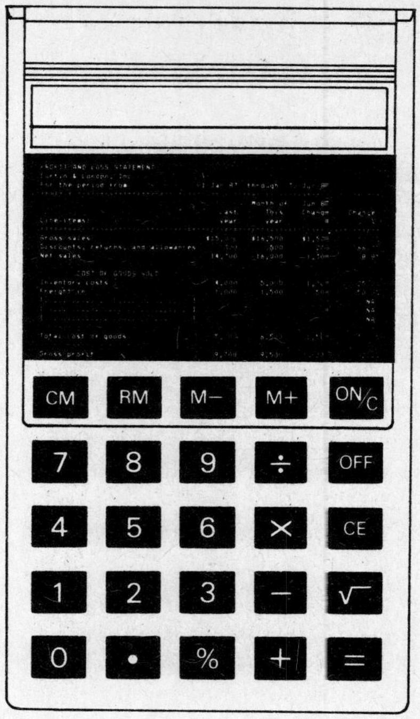

Until the personal computer and electronic spreadsheets came along just a few short years ago, financial analysis was almost more trouble than it was worth. Analyzing the various aspects of a situation was a time-consuming process, and exploring a series of possible outcomes — ranging from the most to the least likely — took even more time. The problem was compounded by the likelihood that one would forget how the analysis was done originally, and so each subsequent analysis would take as much time as the first.

The electronic spreadsheet changed all of this. Although in some cases it may still take as much time to actually build a model, the similarity with the past ends there. If you've never used a spreadsheet before, you can think of it as a calculator with a very fancy display — instead of a paltry eight or nine numbers at a time, it shows a whole financial statement, as wide or as long as necessary. You can enter dollar amounts, labels, column headings, dates, and ruled lines, just like on an accountant's ledger pad; but unlike the pad, a spreadsheet will do all the dirty work for you by calculating the annual totals, percentages of the total by category, and any other figures you need. Better yet, if you change any of the dollar amounts on the spreadsheet, all the totals will be updated automatically and instantaneously. For instance, if you want to see what your annual profit would be if you doubled your monthly sales, all you have to do is enter the new sales figures, and *presto* — all the recalculations are done for you in a split second. This advantage is what makes a spreadsheet more than just a fancy electronic scratch pad, and is also the idea behind the "What If" games we'll play later, beginning in Chapter 3.

## What Do You Use Spreadsheets For?

The possibilities for using spreadsheets are almost endless — but here are a few of the most popular applications:

- ☐ Comparing the current year's sales, expenses, and profits to those of the last year
- ☐ Analyzing the performance of products, salespeople, or dealers
- ☐ Comparing costs and profits on individual products in a product line
- ☐ Exploring alternative investments
- ☐ Calculating prices
- ☐ Budgeting

## The Framework Spreadsheet

| | A | B | C | D | E | F | G | H | [illegible] | J | K | L | M | N |
|---|---|---|---|---|---|---|---|---|---|---|---|---|---|---|
| 1 | CASH BUDGET SUMMARY - FIRST YEAR | Sep 87 | Oct 87 | Nov 87 | Dec 87 | Jan 88 | Feb 88 | Mar 88 | Ap[illegible] 88 | May 88 | Jun 88 | Jul 88 | Aug 88 | Total |
| 2 | [CASH INFLOWS] | | | | | | | | | | | | | |
| 3 | Cash receipts | $20,000 | $15,000 | $30,000 | $40,000 | $10,000 | $10,000 | $15,000 | $1[illegible],000 | $15,000 | $10,000 | $10,000 | $20,000 | $210,000 |
| 4 | [............................] | | | | | | | | | | | | | 0 |
| 5 | [............................] | | | | | | | | | | | | | 0 |
| 6 | [............................] | | | | | | | | | | | | | 0 |
| 7 | [............................] | | | | | | | | | | | | | 0 |
| 8 | [............................] | | | | | | | | | | | | | 0 |
| 9 | [............................] | | | | | | | | | | | | | 0 |
| 10 | [............................] | | | | | | | | | | | | | 0 |
| 11 | [............................] | | | | | | | | | | | | | 0 |
| 12 | ------------ | ------ | ------ | ------ | ------ | ------ | ------ | ------ | ------ | ------ | ------ | ------ | ------ | ------ |
| 13 | Total cash inflows | 20,000 | 15,000 | 30,000 | 40,000 | 10,000 | 10,000 | 15,000 | [illegible],000 | 15,000 | 10,000 | 10,000 | 20,000 | 210,000 |
| 14 | ============ | ====== | ====== | ====== | ====== | ====== | ====== | ====== | ====== | ====== | ====== | ====== | ====== | ====== |
| 15 | [CASH OUTFLOWS] | | | | | | | | | | | | | |
| 16 | Inventory purchases | 7,500 | 15,000 | 20,000 | 5,000 | 5,000 | 7,500 | 7,500 | 7,500 | 5,000 | 5,000 | 10,000 | 12,500 | 107,500 |
| 17 | Space costs | 1,200 | 1,200 | 1,400 | 1,500 | 1,500 | 1,500 | 1,400 | 1,300 | 1,200 | 1,200 | 1,200 | 1,200 | 15,800 |
| 18 | Personnel costs | 3,000 | 3,000 | 4,300 | 4,300 | 3,200 | 3,200 | 3,200 | 3,200 | 3,200 | 3,200 | 3,600 | 3,600 | 41,000 |
| 19 | Other G&A costs | 3,500 | 3,500 | 4,000 | 3,500 | 3,500 | 4,000 | 3,500 | 3,500 | 4,000 | 3,500 | 3,500 | 4,000 | 44,000 |
| 20 | [............................] | | | | | | | | | | | | | 0 |
| 21 | [............................] | | | | | | | | | | | | | 0 |
| 22 | [............................] | | | | | | | | | | | | | 0 |
| 23 | [............................] | | | | | | | | | | | | | 0 |
| 24 | [............................] | | | | | | | | | | | | | 0 |
| 25 | ------------ | ------ | ------ | ------ | ------ | ------ | ------ | ------ | ------ | ------ | ------ | ------ | ------ | ------ |
| 26 | Total cash outflows | 15,200 | 22,700 | 29,700 | 14,300 | 13,200 | 16,200 | 15,600 | 5,500 | 13,400 | 12,900 | 18,300 | 21,300 | 208,300 |
| 27 | ============ | ====== | ====== | ====== | ====== | ====== | ====== | ====== | ====== | ====== | ====== | ====== | ====== | ====== |
| 28 | Opening cash balance | 10,000 | | | | | | | | | | | | |
| 29 | Net monthly cash flow | 4,800 | (7,700) | 300 | 25,700 | (3,200) | (6,200) | (600) | (500) | 1,600 | (2,900) | (8,300) | (1,300) | 1,700 |
| 30 | Cumulative cash before loans | 14,800 | 7,100 | 7,400 | 33,100 | 29,900 | 23,700 | 23,100 | [illegible]2,600 | 24,200 | 21,300 | 13,000 | 11,700 | 11,700 |
| 31 | ============ | ====== | ====== | ====== | ====== | ====== | ====== | ====== | ====== | ====== | ====== | ====== | ====== | ====== |
| 32 | New loans | | | | | | | | | | | | | 0 |
| 33 | Cumulative cash after loans | 14,800 | 7,100 | 7,400 | 33,100 | 29,900 | 23,700 | 23,100 | [illegible]2,600 | 24,200 | 21,300 | 13,000 | 11,700 | 11,700 |
| 34 | ============ | ====== | ====== | ====== | ====== | ====== | ====== | ====== | ====== | ====== | ====== | ====== | ====== | ====== |

As you build the spreadsheets in the following chapters, you will encounter the following expressions:

**1 Labels** are lines of text used as headings for the spreadsheets or to identify individual line items.

**2 Double ruled lines** made up of equal signs divide the spreadsheets into major sections and make them easier to read.

**3 Single ruled lines** made up of dashes are also used to separate sections of the spreadsheets.

**4 Values** are numbers entered directly from the keyboard—for instance, 1000 is a value.

**5 Formulas** can be self-contained, e.g., 10*100, or can refer to the contents of other cells, e.g., 10*D9. Formulas can also use Framework functions—for instance **@SUM(A1:A10)** calculates the sum of cells A1 through A10.

**6 Percentages** are calculated by formulas that divide one value by another, and are displayed as whole numbers followed by a percent sign rather than as decimals. For instance, a decimal like .2 would be displayed as 20%.

The Framework program can format numbers to improve the layout and appearance of your financial statements and reports. Here are just a few of the possibilities:

**7 Global formats** control the way values are displayed, in this case with commas between thousands and with negative numbers in parentheses.

**8 Variable column widths** allow you to set the width of each column individually.

**9 Protected cells** are like a lock on your spreadsheet; they prevent new data from being entered into cells that already contain data or formulas, and thus prevent accidental erasure.

# Using this Book

## Overview of Spreadsheets and Graphs

In the following chapters, you will create a total of eight spreadsheets. You will learn how to develop two main cash budgeting spreadsheets: a cash budget summary spreadsheet (Chapter 3) and a cash budget vs. actuals spreadsheet that facilitates comparisons of your actual performance with your budget (Chapter 6). The cash budget itself is a powerful planning tool. As you will see, it permits you to figure out what your cash position is likely to be at the end of any given month. It also helps you to see—and, therefore, to forestall—the kinds of cash shortfalls that are so often fatal to smaller companies.

The cash budget vs. actuals spreadsheet is designed to be used as a control tool. Its purpose is to let you know when your performance is deviating from your plan and to pinpoint the areas in which the variances are occurring. The underlying notion is that if you can see what is going wrong, you are more likely to be able to fix it.

These main spreadsheets assume you've done a great deal of work on your existing business records, and have given a great deal of consideration to the probable operating characteristics of your business. To help you through these preliminary phases, this book provides you with several other, more detailed spreadsheets.

The first series of spreadsheets is designed to help you to compile all your data and your projections into a form that the cash budget summary can use. We will build three spreadsheets: a cash inflow supplement (Chapter 4), a cash outflow supplement with leads and lags (Chapter 5), and a cash outflow supplement without leads and lags (Chapter 7). Although these are intended to develop data to be fed into the cash budget summary, they are also useful in their own right, as you will see. They permit you to plan and control your cash flows in their natural, separate parts and to focus closely on specific areas that may create problems for your company.

To help you develop or refine the data needed for the detailed worksheets, this book also provides supplemental spreadsheets for three "housekeeping" chores: calculating the economic order quantity (EOQ) for your various inventory items; helping you to age your receivables and develop your normal cash inflow pattern; and analyzing whether to offer or take advantage of trade discounts (Chapter 7). Each of these spreadsheets is simply a handy decision aid, and the results can be fed into your inflow and outflow analyses and, ultimately, into your cash budget summary.

Not all of the spreadsheets in this book may be necessary for your cash planning, but we suggest that you enter them anyway, since important cash budgeting principles and other information are included within the typing instructions. You will enter numbers from typical business situations in each spreadsheet, and when you've tested the formulas and explored the "What Ifs," the sample numbers will be cleared from the spreadsheet so you can enter your own data. You will also create Framework graphs for some of the spreadsheets and save the graphs along with the finished spreadsheets.

We have given names to the frames containing the spreadsheets which reflect their contents: **Cash Summary**, **Trade Discounts**, and so on. These names will be used when you save the files to the disk. It's a good idea to rename the frames containing the blank spreadsheets before saving them—as **E Cash Summary**, **E Trade Discounts**, and so on. That way, you'll have two copies of each spreadsheet: one with the sample numbers and a blank copy for your own data.

When you enter your own numbers into the spreadsheet, we suggest you save the new version with your own initial or number (**A Cash Summary**). When you update your data, the new versions can then be saved with sequential letters or numbers.

## How to Follow the Instructions for Creating Spreadsheets

1 **Row 26**

**Total cash outflows** are calculated on this row by a formula that sums each of the monthly columns in the cash outflows section.

2 *To enter a label:*

3
**Highlight** A26
**Type** **Total cash outflows**
**Press** ⇥

4 **Result** The totals on row 26 should match those shown in the illustration at the beginning of this section (except N26, which will show 0). After we complete the final section in the next step, we will make a month-by-month comparison of total cash inflows on row 13 and total cash outflows on this row.

Before you can begin to create or explore your cash budgets, they must be entered into the computer as Framework spreadsheets and graphs (unless you have the publisher's data disk). The spreadsheets are described in this book step-by-step, or more accurately, row-by-row and column-by-column. The instructions given throughout this book for creating spreadsheets and graphs and exploring "What Ifs" all have the same format: instructions are explained in detail the first time they appear and are abbreviated in any subsequent steps. The instructions follow the format illustrated above.

**1** This section describes the step you are about to complete and, in many cases, the business term or principle being addressed. As you create your spreadsheets and graphs, you'll learn more and more about the Framework program and about the business principles behind what you are doing.

**2** This section describes commands you'll be using, and what you'll be entering, copying, formatting, or otherwise doing in a step.

**3** This section describes the specific Framework commands used and identifies where the cursor should be when using them. In some cases this is a frame border, in other cases a spreadsheet cell. How to get the cursor to where it should be is described in the typing instruction that follows (as are all of the other commands).

**4** This section describes what should have happened on the screen if you followed the instructions correctly. A result is given only when the effect of the commands used isn't immediately apparent from the instructions. If at any time your results don't match those described in the book, you may have a problem! If this happens, retrace your actions back a few steps and try to identify the problem before proceeding any further.

**5** When you explore "What Ifs," the impact of the changes you make on the spreadsheet is discussed in an analysis section (not shown here).

## Terms Used in This Book

When following the instructions in this book, you will encounter certain essential words used over and over again. Here is a brief description of each.

**Cursor** The bright (in some cases) blinking square that identifies your current position: frame border, spreadsheet cell, database field, text character, menu command, disk drive, or file. The cursor can be moved with a variety of keys.

**Highlight** tells you to move the cursor (bright highlight) over item indicated. It can also describe the extension of the cursor indicating area affected by next command.

**Type** tells you what to type on the keyboard, usually a label, number, or formula.

**Press** tells you to press specific command keys, such as (↵), (←), (→), and **Ctrl**, and then release them. **Press Ctrl-(↵)** means to hold down **Ctrl** while you press (↵), and then release **Ctrl**.

**Message** tells you what you should see in the message area at the bottom of the screen — this line "prompts" you to reply.

## The Notation Used in This Book

**Bold** **The bold typeface** indicates the keystrokes to be typed on the computer. Be sure to enter these keystrokes *exactly* as shown, including all punctuation marks and spaces. Entering an extra space, for example, will make some formulas unreadable. Although labels need not be entered exactly as shown, try to get in the habit of duplicating all keystrokes as closely as possible; this will make troubleshooting much easier later on.

Light The light typeface indicates an instruction or cue that appears on the Framework desktop; this includes "messages" which ask for responses, and menu choices.

D29 Framework spreadsheets are made up of cells, which appear at every intersection of a column and a row. Cells are identified by column letter and row number; for instance, cell D29 is in the 29th row and the fourth column, column D.

(SP) This symbol indicates the **Space Bar** on the computer keyboard. We use this symbol only when the need for entering a space might not be obvious.

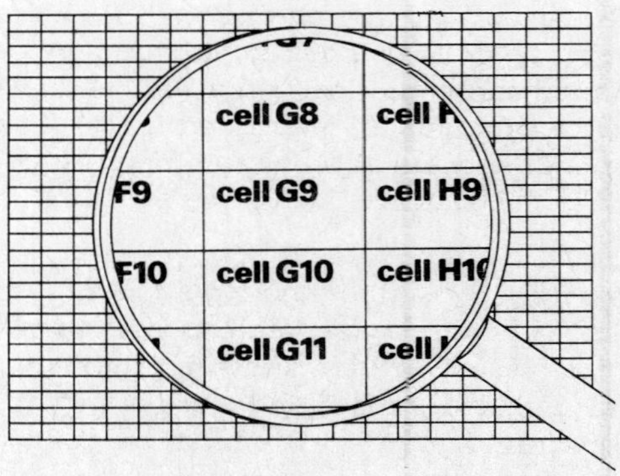

## The Anatomy of a Disk

In this book, you'll be using two different kinds of disks: *data disks* for your spreadsheet files, and the Framework program disks. A typical floppy disk is illustrated at right:

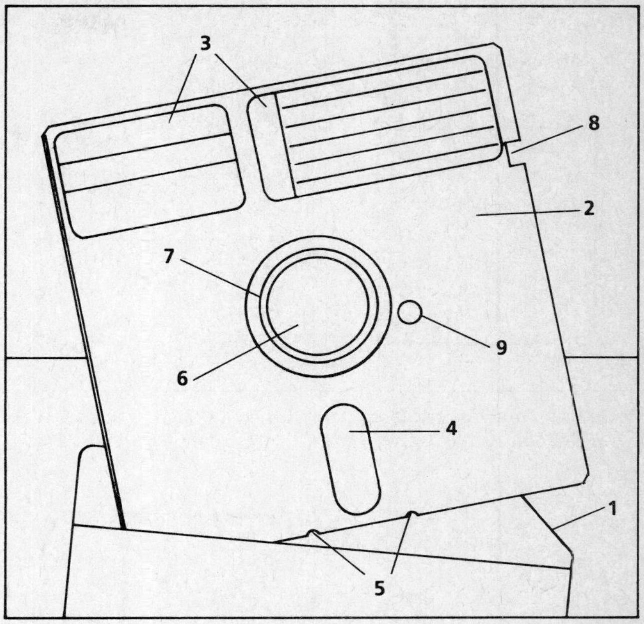


**1 The storage envelope** protects the disk from scratches, dust, and fingerprints. *Always* store your disks in their storage envelopes.

**2 The plastic cover** protects the disk (which is really a record-shaped disk of magnetic material) and allows it to spin smoothly. The cover is permanently sealed and contains lubricants and cleaning agents that prolong the life of the disk.

**3 Labels** identify the manufacturer of the disk and should be used to number and keep track of your own data disks. Always insert the disk in your computer label-side-up, with the oval opening pointed toward the drive.

**4 The oval opening** is where the disk drive head picks up and records information on the disk.

**5 Alignment notches** align the disk over the disk drive head when the disk is inserted into the computer.

**6 The central hole** is used by the disk drive to engage and rotate the disk.

**7 Hub rings** can be glued to the rim of a disk's central hole to prevent wear.

**8 The write-protect cutout** tells the disk drive whether the disk is "write-protected" or not. If you cover the cutout with tape, the disk drive will not allow you to erase files or store new files on the disk.

**9 The recording and reading head** is used by the disk drive to locate disk sectors where information is stored.

### Tips  Cleaning the Disk Drive

This is one of those easily overlooked housekeeping chores, but an important one. The disk drive head, like a tape recorder's head, can pick up debris from the magnetic recording material, and if the debris isn't removed, it can reduce the sensitivity of the head and its accuracy in recording and picking up data.

The easiest way to clean the head is with a special cleaning disk available from your dealer. Insert it into the drive just like a regular disk, and it will clean the disk drive head as it spins.

### Tips  Keeping Track of Disks

When you first buy a computer, keeping track of your disks isn't a problem because you have so few of them. Before long, however, you'll find your desk buried in disks unless you have a system for filing and storing them. Here are some tips for organizing your disks:

1. Assign and label each disk with a number: for instance, Framework #1, Framework #2, etc., for Framework disks.
2. Periodically print out a directory or list of files for each disk, and store the printout along with the disk. Some filing systems and binders even have a place for the directory. Or keep a catalog of your directories, making sure that the number on each directory matches the number on the disk label.

# Disk Handling and Storage

**1** Do not touch disk surface. It is easily contaminated, which causes errors.

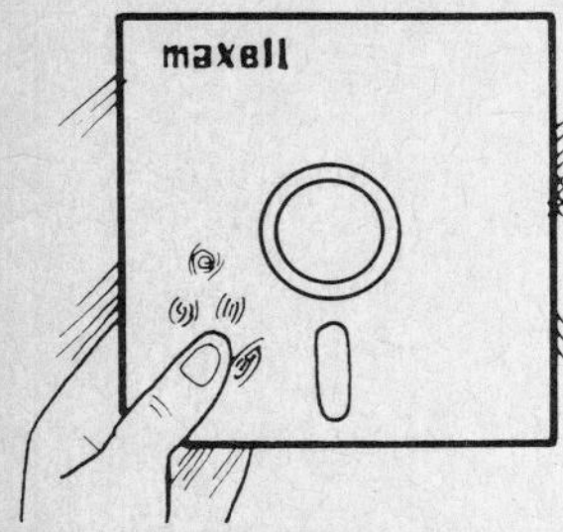


**2** Do not use alcohol, thinners, or freon to clean disk.

**3** Do not use magnets or magnetized objects near the disk. Data can be lost from a disk exposed to a magnetic field.

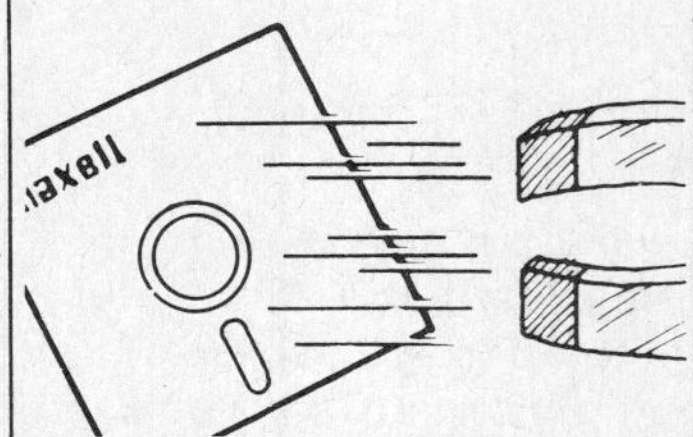

**4** Do not bend or fold the disk.

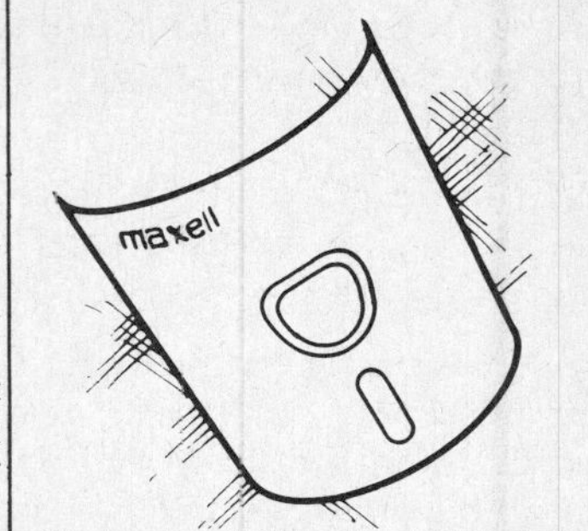


**5** Do not place heavy objects on the disk.

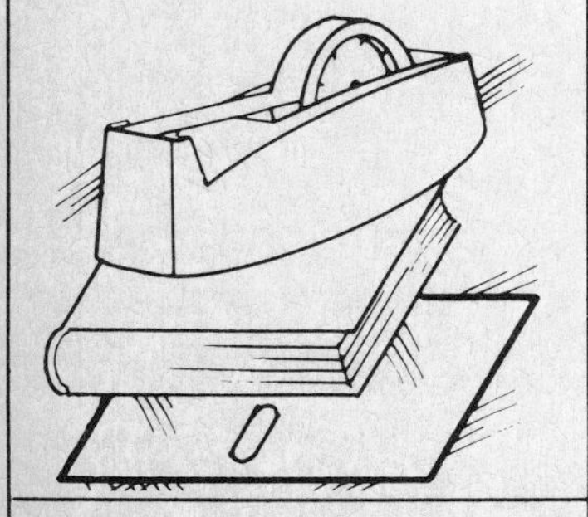

**6** Do not use rubber bands or paper clips on the disk.

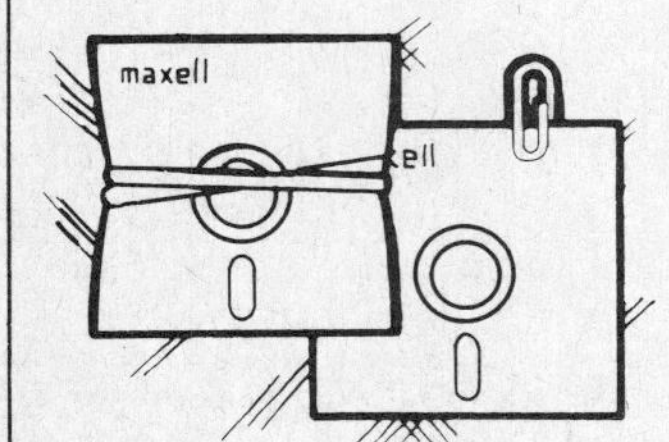


**7** Do not write on disk label with pencil or ball-point pen. Use felt-tip pen only.

**8** Do not use erasers on disk.

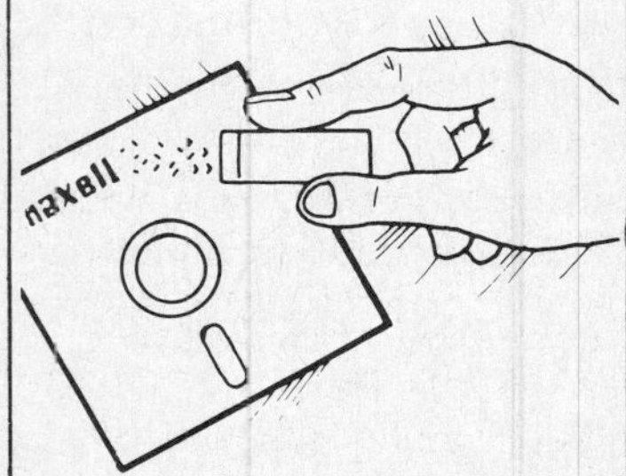


**9** Apply disk label to the right of the label. Do not use labels in layers.

**10** Insert carefully, by grasping upper edge and placing it into the drive.

**11** Keep disk in its protective envelope when not in use.

**12** Disks not being used should be stored vertically in their box.

**13** Do not expose the disk to excessive heat or sunlight.

**14** Operating environment:
- **A** Temperature: 10°C to 50°C (50°F to 122°F)
- **B** Wet bulb temperature: Less than 29°C
- **C** Relative humidity: 20% to 80%

**15** Storage environment:
- **A** Temperature: 4°C to 53°C (40°F to 127°F)
- **B** Relative humidity: 8% to 80%

**16** While in transit the disk should be in its envelope in a protective box within the following ranges:
- **A** Temperature: −40°C to 53°C (−40°F to 127°F)
- **B** Relative humidity: 8% to 90%

Used with permission of Maxell Corporation of America

# 2 Cash: The Basic Business Reality

## Introduction

As many people probably pointed out before you started your company, getting in is easy. It is *staying* in that is the hard part. Clearly, you have managed to accomplish this feat until now. (No mean feat. This makes your company one of a small minority that manages to survive their first years.) And you have undoubtedly discovered by now that the hardest part of the hard part is meeting payroll each week or paying your bills each month.

This book is intended to help you pay your bills. Not, unfortunately, by providing you with direct funding, but by showing you how to control and use the money you already have more advantageously. In a way, though, you can view the extra control and additional benefits you reap by managing your cash better as extra money. As you will discover, you are probably giving away more money now than you would even consider donating to your favorite charities.

The book is designed so that you can use the parts you need when you need them. We do recommend, however, that you read through Chapter 1 and the introductory sections to each chapter first, particularly if you are relatively unfamiliar with accounting or computers or both. These sections present information that will make using the rest of the book much easier and quicker. We have tried to keep this basic material as short and as clear as possible. Give it a try.

## Reality vs. Accounting

Since you are in business, you already *know* why cash is important. Without it, you cannot pay your bills as they come due. If you fail to pay your bills often enough—or if you choose the wrong ones to pay first—you are going to be out of business. It's very simple. Without enough cash at the right times, you're out. And your first objective must be to stay in the game.

Your accountant, or the person who prepares your financial statements and tax returns, knows this as well as you do. He or she simply defines things in terms different from yours—creating some communication difficulties at times. He or she views your business in terms of "profit and loss," a frame of reference that should be of some interest to you, particularly at tax and dividend (or profit-sharing) time.

But this P&L (profit and loss) focus does not really address the issue of cash. Even the financial statement definition of "cash flow" does not really address the cash issues you need to get at. For the purposes of a financial statement, "cash flow" is defined as annual or quarterly net profit plus non-cash expenses (like depreciation which, while it counts as an expense for P&L purposes, does not require that any cash actually leave the company).

Unfortunately, you cannot wait to pay all your bills at the end of the year or at the end of your accounting period. To know how much net cash your business generated for the entire period, then, does not mean that those bills were paid or paid on time. This is why businesses are sometimes in financial trouble despite the fact that, by accounting standards, they are profitable. The way we will consider cash flow, on the other hand, involves the actual movement of cash money into and out of your business over time. *This* is what will ensure that those bills get paid—or, at least, that you know how much you will need to find to get them paid.

**Cash vs. accrual.** To understand why there are such differences between profit and cash, you need to know something about how your accountant arrives at the profit figure shown on your statements. Despite appearances, it is a very logical method. If you are preparing to manage your cash effectively, you will need to understand it.

The key notion in accounting treatments of most businesses is *accrual*. This is the notion that *the expenses of producing an item for sale should be viewed in relation to (matched to) the revenues generated by selling it*. This "matching" principle produces timing differences that underlie cash versus profit issues. Three examples should demonstrate why some companies find themselves profitable, but broke.

**1** In most businesses, a "sale" occurs when the customer signs on the dotted line and walks out with the product or merchandise. It instantly shows up on your P&L as *revenue*. But the business has not yet seen a nickel of that customer's money. You have acquired an *account receivable*; the customer owes you money in exchange for your product. But you cannot pay your bills with your customers' promises; so, if you acquire too many accounts receivable and not enough actual payments, you may be in trouble. You may well be "profitable," but unable to pay your bills.

**2** Suppose that, in October, anticipating the usual Christmas rush, you hire extra production workers, acquire large amounts of raw materials, and manufacture three times the amount that you are likely to sell in the month ahead. You will have added a great deal of cost to your operations this month—more than you expect to get back through October's sales.

But your company can still be highly profitable in October by accounting rules. All you get to show as "Cost" for this month is "Cost of Goods Sold." The matching principle noted earlier dictates that the cost shown for the period is the cost associated with manufacturing the number of items actually sold this month, i.e., your normal volume. The inventory-building costs simply do not show up as October expenses. If your aggregate sales exceed these costs plus the monthly costs of running your operation, you will show a profit for the month.

In *cash* terms, however, your excursion into building inventory may have put you seriously in the hole. Your extra workers will expect their wages. Your suppliers will expect their invoices to be paid. These are reasonable expectations—and these people are unlikely to be prepared to wait until after Christmas for them to be fulfilled. Once again, your company is "profitable," but you may be unable to come up with the cash to cover immediate obligations.

**3** You purchased a piece of equipment a few years ago and are paying principal and interest payments to your bank. You get to take loan interest payments and depreciation on the equipment as expenses on your profit-and-loss statement. You do *not* get to take the repayment of principal to the bank as an expense. Your actual cash outflow each month is interest plus principal. Depreciation neither adds to, nor subtracts from, your actual cash amounts (though it may help your tax position). If your loan repayment and depreciation schedules are such that the principal portion of the repayment is high while interest and depreciation are relatively low, you could show a profit and yet be unable to pay the bank on time.

The purpose of these three examples is not to turn you away from accounting treatments of business data. These treatments are extremely valuable for certain purposes—and, of course, they are required by Uncle Sam. But the examples should show you that:

**1** You are not crazy to worry about paying your bills even if your company is wildly profitable, and,

**2** There is an additional area in which you can control and manage the destiny of your business—cash.

In fact, our purpose is to help ease your worry and to show you how to gain that control of your business cash.

**Businesses at significant risk.** Although all businesses face major cash flow difficulties at one time or another, for some kinds of companies the risk is either fairly constant or predictably seasonal. As you could deduce from some of the examples outlined earlier, these are the businesses with built-in timing differentials between sales and payments, and the businesses that have timing differentials between purchases and sales. Inventory-based companies in high-growth phases generally fall into the latter category. This is why you hear of so many successful companies dying of over-expansion. They look at their profitability (good) and forget that they will have to fund the cash outlays associated with the expansion before they receive the inflows from increased sales.

We can take a quick look at the cash flow patterns of a highly seasonal business in an example. This will permit you to see, immediately, the problems that result from not tracking cash with great care, and the problems that come from considering only the accounting treatment of a business. This example will also demonstrate a major advantage of the kind of cash flow analysis that you will see throughout this book.

## Example Anderson's Boats

Anderson builds small boats intended to be used on lakes in the New England region. In this business, sales to consumers are made mainly during the summer. Boat show models have to be ready in January. Floor models must generally be in dealers' showrooms well in advance of the peak selling season, or the dealers will have nothing to show potential buyers.

A major part of the competition in the small boat business turns on the terms of trade. When a dealer sells an Anderson boat, Anderson's policy allows the dealer 90 days to pay for it. Anderson's suppliers, on the other hand, want payment within 60 days. Obviously, Anderson's workers want to get paid on a regular basis.

**Anderson's Boats**

*Income Statement*
*Year Ending September 30, 1985*

| | | |
|---|---|---|
| Sales (30 boats) | $900,000 | |
| Cost of goods sold (65%) | 585,000 | |
| Gross margin | 315,000 | |
| Selling and general expenses | 250,000 | |
| Interest | 30,000 | |
| Depreciation | 10,000 | |
| Profit before taxes | $ 25,000 | (2.8% Return on Sales) |

As you can see, Anderson's is profitable. Not wildly so, but staying slightly ahead of the game. A look at its cash flow, however, shows serious problems.

| Month | Sales | Inflows (Sale + 90 days) | Outflows (Purchase + 60 days) | Monthly Net Cash |
|---|---|---|---|---|
| October | | | $ 25,000 | $(25,000) |
| November | | | 25,000 | (25,000) |
| December | | | 25,000 | (25,000) |
| January | $ 75,000 | | 74,000 | (74,000) |
| February | 150,000 | | 122,500 | (122,500) |
| March | 150,000 | | 122,500 | (122,500) |
| April | 150,000 | $ 75,000 | 122,500 | (47,500) |
| May | 150,000 | 150,000 | 122,500 | 27,500 |
| June | 150,000 | 150,000 | 122,500 | 27,500 |
| July | 75,000 | 150,000 | 74,000 | 76,000 |
| August | | 150,000 | 25,000 | 125,000 |
| September | | 150,000 | 25,000 | 125,000 |
| Total (rounded) | $900,000 | $825,000 | $885,500 | $(60,500) |

Assume that Anderson's $280,000 in operating expenses (excluding depreciation) are spread equally over the year and that the principal portion of his loan costs $2,000 a month. (These figures are obviously simplified to demonstrate a point.) Excluding his cost of goods sold, then, his monthly cash outflows are about $25,000. Not only has Anderson's shown a negative net cash for the year, he will also have to find more than $440,000 to fund his expenses for the period prior to when his customers begin paying for the boats. If Anderson cannot do this, his boatbuilding venture will not make it to its first sale.

Next year might be better for Anderson's. Anderson can expect to collect the $75,000 that his customers still owe him. He will still, however, have to fund the cost of his manufacturing and general operations until his customers pay up. It does not look good for Anderson's.

What we did in this example—follow the movement of cash into and out of a company over time—forms the basis for all methods of controlling cash. For you to do this effectively in your business, you will have to understand something about how various forms of cash appear in accounting financial statements. It will also help to try to begin to see your business in cash terms. This focus on cash will give you a great deal more flexibility and control than your less-focused competitors.

The next sections address some of the major cash issues and related accounting issues.

## Notions Basic to Cash Flow Analysis

**Working capital.** Perhaps one of the more destructive misconceptions a business owner can have is that "working capital" is synonymous with real cash. Technically, working capital refers to the current portion of a company's balance sheet—those assets and liabilities that will be turned into cash or paid out within an accounting period (generally a year). Working capital is defined as current assets minus current liabilities. *The resulting figure is not usable cash to the business.* This should be clear from a brief examination of the actual balance sheet items.

The current portion of a balance sheet might look like this:

**Balance Sheet for XYZ Corporation**

*As of December 31, 1985*

| ASSETS: | LIABILITIES AND EQUITY: |
|---|---|
| Current assets: | Current liabilities: |
| Cash | Accrued expenses |
| Marketable securities | Accounts payable |
| Accounts receivable (Net) | Notes payable |
| Notes receivable | Current portion of long-term debt |
| Inventory | |
| Prepaid assets | |
| Total current assets | Total current liabilities |

**Working capital = Total current assets − Total current liabilities**

If you examine the items, you will see that most of the assets are definitely *not* cash. Many cannot be turned into the same amount of cash as that figure shown on the balance sheet. For example, if you had to sell off your inventory in its raw state, you would probably get less for it than the number shown. And we have already noted the danger inherent in thinking that an account receivable could be used to pay a bill. Yet people persist in viewing working capital as cash. Clearly separating the two can save some very expensive errors, as the following exaggerated vignette will indicate.

Assume, for a moment, that you have decided to significantly expand your bicycle parts business this quarter. Assume further that, because you really want to get the expansion underway, you extend your payment terms, collecting nothing for sixty days. You also decide to defer paying your suppliers. You make *no* other changes in your business. Your accounts payable will rise because you are not paying invoices (this is not a recommended course of action over an extended period). If all goes very well and you sell all the additional parts inventory you purchased in anticipation of increased sales your accounts receivable will increase by a greater amount (sale price less purchase price times volume). *Voila!* Instant increase in working capital. But, do you have any additional cash?

**In the long run, all costs are variable.** As you can see, following cash is a very different proposition from tracking financial results. And it requires (and encourages) an entirely different attitude toward your business operations. It induces you to consider your company in terms of sources of cash and drains on cash. While most small business owners are concerned only with such income statement (P&L) issues as increasing sales, the cash-focused owner will see that balance sheet items are possibly more promising areas of concentration.

The owner of the bicycle parts business noted earlier, for example, has succeeded in increasing sales. But what value is that, if he has not gotten paid for any of those sales? On an even more basic level, everyone knows that it is easy to create sales by underpricing a product or service. But, if you cannot meet your everyday business needs at those superlow prices, it is an inherently short-term strategy for the business.

Sales are, of course, of major interest to all business owners. However, a balance sheet emphasis lets you consider the cash flowing from those sales, rather than only the sales figures themselves. The key issue becomes whether and when the cash appears, rather than when the merchandise moves off your shelf.

The cost side of your business is also confused by accounting terminology. Consider the notion of "fixed costs." These are defined as those items which recur, usually monthly, as part of your business expenses and which are not directly related to sales volume. For example, to be in the boat manufacturing business, you have to have certain equipment before you can build, and regardless of whether you actually sell a boat in a given month. The cost of this equipment (depreciation or lease costs) is considered a fixed cost.

On your income statement, this cost simply appears month after month. You are not encouraged to see it at all. Seeing the assets on the balance sheet, however, and viewing the balance sheet as a directory of sources and uses of cash might help you to begin to consider whether owning or leasing all that equipment is really the best use of your cash. (Later, we will discuss how to decide.) It might help you to think about alternative approaches to getting the job done.

For example, could you subcontract certain capital-intensive portions of your operation and get rid of some of that equipment? As a specialist, your subcontractor may be able to reduce the unit cost to you of the subcontracted part or process. Even if the cost to you will be the same, you will have increased your cash by selling off some equipment assets and increased your flexibility by reducing your fixed costs. In the longer run, with cash focus, all costs *are* variable. You create additional options for your company.

**Equipment and capital asset accounting.** Another key area in which normal accounting treatment differs markedly from the actual movement of cash is in the area of capital asset accounting. Under accounting rules, when you acquire a piece of capital equipment, you set up a depreciation schedule under which you may write off a certain portion of the cost of the asset each year over the economic useful life of that asset. This depreciation is viewed as an expense in your accounting statements. (You also get to take the Investment Tax Credit as an offset to your taxes.)

The notion of depreciation is closely tied to the principle of "matching" mentioned earlier. The idea is that the cost of a piece of productive equipment should be spread over the period during which you will use it to benefit the business (to produce goods or services). At some point, its useful life in the accounting statements will be over. You are matching the expense to the related revenue. It makes sense within an accounting frame of reference.

But let's look at what is really happening to the way the cash moves in the business. It depends, of course, on how you pay for the equipment in the first place.

Assume, for example, that you acquire a piece of equipment for $10,000. It is expected to be useful for five years with no resale (salvage) value at the end of that period. You decide to take your depreciation on a straightline basis, at $2,000 per year. Assuming a 50% tax rate, you get $1,000 a year off your tax bill.

If you bought the equipment outright, paying cash, your cash outflows would look as follows:

| *Outflows of cash* | *Year 1* | *Year 2* | *Year 3* | *Year 4* | *Year 5* |
|---|---|---|---|---|---|
| (beginning of year) | $10,000 | — | — | — | — |

If, on the other hand, you had gone to the bank for a loan, your cash outflows would look as follows:

| *Outflows of cash* | | | | | |
|---|---|---|---|---|---|
| Down payment | $2,000 | | | | |
| Loan payments | 2,275 | 2,275 | 2,275 | 2,275 | 2,275 |
| Total cash outflow | $4,275 | 2,275 | 2,275 | 2,275 | 2,275 |

Under either approach, your depreciation figures would look the same and so would your investment tax credit. Interest on the loan is, of course, tax-deductible, adding extra benefit to the loan option above. Your net cost of borrowing will be halved. Except for this interest factor, your profit figure will be the same. There is a significant difference between the two in terms of your company's overall financial situation, however, particularly if you are perennially strapped for cash. This difference in the timing of the outflows of cash should be a critical factor in your decision on how to finance the asset.

## Who Cares, Anyway?

The real point of explaining all these differences between accounting definitions and the real movement of cold, hard cash is to let you know that there are really *two* separate, though related, aspects of your business to control. You need to keep tabs on your profitability, the state of your P&L, but you also need to control how your cash is moving if you want to be in full command of your company. Your accountant should be helping you with profitability. He or she may also work on the latter, if you ask.

Once you start tracking your cash, you will find that the knowledge gives you increased ability to manage the business and to plan for its future. You will never be like one small company owner who became a favorite story for his banker. This owner called his banker at home one Thursday evening. He had just discovered that he would be unable to meet his regular Friday payroll and could he please get a hurry-up deal on a loan to get him through? (He did not get it.)

According to the banker, the reason he did not get the loan had nothing to do with the actual operations of the company. The main reason was because the owner was obviously a poor manager, clearly demonstrated by all his last-minute activity. Had he discussed the loan during the preceding month, knowing that there was likely to be a cash shortage, the banker would probably have granted it. Of course, the owner could not have done this because he did not know how to track and forecast his cash position.

I never heard what happened to this company after that fateful Friday. If the owner was able to placate his troops and learn from his Thursday evening disaster, he is probably still in business. If he simply got angry and decided that the banker was rotten for not helping him out when he really needed it, odds are that the company no longer exists. At some point, this owner would surely have been unable to come up with the cash to pay some critical bills—and then the ball game would have been over.

Fortunately, it is reasonably simple to begin to track and manage your business' cash. All it takes is a clear understanding of how the cash flows, a method for forecasting how it will flow, and an understanding of how you can affect those flows. You also need to be willing to do some serious thinking about your business and to put in some fairly tedious work at the beginning.

This book will help you to get on your way by walking you through most of the work at the start, and pointing out the major opportunities for controlling and planning your cash flows. When you have worked through the examples, you will know how to begin to restructure your cash flows in the way you believe is most appropriate for your business. You will have built the spreadsheets which will permit you to use your computer to consider different ways of handling your cash. You will be able to test different courses of action to find out what is likely to happen—without ever risking a nickel!

# 3 The Cash Budget: Your Road Map

## Introduction

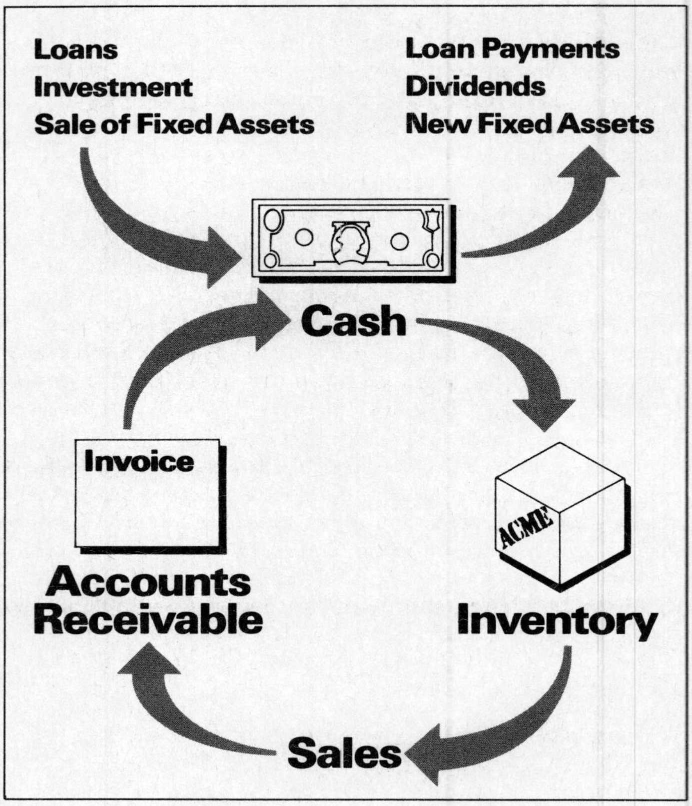


The cash budget is your key document for beginning to gain control of the cash moving through your company. Without a good cash budget, your efforts will be wasted—and none of us has time to waste. View the time it takes to do your initial cash budgets properly as an investment in the future of your company.

If you are going to begin to manage your cash well, you need a very clear understanding of how cash flows through your business now. Happily, there is a relatively simple approach to discovering this, and to tracking and predicting these flows once you've figured out what they are. While it does take some thought, effort, and a willingness to commit to your own estimates, there is nothing inherently difficult about it.

Your cash budget will be a basic tool. In turn, this budget is supported by two other key schedules, a sales budget and an expense plan. All these are simple and logical. Even though they are simple, however, they will probably surprise you. And that is really the idea. Cash-oriented consideration of your business will help you to see the relationships among parts of your business in a new light. Once these relationships are clear to you, you will be able to alter and control them to your advantage.

This chapter focuses on the cash budget. Later chapters address the sales budget and the expense plan in detail.

## What Is a Cash Budget?

At its most basic, a cash budget is a *statement or a projection of the amount of cash that comes into a business and the amount of cash that goes out of a business over a given period of time*. Although there are as many ways of structuring this information as there are people to develop them, the one that we have decided to use is simple and straightforward. It focuses on the amount of cash in your business at any given time—the item that we expect is of most immediate interest to you.

The cash budget format we will use is a simple, four-part document. Its first section requires identification—your business' name and the period the statement covers. The second section shows your cash inflows and the sources of those inflows. The third section shows cash outflows and their destinations. The final section is a status/summary section that will show the cash position for the month and the year-to-date. It also includes space in which you can play with alternative new financings.

Throughout this book, we will talk a great deal about "the amount of cash in your business" or "your business cash" and other phrases that mean just about the same thing. This is *not* the same thing as your net income or your profit or any other accounting line item, as we pointed out earlier. Instead, we mean *money you control during the relevant time period*.

Asking the question "Can you spend it?" is a simple way to identify cash, but it can become fairly complicated depending on what you want to accomplish. For example, for most purposes, you can assume that you gain control of a chunk of cash when you deposit a customer's check in your bank account. Recently, however, newspaper readers have been learning what many bank depositors have learned the hard way. Many banks do not actually release such funds for your use until many business days after your deposit. They claim to need the time to complete the interbank clearing process and assure that the check you deposited is, in fact, a "good" check.

Under most conditions, you can write a check to one of your suppliers against the check you deposited. You control the cash. The underlying assumption you have made, assuming you understand the clearing lags, is that the supplier's bank will be doing the same thing as your bank, and the clearing periods will work out so that your check will not bounce.

(In case you were wondering, the amount of money involved in this clearing process nationwide on any given day is astronomical. *The Wall Street Journal* (3/6/84) estimated this float at $60 billion.)

Sometimes, however, you may need to have actual cash, the bills themselves, in your hands. In that case, you would actually control the cash as soon as your bank releases the funds and will hand you the money. Whatever your particular needs may be, a cash budget can be adapted to reflect them. The key notion, however, is that *cash is only that amount of money over which you can exercise control.* Cash flows in when you gain effective control over it and could spend it if you wanted to. Cash flows out when you lose control by spending it on something or giving it away. A cash budget is a method of tracking or predicting those flows and the cash balances that result from them. It's as simple as that.

## If It's So Simple, Why Bother?

"I know how much money my business has," you are saying to yourself, "why go through all the hassle and all the numbers?"

The answer lies in a matter of degree. If today's balance is all that is important to you, then you can stop reading now. To manage and control the flows in your business over time, however, you will need and use a good deal more information beyond today's balance. If your goal is control, then, read on. In this section, we will note some of the numerous ways in which you can use a cash budget. Many will be discussed in this chapter and others later in this book.

We begin with the assumption that *you have a reliable sense of the account balances of your business holdings*. The issue is understanding *how you got there*. And *what those balances will be by the end of next month*. Not to mention figuring out ways to modify the flows so that you wind up in *better shape*. The cash budget and the process that we outline are designed to highlight the relationships and the dynamics of the elements that affect your business cash flow.

Your level of understanding of cash flows and your ability to affect the elements and the outcomes are of interest to some significant outsiders who can influence your company's health, as well as to you. When you go to the bank for a loan, for example, your banker will want to see your cash flow projections. His or her concern is twofold. First, are you asking for the right amount of money? And, second, but probably more critical to whether you get the loan, have you organized the financial flows of your company so that you will be able to pay the money back—with interest and on schedule?

In addition to the specific numbers on your cash budget, the state of your cash budget—its clarity, its level of detail, and your understanding of it—will tell your banker a great deal about your ability to control and manage your business. And, as you have probably already discovered, bankers like to deal with people whom they believe to be good managers.

If you are in the market for equity, a cash budget will be one item that potential investors will want to see. Since they are unlikely to be prepared to throw their money away through bankruptcy, they will be concerned as much with the cash flows as with the bottom line—if they're smart.

And speaking of bankruptcy, as we pointed out earlier, it is caused by lack of cash. Clearly, then, being in control of the cash position of your company is one of the keys to avoiding such a disaster. Knowing in March that you will run out of cash in July gives you time to plan for how to cover the shortfall. Should July simply arrive, with its disastrous shortfall, it may be too late to do anything useful. Cash budgets prevent bankruptcies.

Cash budgets can be useful planning tools in other cases. If you want to expand your operations or introduce a new product, for example, you know that it will cost money. Wouldn't it be nice to know *how much* money you will probably have to come up with—and when you will need it—*before* you commit your first money and manpower to the project? Your cash budget can tell you.

If you are perpetually short of cash—a problem of epidemic proportions in smaller companies and lots of bigger ones too—wouldn't it be useful to be able to pinpoint problem areas? Once you identify the problem areas, you can begin to shape specific solutions. If you cannot define the problem, you probably won't be able to get a workable solution. Your cash budget can help you define the problem. Because you are working with a computer, you can also use your cash budget to try out various solutions—just by pressing a few buttons.

If you are so far from bankruptcy that you have cash lying around for periods of time, a cash budget can also be useful. If you know in advance how much you will have loose for how long, you can arrange to invest it in the kinds of short-term securities that generally have fixed terms. This would be folly unless you had a good handle on how long you could operate your business without that sum. Your cash budget will tell you when and for how long there will be surpluses of how much cash. It can also give you information that might help you reorganize your cash flows to create surpluses. Viewed this way, cash budgets can actually *make* money for you.

This book will show you how.

## So How Do I Start?

Obviously, building your cash budget begins with an analysis of your cash accounts. If you have been operating your business for awhile, begin by getting out the old checkbook and/or your journal and cash disbursements ledger. If you are new in your business, get out whatever you have that will show when and how much cash came in and went out of the company. If you are still in the planning stage of a business startup (or a purchase), sit down in a quiet room and give yourself some time to think.

Keep in mind that cash is a stream that moves through your business (or prospective business) in a different way from the way it would flow through any other company. This is because your particular combination of products or services, supply arrangements, and your customer payment arrangements is probably unique. Cash flow is so named because cash usually doesn't hold still for even one day. Your objective is to map that flow and to define how your company's flow differs from others which may appear to be similar.

Your stint with checkbook and books is designed to give you the base data you need to begin to build your cash budget. While you can work with pencil and paper, you can use the breakdown schedules and Framework to make your "notes," if you prefer. You are looking for, and listing, every cash inflow and outflow in your business over the last year (or however long you have been operating). If you are doing preopening planning, begin with a list of suppliers and potential customers or categories of customers. For each inflow or outflow, you will need three vital pieces of information:

1 Source or destination of cash

2 Amount of cash moving

3 Date on which the move occurred

Keep firmly in mind that cash moves only when you gain or lose control of it. Thus, if you are given to holding customer checks for weekly deposit rather than running to the bank daily, log the cash moving date as the date of deposit. The date you actually mail a check is the most likely and simple cash moving date for an outflow. (*Note:* If you are using your cash budgets for "money management," you will need to be more concerned with the clearing dates of deposits and checks

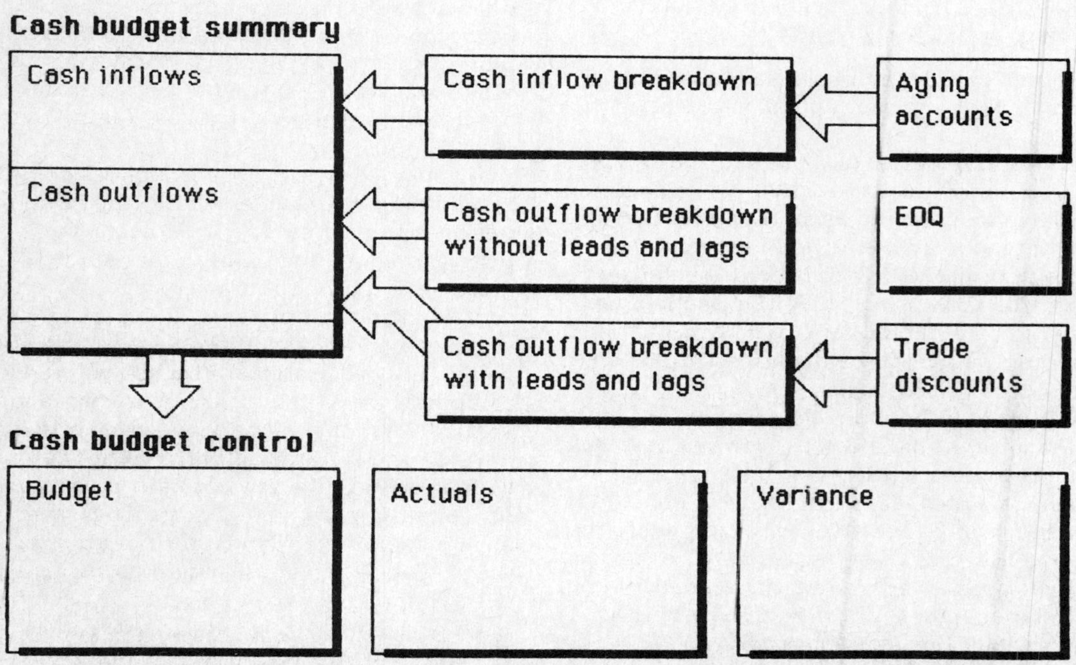


*The spreadsheets that you will develop form a working approach to managing your business cash. The process is shown graphically here. The three spreadsheets at the far right are spreadsheets that will help you build the main breakdown spreadsheets, one for cash inflows and two for cash outflows. These, in turn, provide the information needed to use the basic cash budget effectively. The cash budget summary spreadsheet, shown in the leftmost column, provides the "budget" figures for the "budget-to-actual" analysis represented by the cash budget control section of this diagram.*

since these will affect your investment periods and decisions. For general business use, however, simplicity and convenience should temper absolute accuracy.)

If you are in a preopening phase, work with the terms of trade quoted by each of your suppliers and with the credit terms and options you intend to offer your customers. If you deal in credit card sales, the cash moving date will depend on your arrangement with the bank and the issuing company. Remember, it is only cash to you when you can use it.

(*Note:* A credit card purchase is really two flows, an inflow from the buyer to you and an outflow from you to the bank for administrative costs. *Do not* simply log the net amount as an inflow. This will confuse your projections. You will show both smaller inflows and smaller outflows than there really are. You will also never be able to determine whether accepting credit card sales makes financial sense for your business.)

Once you have your two complete lists, organize each list (separately) by month and by source or use, e.g., inflows from widgets versus inflows from sky hooks, outflows for inventory versus outflows for space rental. The supporting schedules for cash inflows and cash outflows should be detailed. Your summary cash budget, however, is intended to be just that, a summary of both by category. The summary form will help you to spot problem areas and to see the broad picture of how cash works in and through your company.

## Now What Do I Have?

If you are using existing data, you have just built yourself a picture of what last year was really like. If you believe that next year is going to be similar, you now have a pattern for your projections for next year. If you know that next year will be different for specific reasons, consider how those reasons will affect the amount and timing of your inflows and outflows of cash. You can then adjust your projected cash flow to account for those differences. Your cash budget is a very flexible tool for planning and control. When you have projected (or developed) your cash budget for next year, take a look at the status section of the cash budget summary. Right there, for you to look at, will be your projected month-end cash position for each month of the year. The cumulative cash line (row 30) lets you know immediately where you are likely to stand. If this item is negative, check its trend. Is it getting consistently more negative? Or does it begin to get smaller as you move through the year? How large is the largest negative cumulative cash figure for the year? How large is the largest cumulative positive cash balance for the year?

Depending on the answers to these questions, you can begin to consider how to deal with the potential cash issues. If, for example, the flow is negative, but not monstrously so, and you have larger positive balances within the year, you might consider a working capital loan. If the numbers are *very* large and negative, you might want to seek longer-term or permanent financing. If the negatives are fairly small and/or intermittent, you might begin to consider some of the ways of modifying the flows that we will discuss later in this book. If the numbers are all positive and large, you might want to consider some of the investment strategies described later in the book.

In short, what you get for having come this far is a basis for testing your views of problems and potential solutions, and an early warning device. For those of us who really like "no surprises" management, a cash budget is a definite boon.

## Using Cash Budgets in Business Situations

We promised you a working tool to help you control your company better. Until now, we have floated tantalizing possibilities before you. In this section, we will begin to fulfill our end of the deal. Here we will briefly describe some situations in which you can use your cash budget to answer questions that may have or are likely to arise in the normal course of your business life. Some of these situations will be expanded further in later chapters of this book.

### Situation 1 Introducing a New Product

Your company manufactures widgets. One of your designers has come up with an advanced-design widget that is clearly superior to anything on the market—including your own products. You can't wait to get the new widget on the market because you know that it will make your fortune and your company's reputation in the widget field.

There are only two problems with this sure-fire success. The design is so new that your equipment will not be able to produce it. A new frammistat, the machine you need, costs $100,000. You don't happen to have $100,000 free at the moment. Second, there is a curing process required to ensure that the widget casing is sufficiently hard to withstand the stresses placed on it during normal operation. Thus, even with the new frammistat, you will not be able to actually deliver an enhanced widget for three months after the first one comes off your assembly line.

Now obviously, a cash budget cannot make the frammistat magically appear in your shop. Nor can it reduce the length of time the casing takes to cure. But it can tell you how much cash you will have to put up in order to get your enhanced widget to market. And it can tell you when you will begin to get cash out of your new widget line.

To find out this vital information, you simply think through and then enter the additional cash requirements and the additional cash inflows on your existing cash budget. You'll need the frammistat, for example, before you even go into production. And you'll need whatever additional raw materials are required to start the new widget line. No cash will come in from the new line until at least three months after your first enhanced widget is completed. Furthermore, the terms you normally give your customers allow them to come up with cash a full 30 days after their purchases.

Once you have entered all additional inflows and outflows and recalculated the cash budget, your cumulative cash line will show you instantly how much extra cash you will need to launch your new line. Go to the largest negative number on this line. If you extend the cash projection far enough into the future, you can find the point at which the new widget line will begin to generate positive cash. If you use the net cash flow line, you will see when it provides net additions to your company's cash balance on a monthly basis. Using the cumulative cash line, you can find the point at which the new widget generates enough cash to recoup your investment in it.

## Situation 2 Getting a Loan

Given the cost of the frammistat described, it is entirely likely that you will need a loan to finance it. (The bank will probably not be interested in also financing the additional operating costs of your new product—materials, advertising costs, etc.) You know the cost of the machine. Your cash budget can tell you whether you will be able to repay the loan in the installments required and on the terms that are likely.

Simply enter the amount of the loan you are contemplating in the new loans section of your cash budget. Also enter the amounts that you expect to have to come up with monthly to cover principal *and* interest. Your cumulative cash after new loans line will tell you whether you can do it. If you can, go right on down to the bank. If not, try reworking the loan numbers—but stay reasonable! It has been a long time since banks have made loans at 3%, deferring repayment for three years. (You might also try reducing your costs [outflows] or increasing other income.)

Not only does your cash budget serve as a worksheet in this situation, it is also a demonstration document for your bank. It will support your loan application (assuming that it shows that your company is good for the money).

(*Note:* We have used a manufacturing company as our example here. The same principles apply to launching a new sales line or offering a new service. The costs and flows would be different, though. For example, the additional outflows associated with a service might include some investments in high-powered staff as well as in equipment. For a new retail line, the timing of the outflows is likely to be closer to the timing of the inflows. Other differences will exist, just as we noted that no company's cash flow is exactly like another's. *The principles, however, are the same for all companies.*)

## Situation 3 Avoiding Bankruptcy

Your retail garden supplies company is, obviously, highly seasonal. You must purchase your inventory in advance of the sales season for your goods. This year, two things have occurred that are about to make your life miserable. The cost of your normal inventory has risen significantly. You also decided to stock certain new types of garden equipment.

Your projected cash budget shows a massive shortfall for May and June. Working with the cash budget can also show you ways to deal with that shortfall. First, you can talk to your normal suppliers and to new and potential suppliers about deferring the purchase costs of some of your inventory. (In some highly seasonal businesses, such inventory financing plans are common.) Second, you can talk to your bank about a short-term working capital loan, to be repaid in September and October when you expect to have cash surpluses.

Your cash budget will allow you to test the results of each of these approaches. Is a new inventory financing plan adequate? How many of your suppliers have to agree before this becomes a workable solution for you? Which suppliers are key to this approach? Will it work if you combine both approaches? (And the old standby, "How much do you need to borrow, and when can you pay it back?")

(*Note:* Do you see now why we said that you have to be willing to commit to your own projections? Your bank's platform is no place to look or sound shaky about your cash budget projections.)

There are many other situations in which a cash budget will provide you with control and flexibility. Some are described in following chapters. The examples shown here are mainly to let you see that the cash budget is useful and well worth the initial time it will take to develop your first set of numbers—a current year (if one exists) and a year of projection.

We firmly believe that it is worth the time and effort to develop your cash budget. Your gains are not only the ability to see probable results in advance and to test alternative solutions. You will also gain a much better understanding of the underlying structure and operation of your business. While this may merely confirm your "good gut feel" for what is going on and how the business works, confirmation never hurts. A cash budget makes that "gut feel" concrete. And you can't take "good gut feel" to the bank.

# The Cash Budget Summary Spreadsheet

In this chapter you'll use Framework to create the cash budget summary spreadsheet for budgeting and keeping track of your cash inflows and outflows over a twelve-month period. First you'll create the spreadsheet and enter sample numbers for monthly cash inflows and outflows. The annual totals and net and cumulative cash flows will be automatically calculated by formulas that you enter in the spreadsheet. Next, you'll create a second spreadsheet that is linked to the first and that provides data ranges for graphs you will create in the next step. You'll then move the spreadsheets and graphs into a containing frame so they can be saved and retrieved together. Finally, you'll change the sample numbers on the spreadsheet and explore "What If" questions — for instance, "What if your cash inflows increase or decrease?"

After this, you'll be able to call up the cash budget summary whenever you want to explore and graph your own cash flows or ask "What If" questions.

Although the cash budget summary will be adapted later for your own business, we'll use the "case study" approach to guide you as you enter it into the computer. Let's assume that you are the owner or manager of a retail store that does the largest share of its business during the pre-Christmas season, with a second but lower sales peak in the back-to-school period of August and September. We'll enter labels and sample numbers for cash receipts and expenses that reflect this seasonal sales pattern as well as your inventory, accounting, and collection policies.

This approach enables you to check the results of your formulas against those given in this book to make sure you have entered them correctly. More important, the sample numbers demonstrate the structure of the cash budget, and show you how it will behave when you explore "What Ifs." When the budget is finished, you can clear the sample numbers from the spreadsheet to make room for your own data.

## The Cash Budget Summary Spreadsheet

| | | A | B | C | D | E | F | G | H | I | J | K | L | M | N |
|---|---|---|---|---|---|---|---|---|---|---|---|---|---|---|---|
| 1 | 1 | CASH BUDGET SUMMARY - FIRST YEAR | Sep 87 | Oct 87 | Nov 87 | Dec 87 | Jan 88 | Feb 88 | Mar 88 | Apr 88 | May 88 | Jun 88 | Jul 88 | Aug 88 | Total |
| 2 | 2 | [CASH INFLOWS] | | | | | | | | | | | | | |
| | 3 | Cash receipts | $20,000 | $15,000 | $30,000 | $40,000 | $10,000 | $10,000 | $15,000 | $15,000 | $15,000 | $10,[illegible]00 | $10,000 | $20,000 | $210,000 |
| | 4 | [..............................] | | | | | | | | | | | | | 0 |
| | 5 | [..............................] | | | | | | | | | | | | | 0 |
| | 6 | [..............................] | | | | | | | | | | | | | 0 |
| | 7 | [..............................] | | | | | | | | | | | | | 0 |
| | 8 | [..............................] | | | | | | | | | | | | | 0 |
| | 9 | [..............................] | | | | | | | | | | | | | 0 |
| | 10 | [..............................] | | | | | | | | | | | | | 0 |
| | 11 | [..............................] | | | | | | | | | | | | | 0 |
| | 12 | ------------------------------ | | | | | | | | | | | | | |
| | 13 | Total cash inflows | 20,000 | 15,000 | 30,000 | 40,000 | 10,000 | 10,000 | 15,000 | 15,000 | 15,000 | 10,[illegible]00 | 10,000 | 20,000 | 210,000 |
| | 14 | ============================== | | | | | | | | | | | | | |
| 3 | 15 | [CASH OUTFLOWS] | | | | | | | | | | | | | |
| | 16 | Inventory purchases | 7,500 | 15,000 | 20,000 | 5,000 | 5,000 | 7,500 | 7,500 | 7,500 | 5,000 | 5,[illegible]00 | 10,000 | 12,500 | 107,500 |
| | 17 | Space costs | 1,200 | 1,200 | 1,400 | 1,500 | 1,500 | 1,500 | 1,400 | 1,300 | 1,200 | 1,[illegible]00 | 1,200 | 1,200 | 15,800 |
| | 18 | Personnel costs | 3,000 | 3,000 | 4,300 | 4,300 | 3,200 | 3,200 | 3,200 | 3,200 | 3,200 | 3,[illegible]00 | 3,600 | 3,600 | 41,000 |
| | 19 | Other G&A costs | 3,500 | 3,500 | 4,000 | 3,500 | 3,500 | 4,000 | 3,500 | 3,500 | 4,000 | 3,[illegible]00 | 3,500 | 4,000 | 44,000 |
| | 20 | [..............................] | | | | | | | | | | | | | 0 |
| | 21 | [..............................] | | | | | | | | | | | | | 0 |
| | 22 | [..............................] | | | | | | | | | | | | | 0 |
| | 23 | [..............................] | | | | | | | | | | | | | 0 |
| | 24 | [..............................] | | | | | | | | | | | | | 0 |
| | 25 | ------------------------------ | | | | | | | | | | | | | |
| | 26 | Total cash outflows | 15,200 | 22,700 | 29,700 | 14,300 | 13,200 | 16,200 | 15,600 | 15,500 | 13,400 | 12,[illegible]0 | 18,300 | 21,300 | 208,300 |
| | 27 | ============================== | | | | | | | | | | | | | |
| 4 | 28 | Opening cash balance | 10,000 | | | | | | | | | | | | |
| | 29 | Net monthly cash flow | 4,800 | (7,700) | 300 | 25,700 | (3,200) | (6,200) | (600) | (500) | 1,600 | (2,[illegible]0) | (8,300) | (1,300) | 1,700 |
| | 30 | Cumulative cash before loans | 14,800 | 7,100 | 7,400 | 33,100 | 29,900 | 23,700 | 23,100 | 22,600 | 24,200 | 21,[illegible]0 | 13,000 | 11,700 | 11,700 |
| | 31 | ============================== | | | | | | | | | | | | | |
| | 32 | New loans | | | | | | | | | | | | | 0 |
| | 33 | Cumulative cash after loans | 14,800 | 7,100 | 7,400 | 33,100 | 29,900 | 23,700 | 23,100 | 22,600 | 24,200 | 21,[illegible]0 | 13,000 | 11,700 | 11,700 |
| | 34 | ============================== | | | | | | | | | | | | | |

*The cash budget summary spreadsheet has four parts: headings (**1**) identify the spreadsheet and date the monthly columns; the cash inflows section (**2**) records your monthly cash income; the cash outflows section (**3**) records your monthly cash payments; and the summary section (**4**) automatically calculates your net monthly cash flow and cumulative cash balance at the end of every month. You can also enter new loans to see their effect on the cumulative cash balance.*

## The Cash Budget Graph Ranges Spreadsheet

| | | A | B | C | D | E | F | G | H | I | J | K | L | M |
|---|---|---|---|---|---|---|---|---|---|---|---|---|---|---|
| | 1 | CASH BUDGET SUMMARY - FIRST YEAR | Sep 87 | Oct 87 | Nov 87 | Dec 87 | Jan 88 | Feb 88 | Mar 88 | Apr 88 | May 88 | Jun 88 | Jul 88 | Aug 88 |
| 1 | 2 | Total cash inflows | 20,000 | 15,000 | 30,000 | 40,000 | 10,000 | 10,000 | 15,000 | 15,000 | 15,000 | 10,0[illegible] | 10,000 | 20,000 |
| | 3 | Total cash outflows | 15,200 | 22,700 | 29,700 | 14,300 | 13,200 | 16,200 | 15,600 | 15,500 | 13,400 | 12,90[illegible] | 18,300 | 21,300 |
| | 4 | Net monthly cash flow | 4,800 | (7,700) | 300 | 25,700 | (3,200) | (6,200) | (600) | (500) | 1,600 | (2,9[illegible]) | (8,300) | (1,300) |
| | 5 | Cumulative cash before loans | 14,800 | 7,100 | 7,400 | 33,100 | 29,900 | 23,700 | 23,100 | 22,600 | 24,200 | 21,30[illegible] | 13,000 | 11,700 |
| | 6 | Cumulative cash after loans | 14,800 | 7,100 | 7,400 | 33,100 | 29,900 | 23,700 | 23,100 | 22,600 | 24,200 | 21,30[illegible] | 13,000 | 11,700 |
| | 7 | | | | | | | | | | | #GRAPH | #GRAPH | #GRAPH |

*The cash budget ranges spreadsheet pulls together into adjacent rows the key lines (**1**) from the cash budget summary that are to be plotted on graphs. It is linked to the cash budget summary spreadsheet so any changes made are automatically reflected here.*

### Line Graph

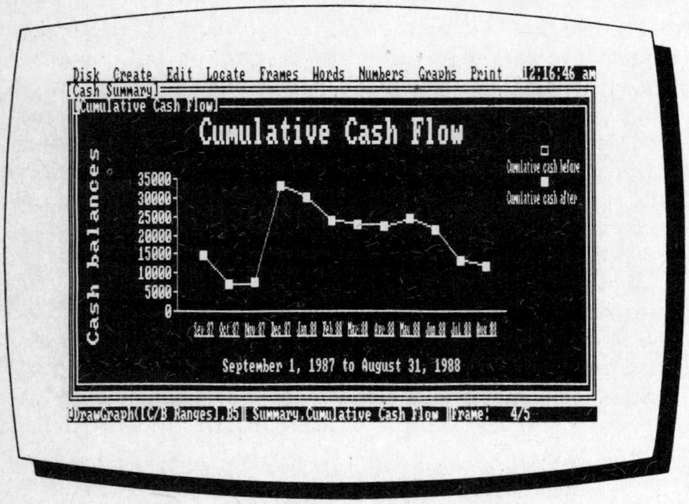


*The line graph shows the cumulative cash balance at the end of every month as well as the cash balance after loans and loan payments.*

### Bar Graph

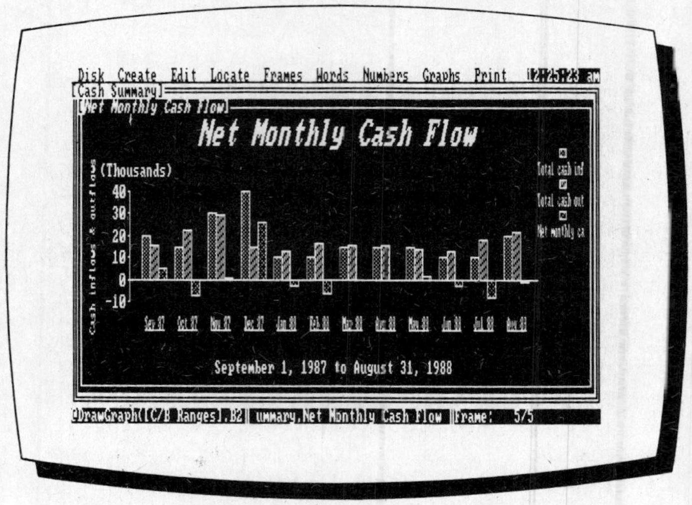


*The bar graph shows the net monthly cash flow—the net result for each month of cash flowing into and out of your business.*

#### Important!

This section has been designed as a tutorial on Framework spreadsheets and graphs. If you are not familiar with Framework, *do not skip this section*; follow all the steps for entering the cash budget summary spreadsheets and creating the graphs. By the end of this chapter, you'll know all you need to know about the Framework program, and you should find the abbreviated instructions beginning in Chapter 4 easy to follow.

If you're already familiar with Framework, feel free to start anywhere you like in this book, although it may be helpful to enter the spreadsheets in the order presented.

A special disk to accompany **Cash Flow Management with Framework** is available. Although the disk is not essential, it will save you time and energy because it contains all the spreadsheets used in this book so you won't have to enter them yourself. If you did not purchase the disk edition of this book, and you want to order the disk, use the Disk Order Form on the last page of the book.

### Pie Chart

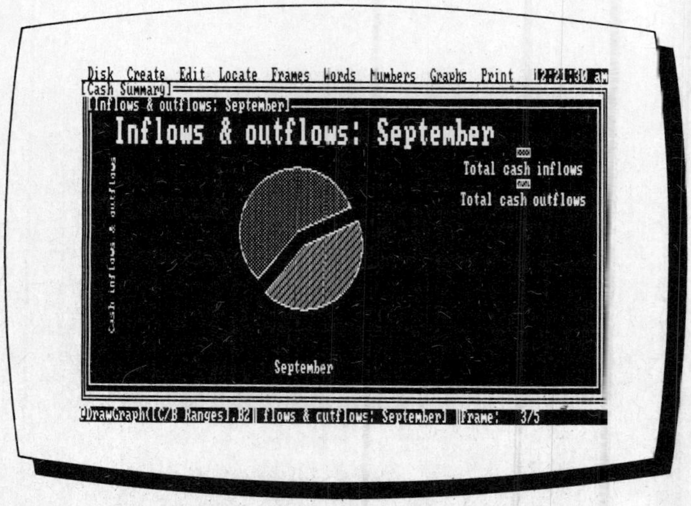


*The pie chart shows cash inflows and outflows for a single month.*

# Entering the Cash Budget Summary

Here are the steps you'll follow in this section:

**Step 1** Load Framework
**Step 2** Create a spreadsheet frame
**Step 3** Enter headings
**Step 4** Enter cash inflows
**Step 5** Enter cash outflows
**Step 6** Enter summary section
**Step 7** Save your work

## Step 1 Load Framework

Framework is easy to load (called "booting") if you have transferred your computer's operating system (COMMAND.COM file), and system (Sys B:), to the disk (see Tips on "Making Framework Self-Booting" on page 30). With these files on the disk you only need to insert System Disk #1 into drive A and turn on the computer (if it's already on, hold down the **Ctrl** and **Alt** keys while you press the **Del** key). You will then be asked to enter the date and time, and in a few seconds a message will appear on the screen asking you to insert System Disk #2, and press ⏎.

Framework can also be loaded from DOS when the system prompt A> is on the screen. Just insert System Disk #1, in drive A, type **FW** (in upper- or lower-case letters) and press ⏎.

If your computer has an internal clock you can add an AUTOEXEC (AUTOmatically EXECuted) file (see Tips on "AUTOEXEC Files" on page 32) to load the program without your having to enter the time and date.

The following step-by-step tutorial on loading the program assumes you have transferred the system to the disk but don't have a clock that is set automatically by an Autoexec file. If you are using a computer with a hard disk drive, see Tips on "Making Framework Self-Booting."

## Get Ready

We are finally ready to sit down at the computer and start building the spreadsheet! But before you begin, be sure you have the following materials.

**1** Framework Program Disks
Framework System Disk #1
Framework System Disk #2
Framework Utility Disk

**2** Blank, formatted double-sided floppy disks to save your work if you aren't using a computer with a hard disk drive. If you are using a hard disk drive, these disks (and labels for them) are optional and could be used for making backup copies of your work. See Tips on "Formatting Framework Data Disks."

**3** Disk labels to identify blank disks. Get in the habit right now of putting clear, informative labels on each disk. Assign each new disk a number or label, such as "Framework #1" or "Framework, Cash Flow." Even light pressure with a ball-point pen can damage the sensitive recording surface of a disk, so fill out the labels *before* you affix them to the disk (or use a felt-tip pen and very light pressure if you must write on a label already on a disk).

**4** An MS- or PC-DOS 2.0 version (or later) system disk. The DOS operating system disk isn't necessary if the operating system has been copied to your Framework disk. You should have it available, however, to copy and format disks and to load the graphics program used to print graphs that appear on the screen.

Now we're ready to load the program.

## Tips Formatting Framework Data Disks

Formatting is the process of preparing a blank disk to work with your specific type of computer. Until a disk has been formatted, it is useless; you cannot store any files on it.

You can format a disk directly from Framework either with the DiskUtil program on the Utility disk or from within a DOS Access frame. If you use a DOS Access frame, copy the FORMAT.COM file from the DOS disk onto System Disk #2 before loading Framework so that you don't have to swap disks.

☐ *On a two-floppy system:* With the system prompt A> on the screen, insert the DOS disk in drive A and the disk to be formatted in drive B. Type **Format B:**.

☐ *On a hard disk system:* With the system prompt C> on the screen, insert the disk to be formatted in drive A and type **Format A:**.

☐ The prompt Insert diskette to be formatted in drive B: and Strike any key when ready will be displayed. Make sure that the disk in drive B is the disk you want to format. Press ⏎ when ready.

☐ The message Formatting will be displayed while the disk is being formatted. When formatting is complete, the number of bytes available will be displayed and you will be asked if you want to format another disk. To format another disk, type **Y**. To return to the operating system, type **N**.

## Tips Making Framework Self-Booting

A self-booting disk loads DOS into memory. It can be used to start the computer without having to use the DOS System Disk. If your Framework System Disk is not already bootable (this is frequently done by the dealer), you can easily make it so. All you need to do is transfer the DOS System and COMMAND.COM files to Framework System Disk #1.

**To make Framework System Disk #1 Self-Booting on a Floppy Disk System:**
**Step 1** Load DOS. Insert the DOS disk into disk drive A and turn the computer on. If the computer was already on, press **Ctrl-Alt-Del**. The system prompt A> will appear on the screen.

**Step 2** Keep the DOS disk in drive A and place Framework System Disk #1 in drive B. Type **SYS B:** and press ↵. In a few moments the message System transferred will be displayed and the DOS prompt A> will reappear.

**Step 3** Now copy the COMMAND.COM file onto System Disk #1. Type **COPY COMMAND.COM B:** and press ↵. When the file is transferred, the message 1 File(s) copied will be displayed and the DOS prompt A> will appear.

**Step 4** Framework System Disk #1 is now self-booting. Remove the DOS disk from drive A and insert System Disk #1 in its place. We can start the computer from System Disk #1 by turning off the computer and turning it back on or by rebooting with the **Ctrl-Alt-Del** sequence. Now DOS is loaded and the system date and time prompts are displayed without using the DOS Disk.

**On a Hard Disk System:**
If you are using a computer that contains a hard disk, chances are that you already boot from the hard disk drive. You can check this by turning on the machine with no disk in the floppy drive. If you receive a DOS prompt, the hard disk is set up with the operating system. If you receive an error message like Non-system Disk or Disk Error, the operating system is not on the hard disk drive. See the DOS manual for the procedures necessary if this is the case.

## Tips Installing Framework

To install Framework on either a two-floppy system or a system containing a hard disk, follow the same basic procedures.

**Step 1** Load DOS. Make sure that the DOS prompt is A>. If you load DOS from a hard disk, type **A:** ↵ to receive the A> system prompt.

**Step 2** Insert Framework System Disk #1 in drive A. Type **Install** and press ↵. A description of the Framework installation procedure will be displayed on the screen. FOR HARD DISK USERS ONLY: If you are using a hard disk, you must first copy the Framework files from all three disks onto it. To do this, type **Harddisk C:** and press ↵, then follow the instructions on the screen. Then continue to Step 3.

**Step 3** Transfer the appropriate drivers. You have three possible driver options to install: Printer drivers, Screen drivers, and Telecommunications drivers. If you are using an IBM PC or PC/XT with a monochrome monitor and a color/graphics adaptor, you will not have to install the screen drivers. To install each driver, type its name, press ↵, and follow the instructions as they are displayed on the screen. For example, to install the printer drivers, at the DOS prompt type **Printer** and press ↵. The instructions for installing the printer drivers will be displayed on the screen.

**Running Framework from a Hard Disk**

- ☐ Framework can be loaded and run from your hard disk provided you keep System Disk #1 in the floppy drive while you are loading the program. This is necessary because System Disk #1 contains a copy-protected sector on the disk that Framework looks for during loading. If the sector is not found (if you don't have System Disk #1 in the floppy drive when loading Framework), you will receive the message Unauthorized duplicate and the program will not load.
- ☐ If Framework is installed in a subdirectory on the hard disk, you must make sure that the proper directory is searched when loading Framework. This can be done either by changing the directory on the hard disk before loading Framework, or by using a DOS CONFIG.SYS file to include the subdirectory in the list of directories that DOS searches when looking for a file. See the DOS manual for the procedures involved in creating a CONFIG.SYS file.

## Insert System Disk #1

Insert Framework System Disk #1 into drive A (usually the drive on the left if the drives are side by side, or the drive on top if the drives are stacked vertically). Keep the label side of the disk on top, and hold the disk by the label as you insert the disk into the drive. Gently close the disk drive door.

If you are using a computer without a hard disk drive, insert a formatted disk onto which you will save your work into drive B (the one on the right or bottom). Gently close the drive door.

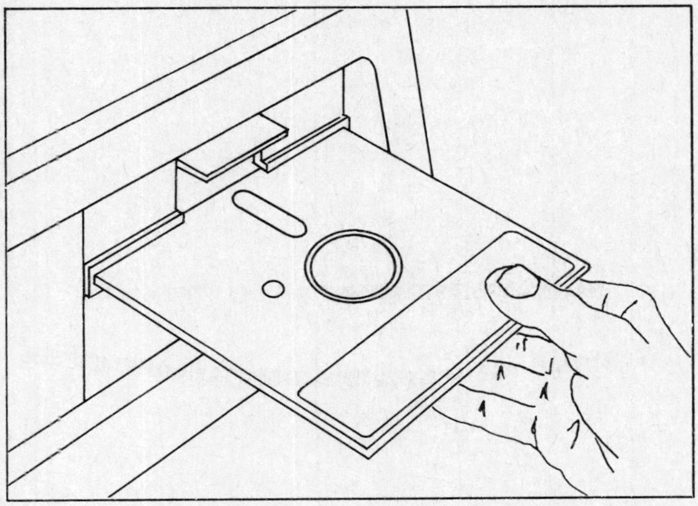

## Load DOS

With the System Disk #1 inserted into drive A, you are ready for the next step. This step, as you have already seen, depends on how your disk has been set up. If you try this step and the program doesn't load, it is not a "self-booting" disk.

**1 If the computer is off,** turn it on.

**2 If you have been working on another program** on an IBM PC, and the computer is on but the system prompt A:> isn't on the screen (be sure you have saved your previous work), then: hold down **Ctrl** and **Alt** keys and press the **Del** (delete) key.

If your computer has an internal clock that automatically enters the time and date, you can skip the next step.

## Enter the Date and Time

If you just turned on the computer, or used the **Ctrl, Alt,** and **Del** keys to load the program, and your computer doesn't have an internal clock, you will now be asked to enter the date and then the time. You can press ↵ to bypass entering each of these, but, since they are used to identify the files that you save on your disks so you can locate the most recent version, you should get into the habit of entering them.

The date is entered by typing the number of the month, a hyphen (-) or slash (**/**), the number of the day, another hyphen (- or slash (**/**), the last two digits of the year, and then pressing ↵.

*To enter the date:*

**Type 6/1/87** (for June 1, 1987) or **6-1-87**

**Press** ↵

The time is entered by typing in the number of the hour and minutes separated by a colon (**:**). Time is given in international terms — 1 PM is entered as 13:00, 2 PM is 14:00, and so on.

*To enter the time:*

**Type 15:30** (for 3:30 PM)

**Press** ↵

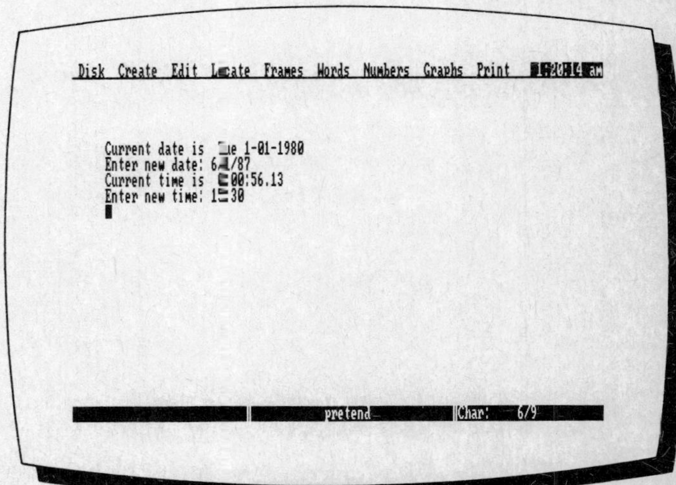

## Load Framework

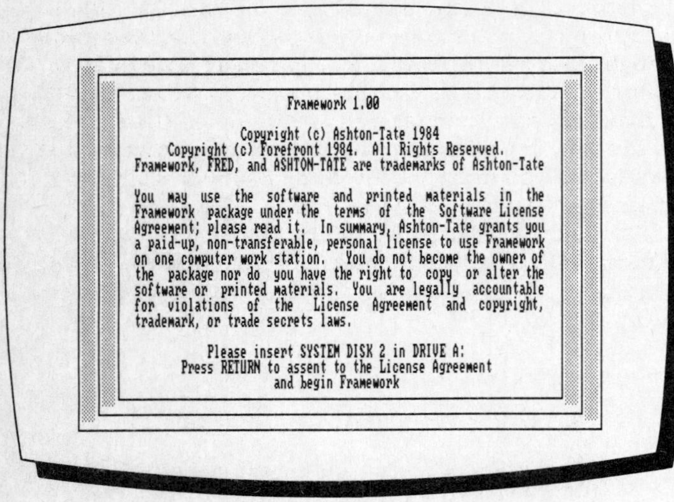


If the system prompt A:> is on the screen, type **FW** (you can use upper- or lower-case letters) and press ↵. The previous display will be cleared from the screen and the disk drive will spin as the Framework program is loaded and the next frame appears. A graphic design appears on the screen briefly and then dissolves into a summary of the Framework copyright notice and license agreement. This frame also identifies the version number of your Framework program.

## Insert System Disk #2

Follow the instructions at the bottom of the frame of text containing the copyright notice and license agreement. Remove System Disk #1, insert System Disk #2 into drive A, and press ↵ to continue. In a few moments the Framework "desktop" will appear on the screen. You are now ready to begin your work.

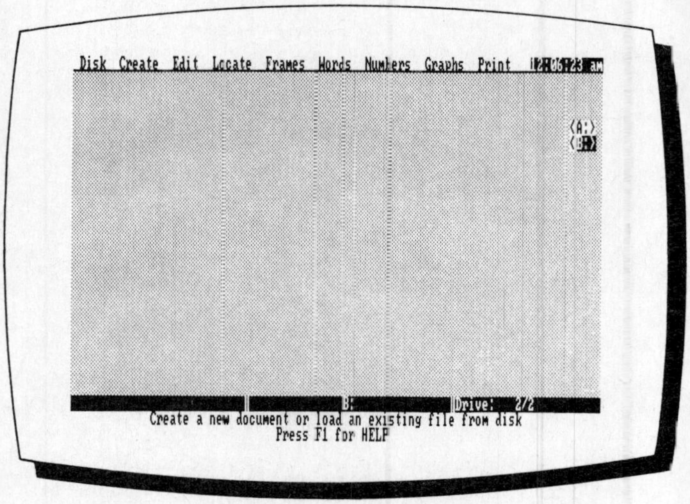


## Tips AUTOEXEC Files

You can load Framework automatically using a DOS AUTOEXEC (AUTOmatic EXECution) batch file. Each time the computer is booted, DOS checks for an AUTOEXEC file. If it exists, the instructions contained in that file will be carried out automatically. If no AUTOEXEC file exists, DOS asks for the date and time and then waits for further input.

- ☐ Use an AUTOEXEC file to perform all the routine tasks you do each time you turn on the computer. For example, if your computer has a built-in clock, you can use an AUTOEXEC file on Framework System Disk #1 to load the clock program and then enter Framework.
- ☐ An AUTOEXEC file is called a batch file because it batches together a series of commands you want the computer to perform automatically.
- ☐ When you load Framework through an AUTOEXEC batch file, quitting the program will cause the next command in the AUTOEXEC file to be carried out. On a two-floppy-disk system, System Disk #2 may be in drive A when you quit Framework, even though you started the AUTOEXEC file from System Disk #1. If this should happen you will receive the message Insert disk with batch file and press any key when ready. Insert System Disk #1 in the drive and press any key. The batch file will finish and you will return to the DOS prompt.
- ☐ To see if you have an AUTOEXEC batch file on a disk, use the DOS command DIR. At the DOS prompt, type **Dir AUTOEXEC.BAT** and press ↵.
- ☐ To view the contents of an AUTOEXEC file, use the DOS command TYPE. At the DOS prompt, type **Type AUTOEXEC.BAT** and press ↵. The contents of the file will be displayed on the screen

## Step 2 Create a Spreadsheet Frame

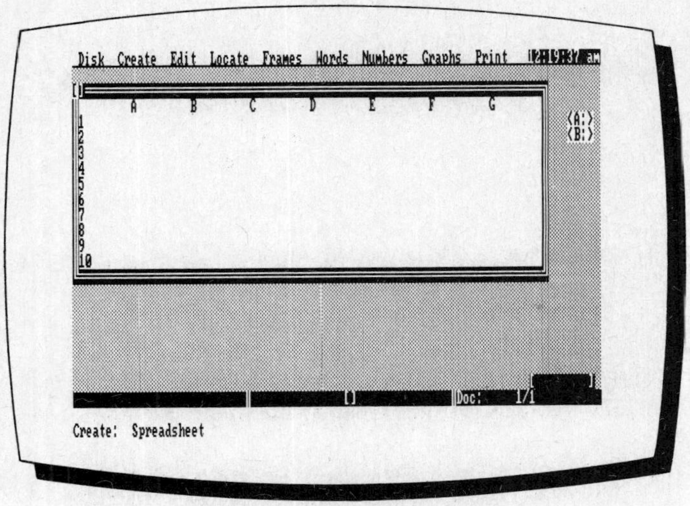


When a spreadsheet frame is created, it rests on the desktop just like other frames. However, the difference between this frame and other types lies in the organization inside the frame. A spreadsheet is much like an accountant's ledger pad with rows and columns forming a grid. As in a ledger pad, you can enter labels and numbers into the squares where rows and columns intersect (in Framework these are called "cells"). Unlike a ledger pad, however, Framework allows you to enter *formulas* in cells: these formulas will automatically calculate and display values based on entries made in other cells on the spreadsheet. For example, you can enter a formula that calculates net monthly cash flow as being equal to monthly cash inflows minus monthly cash outflows; then whenever you make a change to cash inflows or cash outflows, monthly net cash flow will automatically be recalculated.

Before you can create a spreadsheet frame, the Framework desktop must be on the screen. You then create the spreadsheet using the Create menu from the menu bar. If you know the approximate size of the spreadsheet you need, you can specify the dimensions before you create it. If you aren't sure of the size, you can use the *default* setting on the menu; it will create a spreadsheet 14 columns wide and 14 rows deep *or* the same size as your most recently created spreadsheet. You can always change the size of any spreadsheet later by adding or deleting rows and columns.

## Set the Width and Height

The automatic (*default*) settings for the width and height on a spreadsheet are 14 columns across and 14 rows deep. We want to create a spreadsheet that is 14 columns across and 34 rows deep; therefore, we will leave the default setting for width and change the setting for height. To change the number of rows in the spreadsheet before it is created, you use the Height choice on the Create menu.

*To set the height of the spreadsheet to 34 rows:*

**Press** **Ins** to call up the menu bar

**Highlight** Create on the menu bar
Height on the Create menu

**Press** ⏎ to bring the current setting to the edit line

**Type** **34** (for 34 rows)

**Press** ⏎

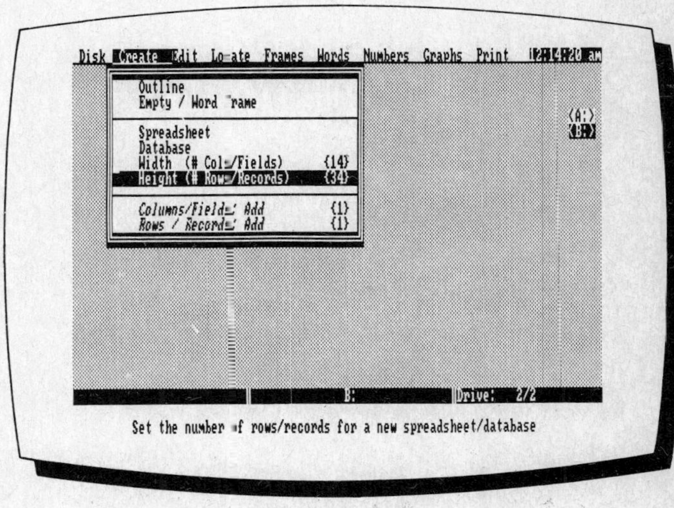


**Result** When Height is selected from the Create menu, the default setting of 14 rows appears on the edit line at the bottom of the screen. When you type in the number **34** and press ⏎, the new setting appears in the curly braces next to the Height choice on the menu.

## Tips Using Pull-Down Menus

There are two ways to pull down menus from the menu bar.

1 Press the **Ins** key to call up the most recently used menu command. If you want to choose another menu, use → and ← to move the highlight along the menu bar to the command you want. As you do so, a brief description of the highlighted command on the menu appears on the message line at the bottom of the screen.

2 Hold down **Ctrl** and press the first letter in the menu name.

If you decide not to make a selection from one of the menus, you can return to the desktop by pressing **Up Level (Gray −)** or **Esc**.

**Keys Used to Pull Down Menus**

| KEYS | EFFECT |
|---|---|
| **Ins** | Calls up most recently used menu. |
| **Ctrl**-first letter | Calls up a specific menu. |
| → | Moves highlight right along the menu bar. |
| ← | Moves highlight left along the menu bar. |
| **Esc** | Clears menu without making a selection. |
| **Up Level (Gray −)** | Clears menu without making a selection. |

## Tips Making Selections from a Menu

When a menu is pulled down, you can select commands in one of two ways:

1 Using ↑ and ↓ to move the highlight over the command and pressing ↵ or the **Ins** key.

2 Typing the first letter of the command (for example, **E** for Empty/Word Frame).

**Keys Used in Pull-Down Menus**

| KEYS | EFFECT |
|---|---|
| ↓ | Moves highlight down to next command. |
| ↑ | Moves highlight up to previous command. |
| **Home** | Moves highlight up to first menu command. |
| **End** | Moves highlight down to last menu command. |
| **PgUp** | Moves highlight up to previous command. |
| **PgDn** | Moves highlight down to next command |
| ↵ | Selects a highlighted choice on menu. |
| **Ins** | Selects a highlighted choice on menu. |
| First letter | Selects from menu without highlighting. |
| **Esc** | Clears menu without making a selection |

## Tips Using Submenus

Commands preceded with a ▶ on the pull-down menus indicate submenus containing additional commands. The submenus can be opened by typing the first letter of their name or by highlighting them and pressing **Ins, Down Level (Gray +)**, or ↵. If you decide not to make a selection, you can exit back to the desktop or to the menu by pressing **Esc** or **Up Level (Gray −)**.

**Keys Used in Submenus**

| KEYS | EFFECT |
|---|---|
| ↵ | Calls up a highlighted submenu. |
| **Esc** | Leaves submenu and returns highlight to main menu. |
| **Up Level (Gray −)** | Leaves submenu and returns highlight to main menu. |
| ← | Leaves submenu and returns highlight to main menu. |
| → | Leaves submenu and returns highlight to main menu. |

## Create the Spreadsheet

In many cases you won't know the exact size of the spreadsheet you want. In those cases you might begin with this step. The resulting spreadsheet will be 14 columns wide and 14 rows deep—or, if you have previously created a spreadsheet it will be the same size as the one most recently created (since the settings are "remembered" by Framework until they are changed or until the program is reloaded).

*To create a spreadsheet:*

**Press** **Ins** and pull down the Create menu (if it is not already on your screen)

**Highlight** Spreadsheet on the Create menu

**Press** ⏎

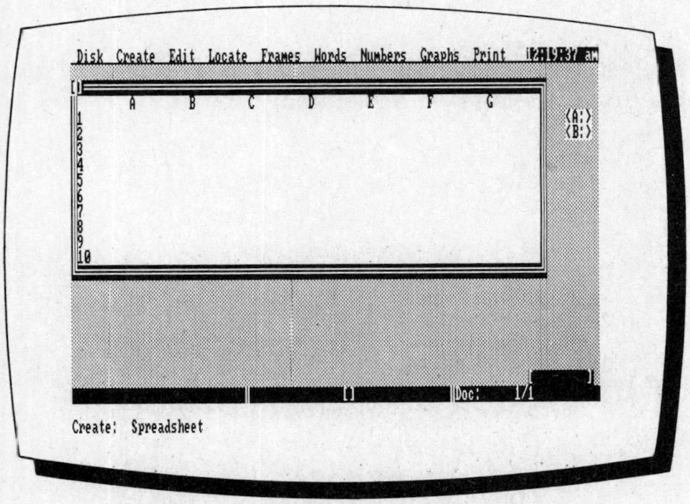


**Result** An empty spreadsheet frame appears on the desktop with column letters across the top and row numbers down the left side. A tray for the frame appears in the lower-right corner of the screen. The cursor is blinking and is on the frame border.

*To label the frame:*

**Type** **Cash Budget**

**Press** ⏎

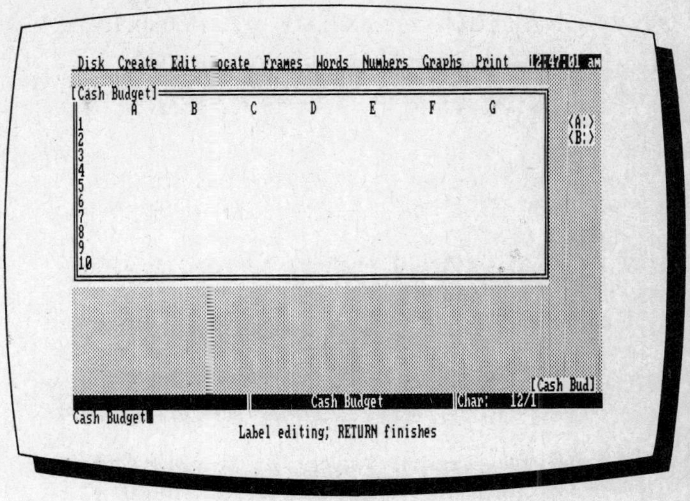


**Result** As you type, the letters appear in the edit line of the message area (so you can correct mistakes), on the frame border, and in the desktop tray in the lower-right corner. When you press ⏎, the label is entered and the cursor moves back to the frame border.

*To move cursor into the frame:*

**Press** **Down Level (Gray +)**

*To enter a sample number (which we'll delete after we practice entering and formatting it):*

**Highlight** A1 (the cursor should already be there)

**Type** **10000**

**Press** ⏎

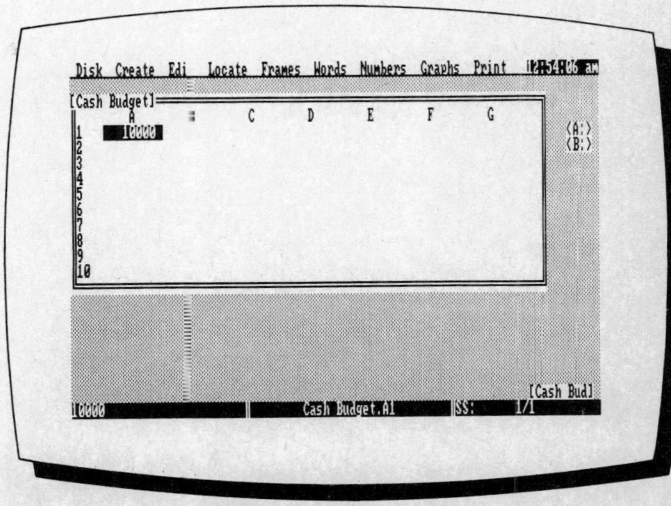

## Tips Entering and Editing Frame Labels

Labels are entered on the frame border by moving the cursor to the border and typing them in (they can be up to 32,000 characters).

To edit a label that has already been entered, highlight the frame and press the **Space Bar** or retype the label.

If you delete a frame label by mistake, you can usually restore it with the Undo command on the Edit menu.

Frame without labels cannot be saved, printed, or referred to by formulas in other frames.

If you change the label on a desktop-level frame and then save it, it will be saved under its new name. If you had previously saved the frame with another name, that version still exists under the old name.

If you change the label on a frame, any formulas in other frames that refer to that frame will no longer work.

Any character can be used in a frame label.

The first eight characters of a frame label are used as the file name, with characters that are unacceptable to the operating system being automatically replaced with underscores. For example, a frame labeled 78% Change will be saved to a file named 78__CHAN.FW.

Formulas in one frame can refer to another frame by entering the name of the frame referred to in the formula. For example, to refer to cell A1 in the spreadsheet frame Example, the formula would be **Example.A1**.

## Tips Entering Text

Framework uses the first character typed in a spreadsheet or database to determine whether the entry will be text or a number. The following characters are interpreted as indicating a number or formula: @ # $ ( – . ". If a label begins with one of these characters or with a number, press the **Space Bar** before entering it.

Unless you specify otherwise, text will align with the left edge of the cell. To change the cell alignment, use the commands on the Numbers menu. Text can be centered, right-aligned, or left-aligned.

If text is longer than the cell is wide, it will overflow into the adjacent cells. If those cells contain data, the text will be cut off on the display (the actual cell entry will not be affected).

Text can be carried to other cells using cell references. For example, if cell A2 contains the word January, using the formula +A2 in cell A4 would copy the word January into cell A4.

## Tips Entering Numbers and Formulas

Numbers preceded by a space will be entered as text and cannot be used in formulas.

Numbers can be entered into a spreadsheet using currency symbols and commas to separate thousands or with percentage signs without affecting the style of the display. For example, a percentage can be entered as .10 or 10%; currency can be entered as 1000, $1000, or $1,000.

To change the format of a number or change the alignment in the cell, you use the Numbers menu.

If you enter a number with commas and without a dollar sign, Framework will ignore all digits preceding the comma. For example, entering the number 1,250 will display only 250.

You can enter numbers quickly using the number keypad on the keyboard. Press the **Num Lock** key to enter numbers instead of using the arrow keys. You can move the cursor using the [↵] and [→|] keys so that you don't have to toggle back and forth with the **Num Lock** key.

Numbers are stored in memory with up to 15 digits precision.

Long numbers can be entered using scientific notation. For example, to enter 1,000,000 you can type 1e6. (The "e" tells Framework to repeat 0 a specified number of times, in this case 6.)

The following symbols, when entered as the first character in a cell, are treated as formula or number values: @ # $ ( – . ".

You can change the type of currency used in a spreadsheet or cell with the @Nationalize formula. Framework has currency specifications for the British Pound Sterling, the Japanese Yen, and a self-defined Unit.

You can enter ranges in formulas in two ways:

**1** You can use the **Extend Select (F6)** key to highlight the range.

**2** You can type the cell coordinates for the upper-left and lower-right corners of the range, separated by a colon.

When you want to refer to the current value of a cell instead of the cell address in a formula, finish the cursor pointing by pressing # instead of [↵] .

You can add comments after formulas by typing a semicolon after the last character in a formula followed by the comment. Comments can be added when you enter the formula or later. Any characters following the semicolon and on the same line will be ignored when the formula is calculated.

## Format the Numbers

Formatting commands on the Numbers menu can change the way words and numbers on a spreadsheet are displayed by adding dollar signs, percent signs, commas between thousands, and by selecting the number of decimal places displayed. You can choose to format only selected cells (after highlighting them with the **Extend Select (F6)** and arrow keys) or you can format the entire contents of a frame by highlighting its border when the format commands are selected. In our spreadsheet, we want numbers formatted to show commas between the thousands, and no decimal places.

Before formatting numbers, the cells containing them must be selected. If more than one cell is to be formatted at the same time, you would use the **Extend Select (F6)** key to highlight a range of cells.

**Press** **Up Level (Gray −)** to highlight the frame border
**Ins**

**Highlight** Numbers on the menu bar
Business in the Numbers menu

**Press** ⏎

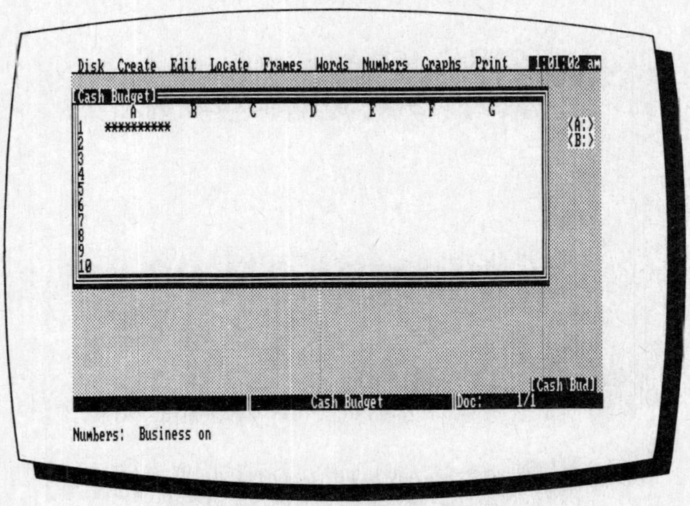


**Result** The pull-down menu disappears and the number you entered in the spreadsheet is displayed as a row of asterisks (********). Don't worry, this indicates that the number and its format together are too large to be displayed in the column width that is currently being used. This can be corrected, and the number displayed, by sizing the column (you'll see how to do this later) or by reformatting the number as you'll do in the next step.

Just as you can add currency symbols (or other formats), you can also control the number of decimal places that are displayed. Although this command changes what you see on the screen, it doesn't change the way Framework recalculates. Numbers out to a maximum of 15 decimal places are stored in memory and used in calculation.

*To change the decimal place setting:*

**Highlight** the frame border

**Press** **Ins**

**Highlight** Numbers
Decimal Places

**Press** ⏎

**Type** **0**

**Press** ⏎

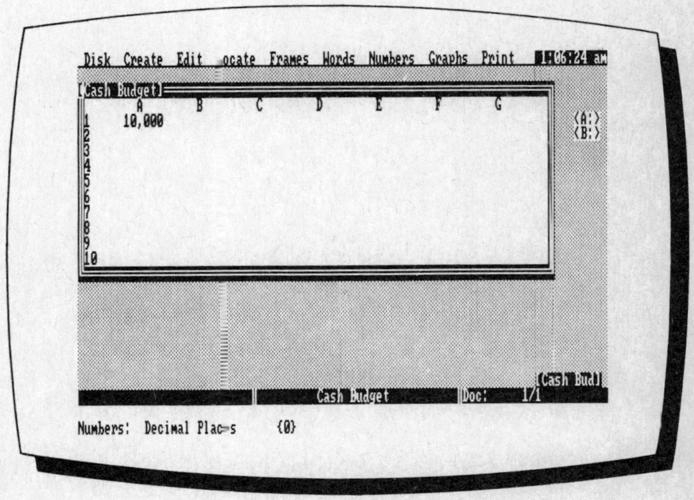


**Result** The number in the spreadsheet is now displayed as 10,000 — a whole number without decimals and in the business format (thousands separated by commas). Highlighting it and pressing the **Del** key deletes the number from the spreadsheet.

*To delete the number:*

**Press** **Down Level (Gray +)** to move the cursor into the frame (it will be in cell A1)
**Del** to delete the number

## Tips Styling and Formatting: Menu Commands

### The Numbers Menu Commands

| MENU CHOICE | DESCRIPTION |
|---|---|
| Decimal Places | Sets the number of decimal places to be displayed. |
| General | Displays numbers with as many decimal places as necessary to show the entire number. If the **Decimal Places** command has been used, the number of digits specified will be displayed. |
| Integer | Displays numbers as whole numbers with no decimal places (e.g., 1001). |
| Fixed Decimal | Displays all numbers with number of decimal places specified by the **Decimal Places** command (e.g., 1001.00 for two decimal places). |
| Currency | Displays numbers as US currency (e.g., $1001.00). |
| Business | Displays numbers with commas separating thousands (e.g., 1,001). |
| Percent | Displays numbers as percentages (e.g., 80%). |
| Scientific | Displays numbers in scientific notation (e.g., 1.00E+3). |
| Words Left/#'s Right | Left aligns labels and right aligns numbers in the highlighted area. |
| Left | Aligns numbers and labels with the left edge of a cell or field. |
| Right | Aligns numbers and labels with the right edge of a cell or field. |
| Middle | Centers numbers and labels in a cell or field. |

### The Words Menu Formatting Commands

| MENU CHOICE | DESCRIPTION |
|---|---|
| Align Left | Aligns selected paragraphs with the left margin. |
| Flush Right | Aligns selected paragraphs with the right margin. |
| Justify | Aligns selected paragraphs flush with both margins. |
| Center | Centers entire paragraph between margins. |
| Left Margin | Used to set the left margin. |
| Right Margin | Used to set the right margin. |
| Paragraph Indent | Used to set the number of characters the first line of a new paragraph is indented. |
| Tab Size | Used to set the number of characters between tab stops. |

## Tips Formatting Text and Numbers

- ☐ Numbers and text are formatted using the commands listed in the Words and Numbers menus. The Words menu is used to change the format of text; the Numbers menu is used to change the format of numbers and to change the alignment within a cell or group of cells.
- ☐ Before formatting text or numbers, the cells must be highlighted using the **Extend Select (F6)** key.
- ☐ To format an entire frame, highlight the frame border. This will change the format of all cells within the frame except those that have been individually formatted.
- ☐ Number formats can be set differently in each cell.
- ☐ Unless otherwise specified, text and numbers are displayed in the default format—Words Left/# s Right and General.
- ☐ The way numbers are formatted doesn't affect the way they are used in formulas; they are always calculated to 15 decimal places. To change the way they are calculated, you use the @Round function.
- ☐ The symbols used to denote currency can be changed to a foreign currency by using one of the tailoring functions (@Nationalize (@Pound), for example) on the frame border. You can also change the currency symbol permanently by adding it to the configuration file.
- ☐ Both the size and the format of a number determine how long it is. If the format is changed in such a way as to make the entry too long for the cell, a row of asterisks may appear in the cell. To display the number, widen the column or field, or change the format (for example, reduce the decimal places from 10 to 5).
- ☐ If you copy or move the contents of a cell, the formats are carried to the new cells.
- ☐ The **Del** key and **Blank All** command do not erase formats entered in cells.

## Set Recalculation to Manual

Framework automatically recalculates the spreadsheet each time you make an entry; while this may not seem like a hindrance at first, you will find that as your spreadsheet becomes larger, the computer will take longer and longer to recalculate. If you find this slowing down your work, you can turn off automatic recalculation, and instead press the **Recalc (F5)** key whenever you want to check your results.

*To set recalculation to manual:*

| | |
|---|---|
| **Press** | **Up Level (Gray –)** to move the cursor to the frame border<br>**Ins** |
| **Highlight** | Numbers<br>Options for Recalc |
| **Press** | ↵ |
| **Highlight** | Manual |
| **Press** | ↵ |

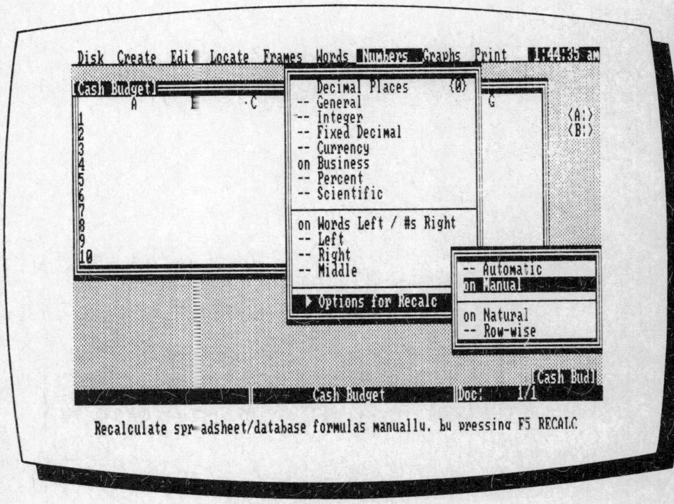


**Result** With recalculation set to manual, there will not be a delay after each entry is made to the spreadsheet. However, you will have to remember to press **Recalc** (**F5**) whenever changes are made.

## Tips Understanding the Status Panel

The status panel (the three-part highlighted strip at the bottom of the screen) provides you with useful information as you work with the Framework program. The information displayed changes depending on what you are doing and on what kind of frame the cursor is on.

**Left Section** Displays formulas in a frame, cell, or data field. Displays formulas and printing functions entered on the frame's border.

**Middle Section** Lists the label of the current frame.

**Right Section** Indicates what special keys are engaged (for instance, **Caps Lock** and **Num Lock**). Also gives information about where you are, depending on where the highlight is:

| CURSOR POSITION | INFORMATION DISPLAYED |
|---|---|
| On disk drives | Drive: 1/2 indicates the number of the highlighted drive and the total number of drives. |
| Inside a disk drive | Dir: 3/10 indicates the number of the highlighted file and the total number of files on the disk. |
| On a document frame border | Doc: 3/4 indicates the number of the highlighted frame (3) and the total number of frames (4) on the desktop at the same level. |
| On a subframe border | Frame: 3/4 indicates the number of the subframe and the total number of other frames on the same level in the same section. |
| In a database | Recs: 5/50 indicates the number of records in the working set and the total number of records. |
| In a spreadsheet | SS: 3/5 indicates the position of the cursor by column (3) and row (5). |
| In a word frame | Char: 49/19 indicates the position of the cursor by column (from the left edge) and line (from the top). |

## Tips Zooming Frames

To return a zoomed frame to normal, you can either press the **Zoom (F9)** key again to leave the cursor in the frame or press **Up Level (Gray –)** to move the cursor to the frame border.

If the frame you zoom contains other frames, the cursor will move down a level to highlight its border. If you continue to press **Zoom (F9)**, you will move successively deeper until you open the lowest frame level. Pressing **Zoom (F9)** again will return you to the starting point, with the cursor remaining inside the lowest frame.

If you get lost while zooming and viewing databases, hold down the **Ctrl** key and press **Up Level (Gray –)**. This moves the cursor back to the document frame border.

## Tips Recalculation Options

**The Options for Recalc Submenu on the Numbers Menu**

| MENU CHOICE | DESCRIPTION |
|---|---|
| **Automatic** | Recalculates a frame automatically whenever a change is made or new data is entered. |
| **Manual** | Recalculates a frame only when the **Recalc (F5)** key is pressed. |
| **Natural** | When a formula is recalculated, all other formulas to which it refers are recalculated first. |
| **Row-wise** | Recalculates a frame starting at the top left cell and proceeding down the spreadsheet's columns, row by row (that is, begins recalculating in cell A1 and recalculates row 1, then row 2, etc.). |

As your spreadsheets grow larger, you will notice that Framework takes a noticeably longer time to enter data. If you find that this is slowing you down, you can change the recalculation from automatic to manual by selecting Options for Recalc on the Numbers menu and selecting Manual.

When circular references are used, set recalculation to Row-wise.

## Zoom the Spreadsheet Frame

Before entering data in a spreadsheet, it helps to zoom it with the **Zoom** (**F9**) key so you can see more of the rows and columns. Frames can be zoomed and unzoomed at any time so you can look at your spreadsheet in different ways. You can zoom the frame with the cursor either on the spreadsheet frame border or down in the frame by pressing the **Zoom** (**F9**) key. To unzoom a frame you just press **Zoom** (**F9**) again.

*To zoom and unzoom a frame:*

**Press** **Zoom** (**F9**)

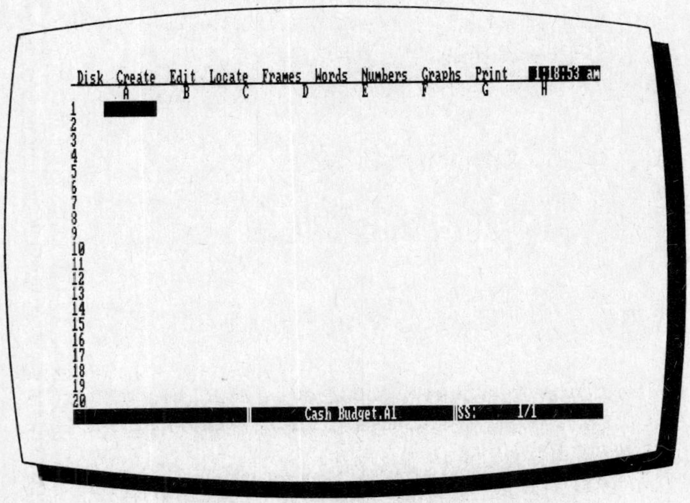


**Result** When you zoom the frame, the spreadsheet expands to fill the desktop. Row numbers now extend to 20. Pressing **Zoom** again reduces it back to the original frame. After experimenting with the **Zoom** key, end with the frame zoomed so your screen matches the following illustration.

## Size the Columns

When a new spreadsheet frame is created, Framework automatically sets all columns at 9 characters wide (the default setting). You can, however, change the width of any columns you choose.

*To select the columns to be changed:*

**Highlight** A1 (your cursor should already be there)

**Press** **Extend Select** (**F6**)

**Message** SELECT: extend selection with cursor keys; RETURN finishes

**Press** **End** to highlight columns A through N
↵ to complete the selection

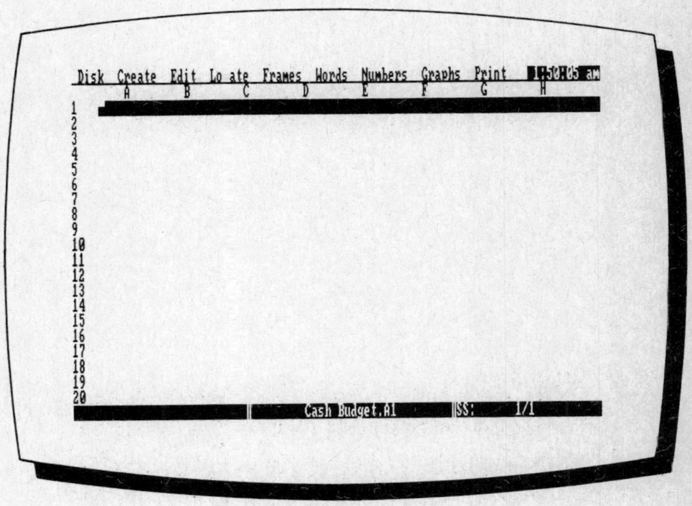


**Result** When you press the **End** key, the highlight stretches to the right to highlight columns A through N.

With the columns to be sized selected, you now use the **Size** (**F4**) key and the cursor movement keys to change the width of the columns. When you press the **Size** (**F4**) key, the current width of the columns is displayed on the rightmost section of the status panel. In this case it displays Size: 9/1, the default setting of 9. As the width is changed with the cursor movement keys, this first number changes.

*To size selected columns:*

**Press** **Size** (**F4**)
→ once (status panel will read **Size: 10/1**)
↵
← once to shrink the cursor

## Tips The Return Key ⏎ in Detail

The Return key ⏎ serves many purposes; its effect depends on where the cursor is in the program.

**Effect of Pressing the Return Key**

| CURSOR POSITION | EFFECT |
|---|---|
| On a menu command | Sets or executes the command. |
| Entering data | Completes the entry. |
| On a disk drive frame | Opens the main directory if closed or closes it if open. |
| On a file in a drive frame | Puts file on desktop. |
| On a subdirectory in a drive | Opens the subdirectory if closed or closes it if open. |
| On a frame border or tray | Opens the frame onto desktop if closed or closes it into its tray if open. |
| In a spreadsheet | Moves the cursor down a row. |
| In a database | Moves the cursor down to the next field. |
| In a word frame | Inserts a carriage return and breaks the line. Cursor moves down to the next line. |
| In a zoomed formula | Inserts a carriage return and breaks the line. Cursor moves down to the next line. |
| When using **Extend Select (F6)** | Completes selection. |
| When using **Move (F7)** | Completes pointing to destination you wish to move to. |
| When using **Copy (F8)** | Completes pointing to destination you wish to copy to. |

## Tips The Home Key in Detail

The **Home** key moves the cursor or highlight to the first item in any sequence. Its effect depends on where the cursor or highlight is positioned when the key is pressed.

**Effect of Pressing the Home Key**

| CURSOR POSITION | EFFECT ON CURSOR |
|---|---|
| On disk drives | To first drive. |
| In an open disk drive frame | To first file or subdirectory listed. |
| On a frame border or tray | To first frame in stack of trays. |
| In a spreadsheet | To far left cell on current row. |
| In a database | To far left field in current record. |
| In a word frame | To first character in current line. |
| On the edit line | To first character. |

## Tips The End Key in Detail

The **End** key moves the cursor or highlight to the last item in any sequence. Its effect depends on where the cursor or highlight is positioned when the key is pressed.

**Effect of Pressing the End Key**

| CURSOR POSITION | EFFECT ON CURSOR |
|---|---|
| On disk drives | To last drive. |
| In an open disk drive frame | To last file or subdirectory listed. |
| On a frame border or tray | To last frame in stack of trays. |
| In a spreadsheet | To far right cell on current row. |
| In a database | To far right field in current record. |
| In a word frame | To last character in current line. |
| On the edit line | To last character. |

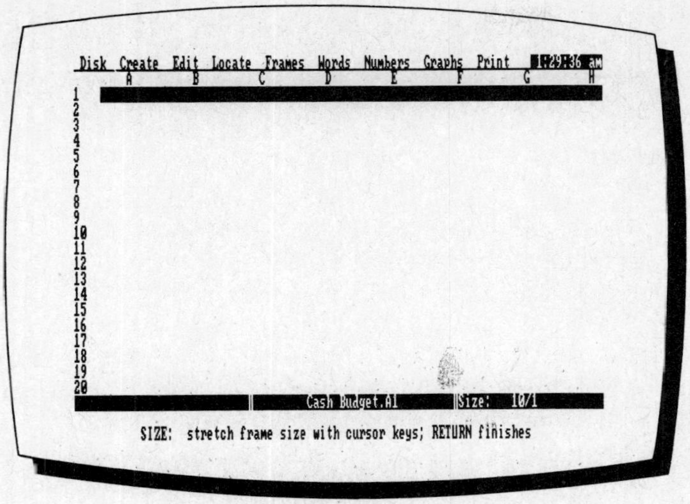


**Result** Each time the arrow key is pressed, the indicator on the status line changes to show the new width. You can experiment with using (←) to narrow the column and (→) to widen it. When you are through experimenting, be sure the indicator reads **Size: 10/1**. Pressing (↵) fixes the column widths. The highlight remains over the 14 columns that were selected until (←) is pressed to shrink it back to one column.

## Tips The Escape Key in Detail

The Escape (**Esc**) key is used primarily to cancel commands in progress whenever you change your mind.

**Effect of Pressing Esc**

| CURSOR POSITION | EFFECT |
|---|---|
| In a menu | Leaves the menu and returns the cursor to the desktop. |
| In a submenu | Leaves the submenu and returns the cursor to the desktop. |
| In Help | Leaves the help screen and returns the cursor to the desktop. |
| In Search and Replace | Terminates the operation. |
| In formula editing | Cancels formula editing without recalculating the formula. |
| In Drag, Size, Extend Select, Move, or Copy | Cancels the operation. |

## Size a Single Column

You will be putting text labels for line items in the first column of the spreadsheet, so you want it to be wider than the other columns (which will contain numbers and formulas). To change the width of individual columns, place the cursor anywhere in the column before pressing the **Size (F4)** key. As you saw in the previous step, the arrow key will change the size of columns in small steps, one character at a time. Here, try holding down the **Ctrl** key while using the arrow key to change the size in large steps, 8 characters at a time.

*To size column A to 32 characters wide:*

**Highlight** A1

**Press** **Size (F4)**
(→) until status panel reads **Size: 32/1**
(↵) to fix the size

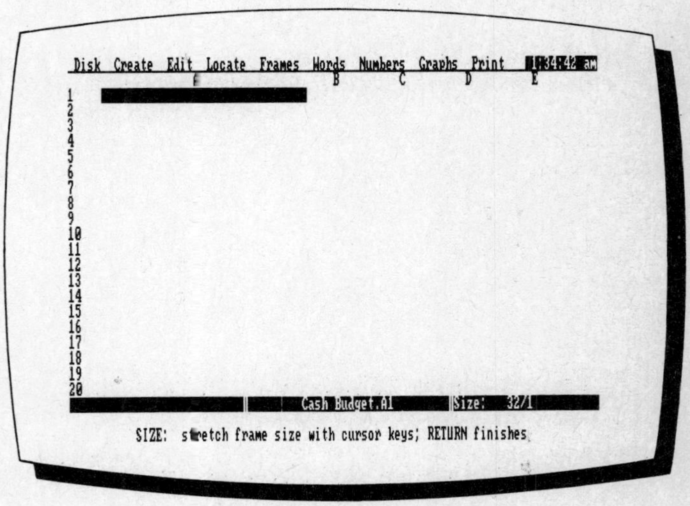


**Result** Pressing the arrow key (and the **Ctrl** key if desired) changes the width of column A. Try experimenting with a combination of movements using just the arrow keys and then the **Ctrl** and arrow keys together. Before proceeding to the next step, be sure the indicator on the status panel reads **Size: 32/1** to indicate that column A is currently set to a width of 32 characters.

## Tips Locking Row and Column Labels

Many spreadsheets use column A and row 1 for titles to identify line items and time periods. When the spreadsheet is larger than the screen display, these important identifying labels will be scrolled off the screen. Locking them in place keeps them displayed on the screen no matter where you are entering data in the spreadsheet.

To lock the first column and row of a spreadsheet frame, use the Lock First Column/Row command on the Edit menu.

When titles are locked they will appear on each page of a multipage printout.

## Tips Framework's Help Facility

Whenever you have a question, press the **Help (F1)** key. The help utility is coordinated with your place in the program. When you press **Help (F1)** in the middle of an operation, the text displayed on the screen is related to what you are doing in Framework at that time. If no command is in progress, a table of contents is displayed, allowing you to select the topic on which you need help. While you use the help utility, you can move back and forth through the screens, choosing the amount of information you need. If you need to refer back to a page, you can move back through the previous screens.

Instructions on finding help topics are always displayed at the bottom of the screen with the current choice highlighted. You can move the highlight around the options using the arrow keys. You select from the options offered by highlighting one and pressing ↵ or by typing the first letter of the option.

When you have found the help you need, quit the help utility by pressing the **Esc** key. Do not try to use Framework commands while still using help.

- ☐ The help options appearing at the bottom of the screen contain the command Key Help. If you use this choice, you will be prompted to Press the key on which you want help—doing so causes a screen of text to appear describing the key.
- ☐ To move around help screens, you can select the option Index of Topics. This displays an index of all the help screens.

## Tips Getting Around the Spreadsheet

The status panel provides detailed information about the location of the cursor in a spreadsheet frame:

- ☐ The left section of the status panel indicates the contents of the highlighted cell if it contains a number or a formula. If the cell contains a formula, the formula is displayed, not the current value.
- ☐ The middle section indicates the frame and the highlighted cell number.
- ☐ The right section indicates the position of the cursor. For example, SS: 3/2 indicates that the cursor is in the third column of the second row (cell C2).

Both the ↵ and ⇥ keys can be used to enter data. The ↵ key enters data without moving the cursor; pressing it again moves the cursor one row down. The ⇥ key enters data and moves the cursor one column to the right; the **Shift-⇥** key enters data and moves the cursor one column to the left.

**Cursor Movement in a Spreadsheet Frame**

| KEY | EFFECT ON CURSOR |
|---|---|
| ↑ ↓ | Up or down one row. |
| ← → | Left or right one column. |
| ↵ | Enters data. Pressing ↵ again moves cursor down one row. |
| ⇥ | Enters data and moves cursor right one column. |
| **Shift-⇥** | Enters data and moves cursor left one column. |
| **PgUp** | To top of screen. If cursor is at top of screen, scrolls up one full screen. |
| **PgDn** | To bottom of screen. If cursor is at bottom of screen, scrolls down one full screen. |
| **Home** | Left to beginning of row. |
| **End** | Right to end of row. |
| **Backspace** | Left one column. |
| **Ctrl-↑** | Up to top cell in column with data. |
| **Ctrl-↓** | Down to last cell in column with data. |
| **Ctrl-←** | Left to first cell in row with data. |
| **Ctrl-→** | Right to last cell in row with data. |
| **Ctrl-Home** | To top-left corner of spreadsheet. |
| **Ctrl-End** | To bottom-right corner of spreadsheet. |

## Step 3 Enter Headings

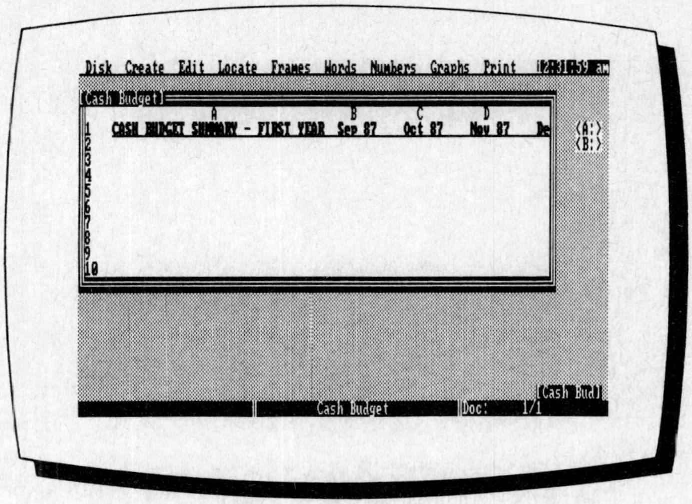


In this step, you'll enter the following: a label identifying the spreadsheet; a label for the total column; dates for the monthly columns.

## Lock the First Column and Top Row

When the cursor is moved around a spreadsheet that is larger than the screen display, the spreadsheet is scrolled as you move the cursor into columns or rows that can't be seen on the screen. This feature allows you to see a large spreadsheet through a small screen display. When scrolling the spreadsheet this way, you can keep the first column and top row of the spreadsheet — the ones used for headings and line item labels — from scrolling off the screen so you can keep better track of where you are.

*To keep the first column and top row from scrolling:*

**Press** Ins

**Highlight** Edit
Lock First Column/Row

**Press** ↵

**Result** No result is immediately apparent, but when you enter the headings and other information on the spreadsheet the first column and top row won't scroll off the screen. Also, when you print the spreadsheet on 8½ × 11 paper this setting will print the row labels and column headings on each sheet when the spreadsheet is too wide, or too long, to be printed on a single sheet of paper.

## Enter Text Labels

Entering text labels is as simple as placing the cursor in a cell and typing your entry. There is one exception — text that begins with numbers or certain mathematical symbols (see Tips on "Entering Text"). Since typing these characters makes Framework think you're entering a number or formula, you have to first press the **Space Bar** to indicate that text beginning with a character normally used for numbers or formulas is being entered. Pressing ↵ completes the entry. You can edit your entries as you enter them, or return them to the edit line for correcting.

*To enter a label identifying the spreadsheet:*

**Highlight** A1 (if your cursor is not already there)

**Type** **CASH BUDGET SUMMARY – FIRST YEAR**

**Press** ↵

**Result** As you type in your entry, it appears both in the cell and on the edit line. The bright highlight on the edit line indicates where the next character you type will be entered. Pressing ↵ completes the command.

## Enter a Date Function

Dates can be entered by typing them in as labels or by using Framework's date functions. The advantage of using date functions is that you can change the way the dates are displayed by using a second function; the disadvantage is that entering them can be a long and tedious process, and the functions can't be copied to other cells. For our purposes on this spreadsheet, we will have you enter the date functions in the first monthly cell on row 1, but then enter labels in the other monthly cells.

The date functions below have two parts; the part that reads **@DATE2** formats the dates so they are displayed as Sep 87, Oct 87, and so on. The function **@DATE(87,9,1)** calculates the date (in this example, September 1, 1987). Dates are entered using the last two numbers of the year followed by the number of the month and then the day, each separated from the next by a comma.

*To enter functions to calculate and format dates:*

**Highlight** B1

**Type** **@DATE2(@DATE(87,9,1))**

**Press** →|

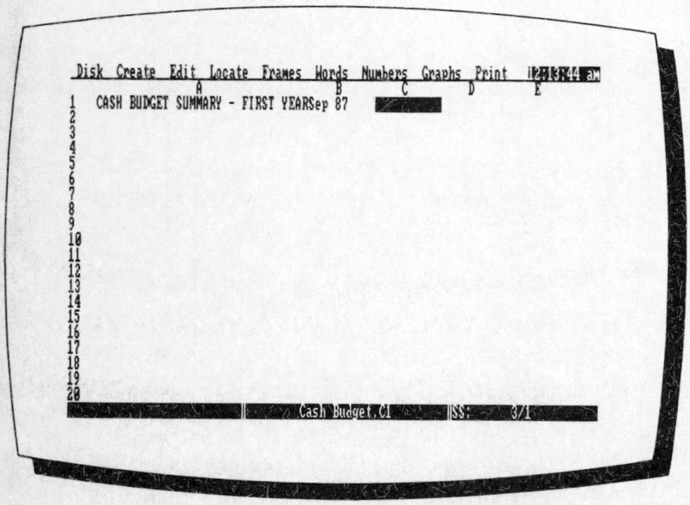


**Result** The date **Sep 87** appears in cell B1 when →| is pressed, and the cursor moves to cell C1.

## Tips Styling Text

Text and numbers can be styled to be italicized, boldfaced, or underlined in any frame, including word, spreadsheet, and database frames. You can combine styles—for instance, key text can be boldfaced and underlined.

**The Words Menu Styling Commands**

| MENU CHOICE | DESCRIPTION |
|---|---|
| Normal | The default setting. Displays and prints highlighted text in normal type. Resets all previous style settings on selected text. |
| **Bold** | Displays and prints highlighted text in boldfaced type. |
| Underline | Displays and prints highlighted text underlined. |
| *Italic* | Displays and prints highlighted text in italicized type. (Some monitors display, and some printers print, text formatted with this command as underlined.) |

To be styled, a frame label has to be on the edit line. To move it there, highlight the frame border and press the **Space Bar**. Use the **Extend Select (F6)** key to select all or part of the label on the edit line. To style it, you can use the choices on the Words menu.

- ☐ To style all text in a frame, highlight the frame border.
- ☐ To change previously styled text, first set it to Normal; otherwise, the newest command will be added to the one used previously.

## Tips Selecting Ranges

Ranges can be changed indirectly or inadvertently by adding rows or columns, deleting rows or columns, or moving the upper-left or lower-right cell boundaries of the range. (For this reason, it's a good idea to include ruled lines as the upper and lower boundaries of a range; this allows you to add or delete rows without any problems.)

Pressing **Esc** when pointing to a range will return the cursor to the cell highlighted before pointing.

In many cases, the highlight remains expanded after selecting a number of cells and completing a command. To return the cursor to one cell, press any arrow key.

## Enter Remaining Dates as Labels

Now that you have seen how the date functions work, we will let you off the hook for the other monthly columns on row 1. We will enter labels in these cells. Note that you could enter date functions for each of these months: you would type in the formulas from cell B1, but you would change the year and month as appropriate. For example, for January 1988 the functions would read **@DATE2(@DATE(88,1,1))**.

*To enter labels for the remaining months in the year, and for the totals column:*

**Highlight** C1 and type **Oct 87** ⇥
At D1 type **Nov 87** ⇥
At E1 type **Dec 87** ⇥
At F1 type **Jan 88** ⇥
At G1 type **Feb 88** ⇥
At H1 type **Mar 88** ⇥
At I1 type **Apr 88** ⇥
At J1 type **May 88** ⇥
At K1 type **Jun 88** ⇥
At L1 type **Jul 88** ⇥
At M1 type **Aug 88** ⇥
At N1 type **Total** ↵

*To move the cursor back to column A:*

**Press** Home

**Result** Each of the monthly columns on the spreadsheet is now dated, and the final column is labeled Total.

## Style Cells

With Framework you can select various styles for both words and numbers: boldfacing, underlining, italicizing, and normal. These choices can be used singly or in combinations. In this example column headings will be boldfaced and underlined so they stand out. (Note that not all computers will print out all the styles you may use.)

*Select the cells to be styled:*

**Highlight** A1

**Press** Extend Select (F6)
**End** to highlight cells A1 through N1
↵ to complete the selection

**Result** The highlight covers cells A1 through N1.

The styles you have to choose from are listed on the Words menu and include Normal (the default setting), Bold, Underline, and Italic. After selecting a style command you style the highlighted cells by pressing ↵.

**Press** Ins

**Highlight** Words
Bold

**Press** ↵

**Result** The menu disappears and the highlighted cells on the spreadsheet are boldfaced. The highlight remains over the selected cells in case you want to use another style.

Framework doesn't limit you to just one style; you can use them in combinations. Now let's add an underline to the headings.

**Press** Ins

**Highlight** Underline (the Words menu has automatically been chosen)

**Press** ↵
← to shrink the cursor

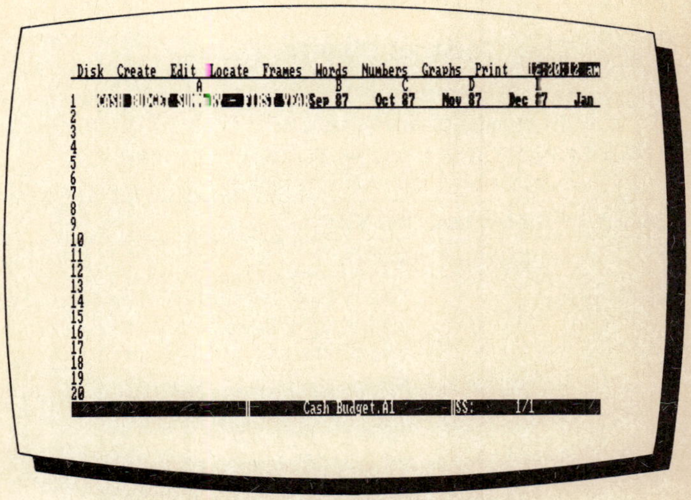


**Result** The cells that were previously boldfaced are now also underlined. If you press **Ins** again to look at the Words menu, you will see that the lines for Bold and Underline are now preceded by the word on.

## Tips The Editing Keys

| EDITING KEYS | DESCRIPTION |
|---|---|
| **Extend Select (F6)** | Select characters for editing |
| | *Moving Entries to the Edit Line for Editing:* |
| **Space Bar** | Labels |
| **Edit Formula (F2)** | Numbers and formulas |
| | *Moving the Cursor While Editing:* |
| ← → | Left or right one character |
| **Ctrl-**← **Ctrl-**→ | Left or right one word |
| **Home** | Left to beginning of line |
| **End** | Right to end of line |
| | *Deleting Characters:* |
| **Del** | Delete highlighted characters |
| **Backspace** | Delete character to left of cursor |
| **Ctrl-Del** | Delete word to right of cursor |
| **Ctrl-Backspace** | Delete word to left of cursor |

## Tips The Control Key in Detail

To use these combination commands, hold down the **Ctrl** key while pressing the second key listed.

**Effect of Using the Ctrl Key**

| KEY COMBINATION | EFFECT |
|---|---|
| **Ctrl-**↵ | Saves selected frames in or on which the cursor is positioned and all frames contained within them. |
| **Ctrl-**first letter | Calls up a specific pull-down menu. |
| **Ctrl-**arrow keys | Moves the cursor farther than if the arrow keys were pressed by themselves. Also used to select text, cells, or fields. |
| **Ctrl-Backspace** | Deletes the word to the left of the cursor in a word frame. |
| **Ctrl-Del** | Deletes the word to the right of the cursor in a word frame. |
| **Ctrl-Break** or **Ctrl-Scroll Lock** | Stops certain commands in progress, including recalculation and printing. |
| **Ctrl-**number (0-255) | Causes the next character typed to be repeated the indicated number of times. |

## Tips Editing and Correcting Mistakes

If you need to correct a mistake, there are a number of keys that make it easy and that work the same in all frames. When working in any kind of frame or when entering data on frame borders, you can delete entries, type over them, or return them to the edit line for editing. Selecting Undo on the Edit menu can restore many deletions if used immediately—*before* executing any other commands.

**Keys Used in Editing**

| KEYS | EFFECT |
|---|---|
| **Space Bar** | Moves frame labels and spreadsheet headings to the edit line. |
| **Edit Formula (F2)** | Moves numbers and formulas to the edit line. |
| **Esc** | Cancels edit command without making changes. |
| **Del** | Deletes highlighted character(s), cell(s) or field contents, frames, or files on the disk. |
| **Backspace** | Deletes character to left of cursor. |
| **Ctrl-Del** | Deletes word to right of cursor. |
| **Ctrl-Backspace** | Deletes word to left of cursor. |
| **Extend Select (F6)** | Selects characters for editing. |

## Align Text and Numbers

If you place the cursor in cell B1, you will notice that the date is aligned with the left edge of the cell. When numbers are entered later, they will be aligned with the right edge. To keep the heading and numbers more closely aligned, the headings can be aligned so they are in the middle of their cells. The Numbers menu lists your alignment choices: your entries can align with the left or right edges or they can be centered. Before aligning, you must select the cells to be affected. If you wish to affect more than one cell, use the **Extend Select (F6)** key to highlight the range of cells.

*To select cells to be aligned:*

**Highlight** B1

**Press** **Extend Select (F6)**
**End** to highlight cells B1 through N1
⏎ to complete the selection

*To align cells:*

**Press** **Ins**

**Highlight** Numbers
Middle

**Press** ⏎
← to shrink the cursor

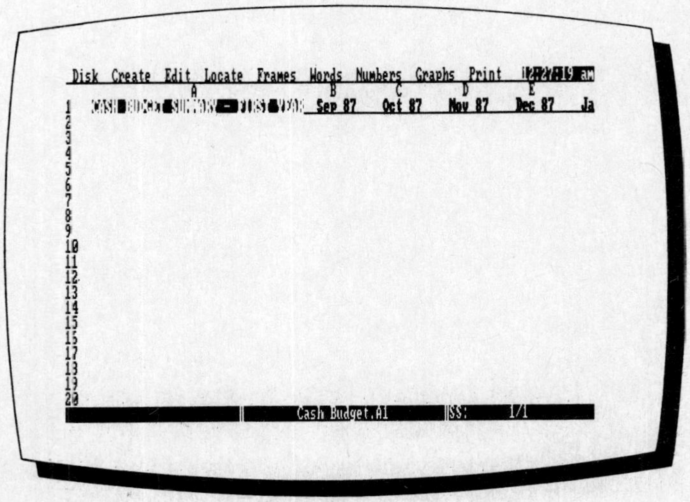


**Result** The menu disappears and the date and total labels are aligned in the center of their cells.

## Step 4 Enter Cash Inflows

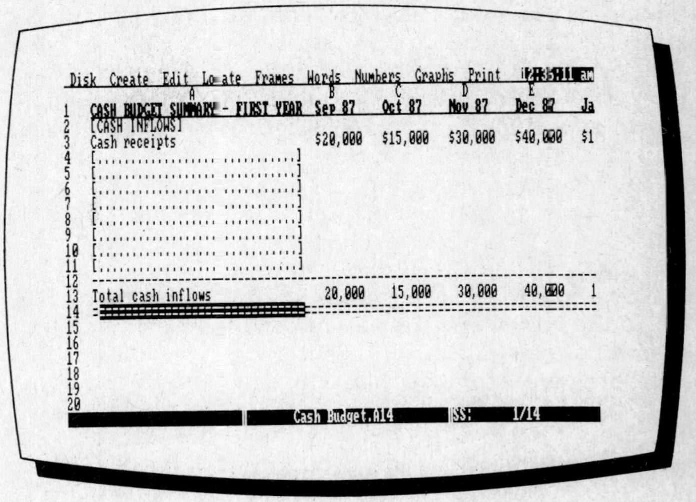


As we mentioned earlier, a cash inflow is cash coming into a business from any source. This part of the spreadsheet — rows 2 through 14 — is where you will break down your cash inflows, and enter the monthly amounts you expect to receive from each source. In this section you'll enter the following: labels to identify this section of the spreadsheet and the line items; sample "case study" numbers to check your formulas and create graphs and explore "What Ifs" later in this chapter; formulas in row 13 that add the monthly amounts in each column and give you a grand total for your cash inflows over the twelve-month period covered by the budget; a formula in column N that calculates the annual totals from each source.

### Row 2

**A heading** to identify the cash inflow section of the budget is entered.

**Highlight** A2

**Type** **[CASH INFLOWS]**

**Press** ⏎ twice to complete the entry and move the cursor down one row

## Row 3

**Cash receipts** are the first key line item in our case study. Let's assume that our store does most of its business on a cash basis. Although it accepts the major bank credit cards, MasterCard and VISA, these charges are paid so quickly that they are effectively "cash" sales as well. Our business is typical of many retail operations — it does the largest share of business during the pre-holiday season in December, but also has good "back-to-school" sales in August and September, and lower but still good sales in the spring.

Numbers are entered just like text. You move the cursor to the cell in which you want them entered and type them in. Percentages can be entered as decimals or as percentages — for example, 10% can be entered as .1 or 10%.

*To enter a label:*

**Highlight** A3
**Type** **Cash receipts**
**Press** ⇥

*To enter numbers:*

**Highlight** B3 and type **20000** ⇥
At C3 type **15000** ⇥
At D3 type **30000** ⇥
At E3 type **40000** ⇥
At F3 type **10000** ⇥
At G3 type **10000** ⇥
At H3 type **15000** ⇥
At I3 type **15000** ⇥
At J3 type **15000** ⇥
At K3 type **10000** ⇥
At L3 type **10000** ⇥
At M3 type **20000** ↵

*To move the cursor back to column A:*

**Press** **Home**

**Result** Your results should match those in the illustration on page 27. All of the numbers should be displayed in the format you selected earlier, commas separating thousands and no decimal places.

(*Hint*: Numbers with many zeros can be entered much faster if you use scientific notation. For instance, to enter **300,000**, you type **3** and then **e** (for "exponent") and then **5** for the number of zeros; **15,000** can be entered as **15e3**.)

## Tips Copying Data

Don't copy from a range to a range. Instead, copy from a cell to a range, a column to a range, or a row to a range.

Don't copy into a range that contains data. The original contents will be erased and replaced with the new data.

Only data that will not fall outside the boundaries of the spreadsheet will be copied.

Always point to the upper-left cell in the range you are copying to.

You can copy data from a spreadsheet into another part of the same spreadsheet, into another spreadsheet, or into a database. You cannot copy data from a spreadsheet into a word frame.

## Tips Moving Data

You can move cell contents to other cells on the same spreadsheet, to another spreadsheet, or to a database. The original cell retains the format of the data that was moved. For example, if the cell had been formatted for currency, any future data entered into that cell after moving the original contents will be formatted as currency also.

You cannot move data from a spreadsheet frame into a word frame.

If the cell being moved is the upper-left or lower-right corner in a range, the range will expand or contract with the moved cell. Moving any other cells in a range leaves the range intact.

Don't move into a range that is already occupied unless you want the cells in that range to be erased by the new cell contents.

When cells are moved, all formulas referring to them in the same frame will automatically adjust to refer to the new position.

If a cell is moved to another frame, all formulas referring to it in the original frame will automatically adjust to refer to the new position.

You can use the Ascending Sort and Descending Sort commands on the Locate menu to sort the rows in a spreadsheet. To sort selected rows, use the **Extend Select (F6)** key to select them before sorting. You can use any column as the criterion to be sorted by pointing to that column.

You can restore a sort with the Undo command on the Edit menu.

## Rows 4–11

**Blank data entry spaces** for your own cash inflow breakdown are entered in rows 4 through 11.

*To enter a blank data entry space in row 4:*

**Highlight** A4

**Type** [30 periods]

**Press** ↵

*To copy the entry space to rows 5 through 11:*

**Highlight** A4

**Press** **Copy** (**F8**)
↓ to move the cursor to A5
**Extend Select** (**F6**)
↓ 6 times to highlight rows 5-11
↵ to complete the selection
↵ to complete the copy command
↓ to shrink the cursor

## Row 12

**Ruled lines** are frequently used on spreadsheets to separate major sections and subsections to make them easier to read and more attractive when printed out. With Framework there are three ways to enter ruled lines: entering them as text (i.e., press the hyphen key until you have the necessary number of hyphens); using the **Ctrl** key to repeat a symbol (in this case the hyphen); and using Framework's repeat function. After you enter a ruled line, you can copy it elsewhere on the spreadsheet where needed.

We will show you both ways to enter the lines as *formulas:*

*To enter a ruled line with the @REPT function:*

**Highlight** A12

**Type** **@REPT("–",32)** (the 32 indicates how many times the hyphen is to be repeated)

**Press** ↵

**Result** A string of hyphens, 32 characters long, will appear in cell A12 when ↵ is pressed.

Ruled lines can also be entered by using the **Ctrl** key to repeat a symbol — in this case, the hyphen.

*To repeat a character using the **Ctrl** key:*

**Highlight** B12

**Press** **Space Bar** (since we are using an arithmetic symbol as a text label)

**Press** **Ctrl**

**Type** **10**

**Release** **Ctrl**

**Type** – (the hyphen)

**Press** ↵

**Result** Cell B12 should be filled with hyphens appearing as a single ruled line.

You can easily copy text, numbers, or formulas by using the **Copy** (**F8**) key. Copying is a very useful spreadsheet feature; if you are preparing an annual budget broken down by months, for instance, just enter the formulas in the first monthly column and then copy them to the other monthly columns.

*To copy the ruled line to cells across the row:*

**Highlight** B12

**Press** **Copy** (**F8**)

**Message** COPY: cursor to the copy destination; RETURN finishes

**Highlight** C12

**Press** **Extend Select** (**F6**)
**End**
↵ twice
← to shrink the cursor

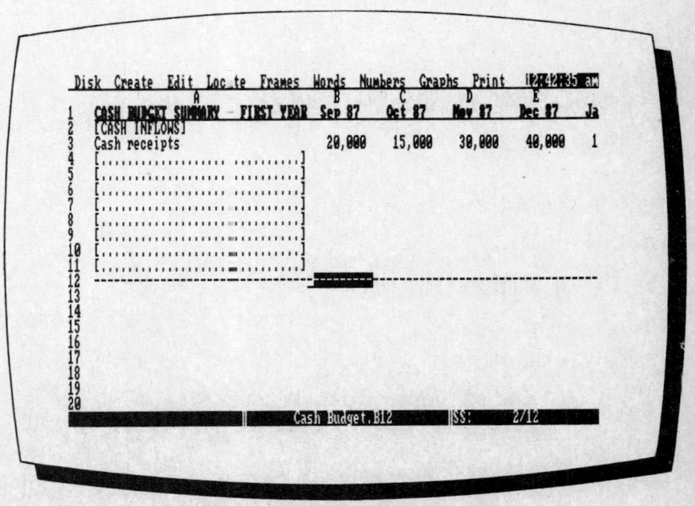


**Result** The ruled line in cell B12 is copied to other cells on the row.

## Row 13

**Total cash inflows** are calculated on this row by formulas that sum each of the monthly columns on the cash inflows section. Although you can type in the coordinates of cells referred to in formulas, it is usually faster and easier to use cursor pointing to point to the cells. In the next and all subsequent sections the formulas will be shown as they would be typed in (to save space and simplify the instructions), but you can use cursor pointing to enter those formulas and become more familiar with the process.

The @SUM formula used to total entries in each column includes a range of cells. Although the entries are actually made on rows 3 through 11, the range you will enter will be rows 2 through 12 so that if you insert new rows into this section, they will automatically be included in the range.

*To enter a label:*

**Highlight** A13
**Type** **Total cash inflows**
**Press** ⇥

*To enter a formula, using cursor pointing, that totals cash inflow entries in column B:*

**Highlight** B13
**Type** **@SUM(**
**Press** ↑ once to begin cursor pointing
↑ to point to cell B2
**Type** : (the colon indicates that you are specifying a range of cells to be included)
**Press** ↑ once to call up cursor pointing again
↓ to point to cell B12
**Type** **)** to complete the formula
**Press** ↵

*To copy the formula:*

**Highlight** B13
**Press** **Copy** (**F8**)
**Highlight** C13
**Press** **Extend Select** (**F6**)
**End** to highlight out to cell N13
↵ twice
← to shrink the cursor

**Result** Since we have entered only one row of cash inflows, the totals on row 13 should match the cash receipts on row 3.

## Row 14

**A double ruled line** is created by using the equal sign repeated across the cells on a row. Here we will use the formula that repeats a character with the **Ctrl** key.

*To repeat a character using the* **Ctrl** *key:*

**Highlight** A14
**Press** **Space Bar**
**Press** **Ctrl**
**Type** **32**
**Release** **Ctrl**
**Type** = (the equal sign)
**Press** ↵

**Result** Cell A14 should be filled with equal signs appearing as a double ruled line.

*To copy the ruled line to cells across the row:*

**Highlight** A14
**Press** **Copy** (**F8**)
**Highlight** B14
**Press** **Extend Select** (**F6**)
**End**
↵ twice
← to shrink the cursor

**Result** The double ruled line in cell A14 is copied to other cells on the row.

### Tips Using English Language References

When a cell containing a formula is highlighted, the cell coordinates are displayed in the center section of the status panel. If you type **!**, you can switch this display to show English language references to the cell. The English language reference shows the text entries in the first cell in the same row and column instead of the cell coordinates.

The English language references will continue until **!** is typed again.

To keep you from getting confused, all labels on the first row and column should be different.

## Column N

**Row totals** are calculated in column N. When your cash inflows are broken down into specific categories, the formulas in column N will calculate totals for each line in the breakdown. Try entering the formula by just typing it in instead of pointing with the cursor.

*To enter a formula that totals the cash receipts entered on row 3:*

**Highlight** N3

**Type** **@SUM(B3:M3)**

**Press** ↵

*To copy the formula to other rows:*

**Highlight** N3

**Press** **Copy** (**F8**)

**Highlight** N4

**Press** **Extend Select** (**F6**)
↓ to point to cell N11
↵ twice
↑ to shrink the cursor

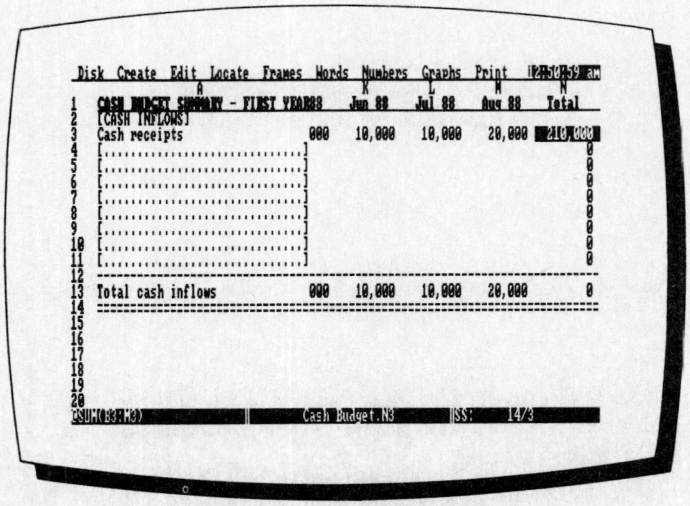

**Result** The calculated value of 210,000 appears in cell N3; the formula is displayed in the left section of the status panel. When the formula is copied, the results should match those in the illustration.

We would like the first row of numbers in this spreadsheet to appear as currency; therefore we will format row 3.

*To select the cells to be formatted:*

**Highlight** B3

**Press** **Extend Select** (**F6**)
**End**
↵
**Ins**

**Highlight** Numbers
Currency

**Press** ↵
← to shrink the cursor

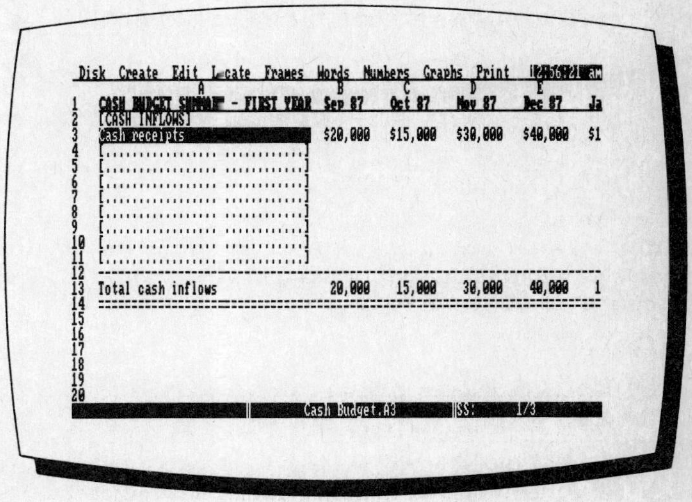

**Result** The numbers on row 3 will now appear with dollar signs, commas between thousands, and no decimal places.

## Step 5 Enter Cash Outflows

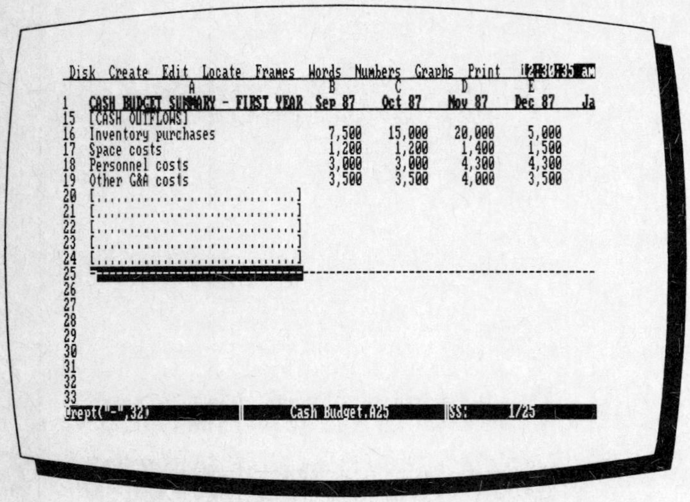


As we discussed earlier, a cash outflow is cash going out of the business for any purpose. Rows 15 through 24 of the spreadsheet are for your breakdowns of cash outflows; formulas will be entered on row 26 to sum the monthly amounts in each column, in column N to total each row, and cell N26 will give a grand total for all cash outflows.

### Row 15

**A heading** to identify the cash outflow section of the budget is entered.

**Highlight** A15

**Type** **[CASH OUTFLOWS]**

**Press** ⏎ twice

### Row 16

**Inventory purchases** are the first of the four cash outflow categories in our case study. We're assuming that we can have inventory delivered by our suppliers and then pay for it exactly one month before it is sold, which means that we must accurately predict how much inventory we'll need in the coming month. We also expect to maintain a 100% markup on our inventory costs; in other words, our inventory cost for any month will be 50% of the cash receipts figure for the following month. (This is obviously a hypothetical example — if you find someone who can target inventory levels this precisely, hire that person immediately!)

The formula to be entered begins with a letter, so you have to press the **Edit Formula (F2)** key before typing the letter. This tells Framework that you are entering a formula rather than text. Since the formula used to calculate inventory purchases refers to the next month's sales, the value in the last column has to be entered as a number since there is no "next month" on the spreadsheet to which it can refer.

*To enter a label:*

**Highlight** A16

**Type** **Inventory purchases**

**Press** ⇥

*To enter a formula in column B:*

**Highlight** B16

**Press** EDIT (the **Edit Formula (F2)** key)

**Type** **C3*50%** (or **C3*.5**)

**Press** ⏎

*To copy the formula:*

**Highlight** B16

**Press** **Copy (F8)**

**Highlight** C16

**Press** **Extend Select (F6)**
**End**
← twice to move the cursor back to L16
⏎ twice
→ to shrink the cursor and move it to M16

*To enter a value in the last monthly column:*

**Highlight** M16

**Type** **12500**

**Press** ⏎

**Result** Inventory purchases should begin at 7,500 in the first month and reach 12,500 in the last month. Each month's inventory purchases should be one-half of the next month's cash receipts on row 3.

## Row 17

**Space costs,** which include rent and utilities, are entered next. These costs are fairly consistent over the course of the year, but there are increases for extra lighting and heating during the winter months.

*To enter a label:*

**Highlight** A17
**Type** **Space costs**
**Press** →|

*To enter "case study" numbers for space costs:*

**Highlight** B17 and type **1200** →|
At C17 type **1200** →|
At D17 type **1400** →|
At E17 type **1500** →|
At F17 type **1500** →|
At G17 type **1500** →|
At H17 type **1400** →|
At I17 type **1300** →|
At J17 type **1200** →|
At K17 type **1200** →|
At L17 type **1200** →|
At M17 type **1200** ↵

## Row 18

**Personnel costs,** which include salaries and benefits, are entered. These are also fairly consistent, but we anticipate the need for extra help to handle the pre-holiday rush in November and December, and during the smaller peak periods in the spring and fall. We also budget some salary raises over the course of the year — one in January and the other in June.

*To enter a label:*

**Highlight** A18
**Type** **Personnel costs**
**Press** →|

*To enter "case study" numbers for personnel costs:*

**Highlight** B18 and type **3000** →|
At C18 type **3000** →|
At D18 type **4300** →|
At E18 type **4300** →|
At F18 type **3200** →|
At G18 type **3200** →|
At H18 type **3200** →|
At I18 type **3200** →|
At J18 type **3200** →|
At K18 type **3200** →|
At L18 type **3600** →|
At M18 type **3600** ↵

## Row 19

**Other G&A costs** are entered. These costs are grouped together to simplify the case study: a complete breakdown of possible costs for G&A and other categories is included in Chapter 5. In this example, these G&A costs remain at $3,500, except during the four months when quarterly insurance payments are due.

*To enter a label:*

**Highlight** A19
**Type** **Other G&A costs**
**Press** →|

*To enter "case study" numbers for other G&A costs:*

**Highlight** B19 and type **3500** →|
At C19 type **3500** →|
At D19 type **4000** →|
At E19 type **3500** →|
At F19 type **3500** →|
At G19 type **4000** →|
At H19 type **3500** →|
At I19 type **3500** →|
At J19 type **4000** →|
At K19 type **3500** →|
At L19 type **3500** →|
At M19 type **4000** ↵

Rows **20-24**

*To enter a formula that totals cash outflows:*

**Highlight** B26

Entering the Cash Budget Summary

## Step 6 Enter Summary Section

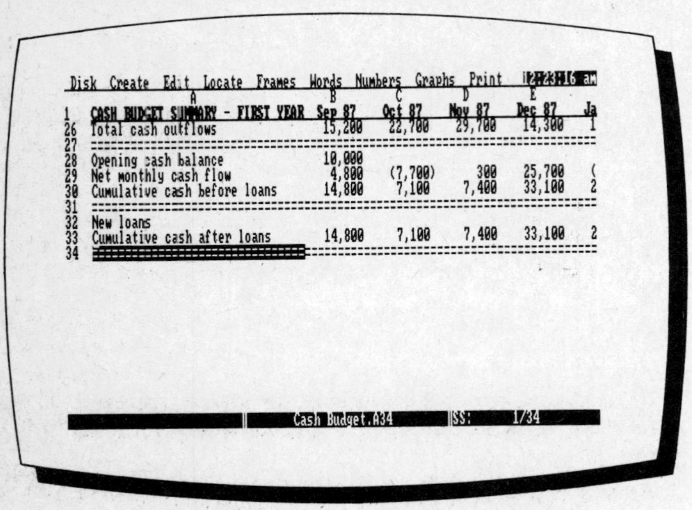


This part of the spreadsheet uses the cash inflows and outflows to calculate the monthly cash flow and cash balances. You will enter the following: an opening cash balance on row 28; formulas on row 29 to calculate the net monthly cash flow; formulas on row 30 to calculate the cumulative cash balance, the amount of cash you have on hand at the end of each month; formulas on row 33 to calculate the cumulative cash balance after loans (if entered on row 32, which we are leaving at 0 for now) at the end of each month; and formulas in cells N29 and N32 to calculate net cash flow for the period.

### Row 28

**The opening cash balance** carries forward the closing cash balance from the end of the last operating period, in this example a closing cash balance of $10,000 from the previous August.

*To enter a label:*

**Highlight** A28
**Type** **Opening cash balance**
**Press** (→|)

*To enter an opening cash balance:*

**Highlight** B28
**Type** **10000**
**Press** (↵)

### Row 29

**Net monthly cash flow** is calculated on this row by subtracting each month's total cash outflows from the month's total cash inflows. The last column on this row is used to enter a formula that calculates the net cash flow for the twelve-month period.

*To enter a label:*

**Highlight** A29
**Type** **Net monthly cash flow**
**Press** (→|)

*To enter a formula that calculates net monthly cash flow:*

**Highlight** B29
**Press** **Edit Formula** (**F2**)
**Type** **B13−B26**
**Press** (↵)

*To copy the formula to other columns:*

**Highlight** B29
**Press** **Copy** (**F8**)
**Highlight** C29
**Press** **Extend Select** (**F6**)
**End**
(←) to move the cursor back to cell M29
(↵) twice
(→) to shrink the cursor and move it over to cell N29

*To enter a formula that calculates net cash flow:*

**Highlight** N29
**Type** **@SUM(B29:M29)**
**Press** (↵)

**Result** The net monthly cash flows and the net cash flow for the period should match the illustration at the beginning of this section.

## Analysis

As you can see, the totals on this row vary widely, from −$8,300 (in July) to $25,700 (in December). A closer look will reveal that this variation is caused largely by inventory buildups for anticipated higher sales in the following months: for instance, the negative cash flow of −$7,700 in October is offset by an overwhelmingly positive cash flow during the December peak sales season. As long as we can cover the negative monthly cash flows with our cumulative cash balance, we shouldn't have any problem.

## Row 30

**Cumulative cash before loans** is essentially a running total of our cash on hand at the end of each month. At the beginning of the operating period covered by the budget, it is carried over from the closing balance of the previous period as the opening cash balance. Then we simply add (or subtract) our net monthly cash flow to get the new cumulative cash balance. (The result should match our bank balance.) The cumulative balance is particularly useful for predicting cash surpluses or shortfalls, and is thus a key indicator for cash management.

*To enter a label:*

**Highlight** A30
**Type** **Cumulative cash before loans**
**Press** ⇥

*To enter a formula to calculate cumulative cash flow in the opening period:*

**Highlight** B30
**Press** **Edit Formula** (**F2**)
**Type** **B28+B29**
**Press** ⇥

*To enter a formula to calculate cumulative cash flow in subsequent months:*

**Highlight** C30
**Press** **Edit Formula** (**F2**)
**Type** **B30+C29**
**Press** ↵

*To copy the formula to other columns:*

**Highlight** C30
**Press** **Copy** (**F8**)
**Highlight** D30
**Press** **Extend Select** (**F6**)
**End**
← to move the cursor back to cell M30
↵ twice
→ to shrink the cursor and move it over to cell N30

*To enter a formula to carry the last month's closing cash balance to the total column:*

**Highlight** N30
**Press** **Edit Formula** (**F2**)
**Type** **M30**
**Press** ↵

**Result** The cumulative cash balances should match the illustration at the beginning of this section.

## Analysis

We find that we do in fact have sufficient cash to cover the months that have negative cash flows. We won't need a new loan this year — assuming everything goes as planned. But a closer look at this row reveals that the business is not providing a large enough cash surplus, at least not at the beginning of the year: the only thing keeping us out of the loan office is our $10,000 opening cash balance. Furthermore, if you follow this row to the last column (N), you'll see that during the year of operations, the business has added only $1,700 to its original cash balance of $10,000.

At this point, several questions should be asked. If this is a new business, when do we expect sales to reach their normal operating level? If we hope to see sales rise as the business establishes itself, then perhaps it might be prudent to prepare cash budget projections for the second and third years. If the business is already established however, we might take a look at the cash budget and ask ourselves if the effort of running the business is worth it.

In short, the cash budget tells us that there will likely be a problem unless some aspects of the operation are changed. Some possibilities might be raising prices, changing the product lines, or cutting expenses. With Framework's instant recalculation feature, you can try various approaches on the spreadsheet. We will test some of these possibilities at the end of the chapter in the "What If" section.

## Rows **31** and **34**

**The double ruled line** is copied from row 27 to rows 31 and 34.

*To select the cells to be copied:*

**Highlight** A27

**Press** **Extend Select** (**F6**)
**End** to highlight cells A27 through N27
↵

*To copy the ruled line to row 31:*

**Press** **Copy** (**F8**)

**Highlight** row 31

**Press** ↵

*To copy the ruled line to row 34:*

**Press** **Copy** (**F8**)

**Highlight** row 34

**Press** ↵
← to shrink the highlight

## Row **32**

**New loans** are entered on this row. (Payments against existing loans are regular cash outflows, and would be listed in the cash outflows section of the spreadsheet.) In our example, we don't need any new loans since our cumulative cash covers negative net monthly cash flows. However, if you wanted to take out a new loan for your business, you would simply enter the cash received as a positive number on this row and any loan repayments as a negative number.

*To enter a label:*

**Highlight** A32

**Type** **New loans**

**Press** ↵

*To enter a formula in the total columns:*

**Highlight** N32

**Type** **@SUM(B32:M32)**

**Press** ↵

## Row **33**

**Cumulative cash after loans** calculates the cumulative cash balance after any new loans or loan repayments. This row, in conjunction with the row above, lets you try out various combinations of loans, interest rates, and repayment schedules, and helps insure that if you do take out a new loan, you'll have enough cash on hand to pay back the loan (and the interest) when payments come due.

If a formula in Framework refers to a cell containing no value, it will display a #VALUE! error message. To prevent such messages from being displayed on row 33 when no values are entered on row 32, we'll use a version of the @SUM function that ignores cells that are referred to when they are blank.

*To enter a label:*

**Highlight** A33

**Type** **Cumulative cash after loans**

**Press** ⇥

*To enter a formula that adds the first month's cumulative cash balance to new loans:*

**Highlight** B33

**Type** **@SUM(B30:B32)**

**Press** ⇥

*To enter a formula that adds the first month's cumulative cash balance after new loans to the net cash flow and new loans:*

**Highlight** C33

**Type** **@SUM(B33,C29,C32)**

**Press** ↵

*To copy the formula:*

**Highlight** C33

**Press** **Copy** (**F8**)

**Highlight** D33

**Press** **Extend Select** (**F6**)
**End**
← to point to cell M33
↵ twice
→ to shrink the cursor and move it over to cell N33

*To enter a formula in column N that carries the last month's closing cash balance to the total column:*

**Highlight** N33

**Press** **Edit Formula** (**F2**)

**Type** **M33**

**Press** ↵

**Result** Since no new loans were entered on row 32, row 33 should be the same as row 30.

## Tips Clearing the Desktop and Frames

If you want to clear your desktop of data that you are finished with, you can do so in several ways.

- ☐ The Put Away command on the Disk menu saves highlighted files on the default drive and directory and removes them from the desktop.
- ☐ The Clean Up Desktop command on the Disk menu closes all open frames on the desktop into their trays. This command also closes any drive frames that are open.
- ☐ An entire frame (including any frames it contains) can be deleted from the desktop (if you haven't saved it, the frame and its contents will be lost) by highlighting the frame border or tray and pressing the **Del** key. Only frames that have been protected using the Protect from Editing command on the Edit menu will remain when you use this command.
- ☐ The contents of the frame (including any frames it contains) can be deleted while retaining the frame itself by using the Blank All command on the Frames menu. Only cells or fields that have been protected using the Protect from Editing command on the Edit menu will remain in the frames when you use this command. If you select Blank All by mistake, don't worry. Framework will ask you if you are sure you want to blank the frame (since blanking is undoable).
- ☐ If you press **Del** by mistake, you can usually undo deletions provided you don't execute any other commands. The Undo selection on the Edit menu will undo only the most recently used command.
- ☐ The contents of deleted or blanked frames may not be recoverable with the Undo command; be sure to *save your work* before using these commands.
- ☐ You can use the **Extend Select (F6)** key to select several adjacent frames before using the commands described above.

## Step 7 Save Your Work

At this point, your spreadsheet exists only in the memory of your computer. If you accidentally erase the spreadsheet, or if your power fails, the spreadsheet will be lost. To avoid this unhappy fate, make it a habit to save your work onto a disk whenever you finish a major section. It takes only a few seconds, and does not affect the spreadsheet on your screen in any way.

Note that the spreadsheet will be saved to the disk in exactly the same manner that it now appears on the screen. So if the cursor is currently in cell A1, that is where it will be when you retrieve the file from the disk later on. Therefore we recommend that when you save the spreadsheet, you place the cursor in cell A1 or on the frame border.

You will be saving the spreadsheet on a blank formatted disk in drive B. Make sure you have a disk in drive B before you start.

*To save the spreadsheet:*

**Highlight** A1 (or the frame border)

**Press** **Ctrl-**↵

**Message** SAVING
Document saved

**Result** The spreadsheet will be saved to the disk in drive B; you will now be able to retrieve it from the disk at any time.

## Tips Saving Files

- A frame must have a label before it can be saved. The first eight characters of the frame label are used as the file name for the saved frame, with any unacceptable characters being replaced with the underscore (_) character. For example, a frame labeled "File Name" would be saved on the disk as "FILE_NAM.FW."
- There are several different ways to save a frame:

  **Ctrl-(↵)** will save the frame highlighted or currently being used. If the cursor is in a subframe, the containing frame will also be saved. Other frames that have their own desktop trays will not be saved unless they have been included in the highlighted area with the **Extend Select (F6)** key.

  The Save and Continue command from the Disk menu will save all highlighted frames and leave them exactly as they were on the desktop and in memory, so that you can continue working.

  The Put Away command from the Disk menu will save all highlighted frames and remove them from the desktop and from memory. This will free up memory and allow you to create or retrieve additional frames.

  The Write DOS Text File command from the Disk menu will save a picture of the frame exactly as it appears on the screen in a text file. The text file will have a .TXT extension (to distinguish it from the Framework file with the same name) and is in standard ASCII text. Copying a file with this command will ignore all special Framework attributes (like boldface or italics).

  The Quit Framework command from the Disk menu will prompt you to save the current file if it is new or modified: Document new or modified: SAVE IT (y/n)?. Type **Y** to save the file, **N** to quit without saving changes.

  The **Copy (F8)** and **Move (F7)** keys can be used to copy a frame to a different frame or subframe which could be saved separately.
- If you change disks in the drive from which you have retrieved a file and then attempt to save that file, the prompt Diskette has been changed, store anyway (y/n)? will be displayed. Typing **Y** will save the file on the new disk, **N** will cancel the save command.
- You can use the **Move (F7)** and **Copy (F8)** keys to save a frame after moving its home disk to another drive.
- To save or copy only a subframe within a containing frame, you must copy or move it to its own frame on the desktop.
- If a file with the same name is already on the disk to which you are copying or moving it, the message File exists, do you wish to overwrite it (y/n)? will be displayed.
- Sometimes when Framework is saving a long file, it will pause during the save operation. Be sure you don't open the drive until the message Document saved appears on the message line.

**Possible Problems When Saving Files:**

- When a file is saved, Document saved is displayed on the message line of the screen. If a problem is encountered while Framework is attempting to save a file, a message will be displayed that should help you identify and solve the problem. When a file is not saved to the disk, for whatever reason, the message Frame NOT Stored is displayed. The following is a list of some of the common problems encountered when saving files

  The message File exists, do you wish to overwrite it (y/n)? is displayed when you attempt to save, copy, or move another file to a disk containing a file with the same name. Type **Y** to overwrite the existing file or **N** to cancel the command.

  The message Diskette has been changed, store anyway (y/n)? is displayed when you attempt to save a file after changing the disk in the drive that originally contained that file.

  The message Disk in drive is write protected is displayed when the tab covering the write-protect notch on the disk you are saving to has not been removed. Remove the tab and try again.

  The message Not enough free space on destination disk is displayed when there is not enough room on the disk to save the file. You must delete some files from the disk or insert a different disk and try again.

  The message Read error while trying to sync diskette—retry (y/n)? is displayed when no disk is in the drive or the drive cover is open.

  The message Drive frame now reflects actual drive contents, finish saving (y/n)? is displayed if you have opened a drive frame and then put a different disk in that drive before issuing a save command. When the save command is issued, Framework displays the new directory and this message. Type **Y** to save the file or **N** to cancel the command.

# Linking Spreadsheets

Spreadsheets don't have to be gigantic to be very useful. In fact, smaller spreadsheets can be easier to understand and use. In this section you'll see how to overcome the only limitation of smaller spreadsheets — their size. Framework allows you to link spreadsheets so changes in one are reflected in others. This ability to link smaller spreadsheets into chains gives you an incredible amount of flexibility. For example, an inexperienced operator can be assigned to enter data into a single frame with the results being totally hidden; the manager can then bring the related frames to the desktop to complete the analysis. Or, in another case, separate frames can contain values to be compared — for instance, this year's and last year's P&L — and then a third frame can contain the formulas that calculate variations.

The spreadsheet you will create in this section will be linked to the cash budget spreadsheet created in the last section. If you haven't already created that spreadsheet, take a few minutes now to do so. This new spreadsheet serves two purposes: first, it demonstrates how to link one spreadsheet to another; and second, it provides you with a unique way to set up graph ranges that will be used to create graphs in the following section.

## The Ranges Spreadsheet

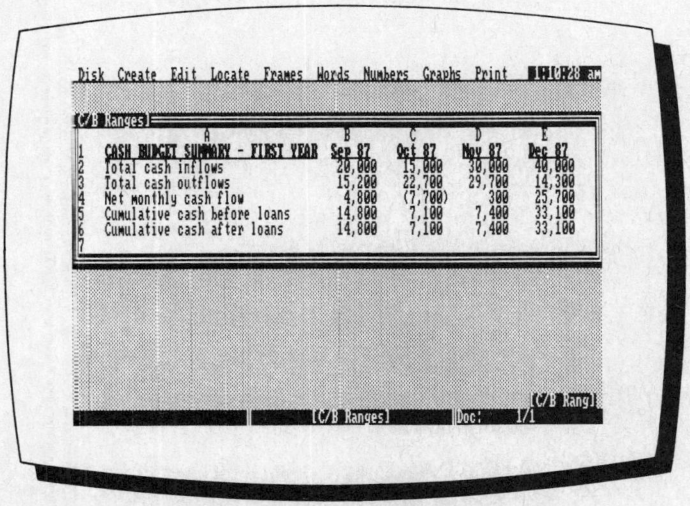


The spreadsheet created in this section will work in conjunction with the cash budget spreadsheet created in the previous section. The spreadsheet is designed so that changes in any of the cells in the cash budget spreadsheet cause this spreadsheet to change — they are linked together. Here's how it works: formulas in this spreadsheet will refer to key cells in the cash budget — for instance, the total cash inflows and outflows rows. Any numbers or values calculated by numbers on those rows will be automatically carried to this spreadsheet.

Here are the steps you'll follow in this section:

**Step 1** Getting ready
**Step 2** Create a new spreadsheet
**Step 3** Link the spreadsheets
**Step 4** Create a containing frame
**Step 5** Save your work

## Step 1 Getting Ready

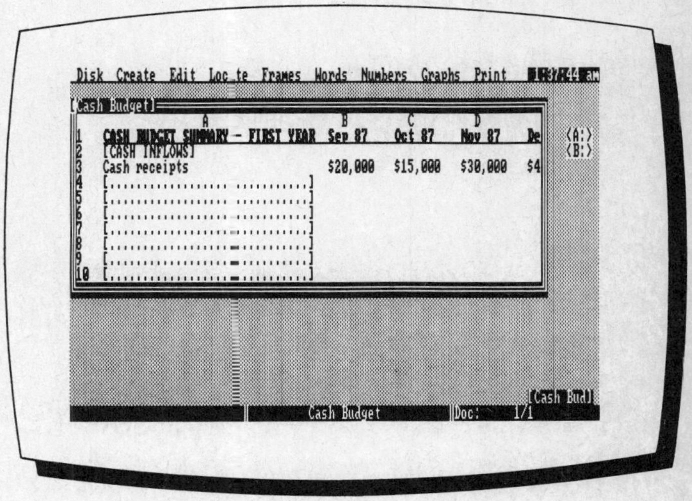


Before creating a new spreadsheet that is linked to the cash budget frame, that frame has to be on the desktop. We will then size it and drag it to make room for the new spreadsheet. (For more information, see Tips on "Sizing Frames" and "Dragging Frames.")

Frames can be laid out on the desktop to suit your own tastes. Generally, when you have only one frame you'll want to zoom it to fill the screen (using the **Size (F4)**) key so you can see the maximum amount. When there is more than one frame on the desktop, you can arrange them so they are next to each other or overlapping. This will give you a better idea of where they are, especially when you move from one frame to another.

## Retrieve the File

If the cash budget spreadsheet frame isn't already on the desktop, you must retrieve it from the disk by opening the drive and selecting the file. The file will appear on the desktop exactly as it was when last saved.

*To retrieve the file containing the cash budget spreadsheet:*

**Press** **Scroll Lock** to move the cursor to the disk drive

**Select** <B:> (or the disk on which you saved the file)

**Press** **Down Level (Gray +)** to open the drive frame and move the cursor into it

**Highlight** CASH_BUD.FW

**Press** ↵

**Result** The drive spins and in a few moments the file appears on the desktop exactly as it was when it was saved. If the file was closed in its tray when it was saved, that is the way it will be retrieved. To open it, highlight the tray and press ↵.

## Tips Retrieving Files

You can retrieve files that are stored on a disk in one of three ways:

- ☐ If you know the name of the file you want, you can retrieve it using the Get File By Name command on the Disk menu. If the file is not on the default drive or current subdirectory (if one is being used), you must specify the full file name, including drive and/or subdirectory names. For example, if the default drive is C and you want to retrieve the file TEST.FW from drive B, you would type **B:TEST.FW**.
- ☐ Use the **Scroll Lock** key to move the cursor to the drive letters from the desktop. Open the drive on the desktop by placing the highlight on the drive letter, and pressing ↵. Then press **Down Level (Gray +)** to enter the directory. Once the highlight is in the directory, you can retrieve files one at a time by using the arrow keys to move the highlight onto the desired file and pressing ↵. If you want to retrieve more than one file, use the **Extend Select (F6)** key to highlight a range of file names and press ↵.
- ☐ You can retrieve files automatically when you load Framework. When you type the command that loads Framework from the operating system, include the names of the files you want to retrieve. If you want to retrieve more than one file, separate the file names with commas. If the file you are retrieving contains a program or function routine, it can be retrieved and run automatically by following the file name with the characters /X. Using /X will run any program contained within the file, just as if it had been retrieved from the desktop and the **Recalc (F5)** key had been pressed. Be sure to include the file extension .FW when you retrieve files automatically, and specify the drive or subdirectory name if the file is not on the default data drive. For example, to retrieve the file TEST.FW automatically, you would type **FW TEST.FW** from the DOS prompt.

If frame is closed in its tray when saved, it will also be closed when it is retrieved.

Files can be retrieved directly into an outline or containing frame by opening the file and using the **Move (F7)** or **Copy (F8)** command from within the disk drive frame to transfer the highlighted file.

**Step 1** Open the outline or containing frame onto the desktop.

**Step 2** Open the disk drive containing the file to be retrieved and highlight the file name.

**Step 3** Press **Move (F7)** or **Copy (F8)**.

**Step 4** Press **Scroll Lock** to return to the desktop, move the cursor into the outline or containing frame, and press ↵.

You can use the **Down Level (Gray +)** key to simultaneously open a highlighted drive and move into that drive's frame. The highlight will automatically go to the first file in the disk drive directory.

## Size the Frame

To size a frame, highlight the frame's border, press the **Size (F4)** key, and then use the cursor movement keys to move the right side in and out and the bottom up and down.

*To size the cash budget frame:*

**Highlight** the frame border

**Press** **Size** (**F4**)
(→) until right part of status panel reads Size: 78/11
(↓) until status panel reads **Size: 78/12**
(↵) to fix the frame's size

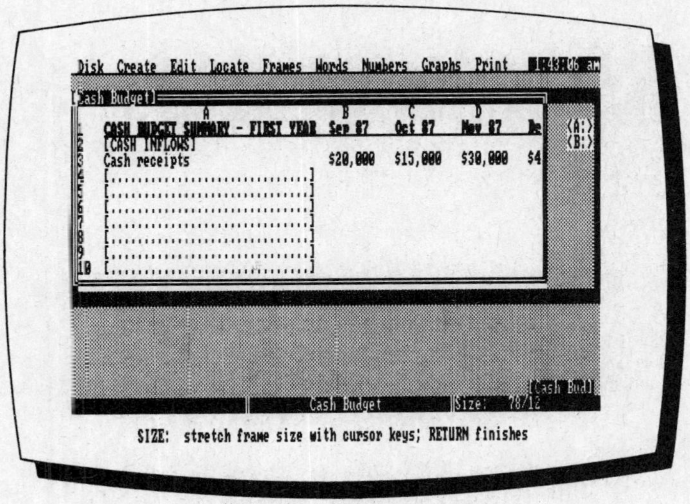


**Result** As you change the size, a ghost highlight shows the new size, and the status panel indicates the column where the right edge falls and the row where the bottom falls. When the size is fixed, the ghost highlight disappears and the new frame size appears on the desktop.

## Drag the Frame

Frames are dragged around on the desktop by highlighting the frame border, pressing the **Drag (F3)** key, and using the cursor movement keys to drag it. In this step we'll drag the frame into the upper-left corner of the screen.

*To drag the frame:*

**Highlight** the frame border

**Press** **Drag** (**F3**)
(↑) until right part of status panel reads Drag: 1/1
(↵) to fix the frame in place

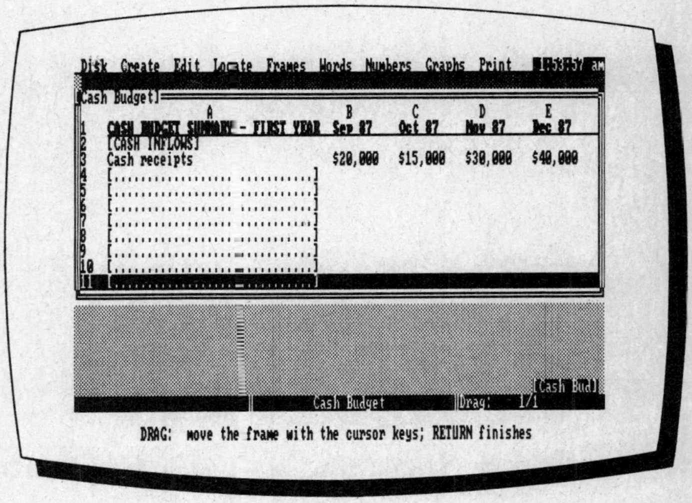


**Result** The ghost image of the frame disappears and the frame is positioned in the upper-left corner of the screen.

## Tips Sizing Frames

If a frame is closed in its tray, open it onto the desktop before sizing it.

Pressing the **Size (F4)** key twice and then presing ↵ will size a frame to fill the desktop or the frame within which it is contained. Unlike zooming, this size will remain fixed unless you resize it.

You can use the **Extend Select (F6)** key to select a group of adjacent frames to size at the same time.

**Keys Used to Size Frames**

| KEY | EFFECT ON FRAME |
|---|---|
| **Size (F4)** | Begins sizing a highlighted frame. |
| ← | Moves right edge in one column. |
| → | Moves right edge out one column. |
| ↑ | Moves bottom edge up one row. |
| ↓ | Moves bottom edge down one row. |
| **Ctrl-**← | Moves right edge in eight columns. |
| **Ctrl-**→ | Moves right edge out eight columns. |
| **Ctrl-**↑ | Moves bottom edge up four rows. |
| **Ctrl-**↓ | Moves bottom edge down four rows. |
| **Home** | Moves right edge to far left of desktop. |
| **End** | Moves right edge to far right of desktop. |
| **Ctrl-Home** | Moves frame to top-left corner of screen. |
| **Ctrl-End** | Moves bottom of frame to bottom of screen, and right edge to far right of desktop. |
| ↵ | Enters the size of the frame. |

## Tips Dragging Frames

If the frame you want to drag up or down is inside another frame, you must choose Allow Free Dragging from the Frames menu.

If you drag a containing frame past the bottom or right edge of the desktop, it will be resized.

You can use the **Extend Select (F6)** key to select a group of adjacent frames to size.

**Keys Used to Drag Frames**

| KEY | DESCRIPTION |
|---|---|
| **Drag (F3)** | Begins dragging a highlighted frame. |
| ← → ↑ ↓ | Drags the frame left, right, up, or down one row. |
| **Ctrl-**← **Ctrl-**→ | Drags the frame left or right eight columns. |
| **Ctrl-**↑ **Ctrl-**↓ | Drags the frame up or down four rows. |
| **Home** | Drags the frame to the far left of the desktop. |
| **End** | Drags the frame to the far right of the desktop. |
| **Ctrl-Home** | Drags the frame to the top left corner of the screen. |
| **Ctrl-End** | Drags the frame to the bottom right corner of the screen. |
| ↵ | Fixes the new position of the frame. |

## Step 2 Create a New Spreadsheet

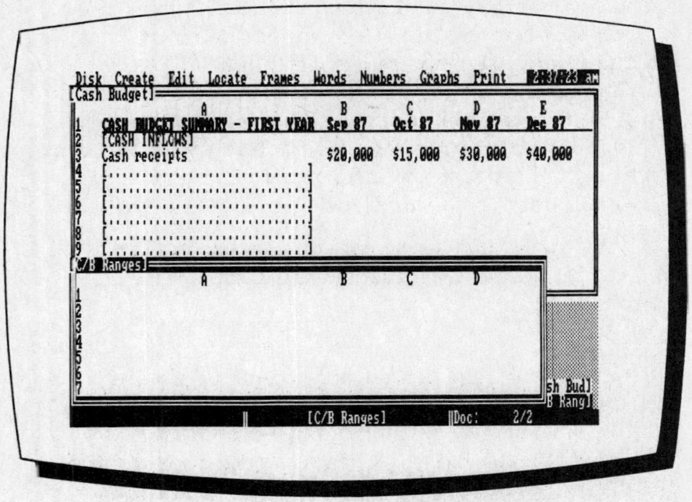


Now that the cash budget spreadsheet frame has been placed on the desktop and positioned, we'll create a new frame so we can enter formulas linking the two frames.

### Set the Width and Height

The spreadsheet we'll be creating will be 13 columns wide and 7 rows deep.

*To set the width of the spreadsheet:*

**Press** **Ins**

**Highlight** Create<br>Width

**Press** ↵

**Type** **13**

**Press** ↵

*To set the height of the spreadsheet:*

**Highlight** Height

**Press** ↵

**Type** **7**

**Press** ↵

### Create the Spreadsheet

Now we'll create and label the new spreadsheet. We'll call this spreadsheet *C/B Ranges*. (*Remember:* Two files with the same name cannot be saved on the same disk: one would overwrite the other. And, since Framework uses only the first 8 characters of a file name when saving, you must be careful to give a new frame a different name within those first characters.)

*To create a spreadsheet:*

**Highlight** Spreadsheet on the Create menu

**Press** ↵

*To label the frame:*

**Highlight** the frame border

**Type** **C/B Ranges**

**Press** ↵

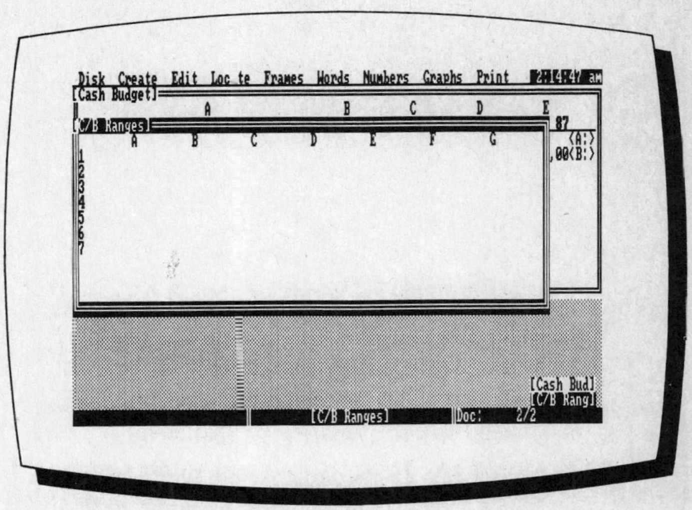


**Result** A new frame appears on the desktop on top of the old one, and a tray for the frame appears in the lower-right corner of the screen. We have named the frame C/B Ranges.

## Tips Linking Spreadsheets

There are two ways to refer to cells in another spreadsheet in a formula:

**1** References can be made using the ↑ key to start pointing, and then using the **Up Level (Gray −)** and **Down Level (Gray +)** keys to refer to the cell in another spreadsheet.

**2** The other spreadsheet cell can be referred to by typing the name of the spreadsheet (preceded by @) and the specific cell. For example, to refer to cell B5 in the spreadsheet Sales, you would type **@Sales.B5** in the formula.

If you change the values in a spreadsheet that is linked to others, you may also need to recalculate the other spreadsheets. This is done by highlighting the borders of the other frames and pressing **Recalc (F5)**.

To automatically recalculate all linked spreadsheets, you place a reference to the linked frames on the frame border of the spreadsheet you are changing. The function @(frame name) is used. Each time the frame border is highlighted and the **Recalc (F5)** key is pressed, the linked spreadsheets will automatically be recalculated.

To avoid confusion, place linked spreadsheets in a containing frame. Saving the containing frame will save all subframes within it. Grouping related frames in containing frames keeps the disk directories less cluttered.

It is easier to see the frames within a containing frame if Outline View is used. Setting on Number Labels and Reveal Type on the Frames menu also makes the outline display easier to read.

To open a subframe while you are in Outline View, use the **Zoom (F9)** key. To close it, press **Zoom (F9)** again.

Close the subframes that you are not currently using to keep the desktop from becoming too cluttered.

## Step 3 Link the Spreadsheets

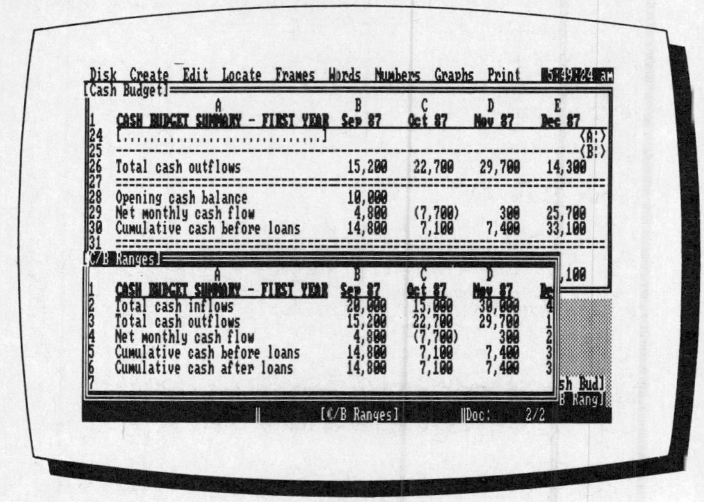


You'll now enter formulas in the first column of this new spreadsheet that refer to cells on the cash budget spreadsheet.

### Row 1

**Headings** on this spreadsheet are carried down from the cash budget spreadsheet. Formulas will refer to the cash budget frame, so that changes made in that frame will be reflected here. You can just type in the formulas (including the name of the frame), but generally it's faster and more accurate to point to cells when building formulas across two spreadsheets. Here you'll see how.

*To build formulas by pointing to cells:*

**Highlight** A1

**Press** **Edit Formula (F2)**
↑ to begin cursor pointing
**Up Level (Gray −)** to highlight the frame border
↑ to move the highlight to the cash budget frame and tray
**Down Level (Gray +)** to enter the frame (cell A1 will be highlighted)

**Result** The formula reading **Cash Budget.A1** is displayed on the edit line; the one on your screen should match that shown in the illustration.

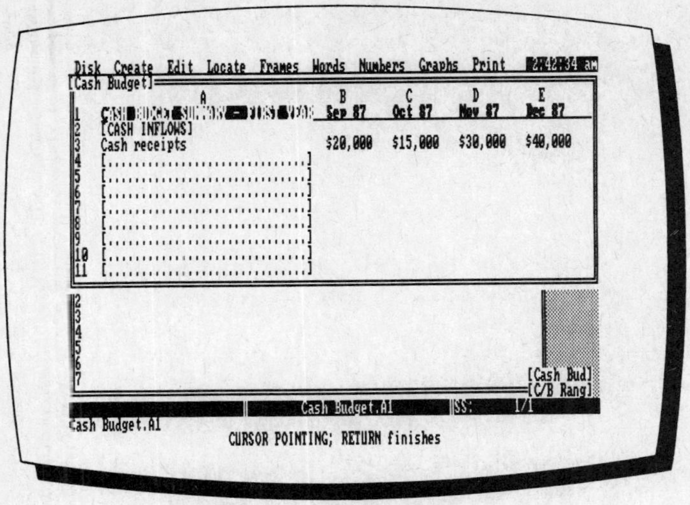


Now that the formula has been completed, it can be entered by pressing (↵).

*To enter the formula:*

**Press** (↵) twice

**Result** The label (called a "string") is carried from the cash budget frame to the C/B Ranges frame. *Note:* If you get a #N/A message in cell A1 of the C/B Ranges spreadsheet, it may be because you have more than one cash budget tray on the desktop. Delete the extra tray(s) and try again. Framework needs to know it is referring to only *one* frame.

## Row **2**

**Total cash inflows** will be carried down from the cash budget spreadsheet. The formula on this row will refer to the total cash inflows row on the Cash Budget frame.

**Highlight** A2

**Press** **Edit Formula** (**F2**)
(↑) to begin cursor pointing
**Up Level (Gray −)** to highlight the frame border
(↑) to move the highlight to the cash budget frame and tray
**Down Level (Gray +)** to enter the frame

**Highlight** A13 of the Cash Budget frame

**Press** (↵) twice

**Result** The label is carried from the Cash Budget frame to the C/B Ranges frame.

## Row **3**

**Total cash outflows** are now carried down. The formula on this row will refer to the total cash outflows on the Cash Budget frame.

**Highlight** A3

**Press** **Edit Formula** (**F2**)
(↑)
**Up Level (Gray −)**
(↑) move the highlight to the cash budget frame and tray
**Down Level (Gray +)** to enter the frame

**Highlight** A26

**Press** (↵) twice

## Row **4**

**Net monthly cash flow** is carried down. The formula on this row will refer to the net monthly cash flow row on the Cash Budget frame.

**Highlight** A4

**Press** **Edit Formula** (**F2**)
(↑)
**Up Level (Gray −)**
(↑)
**Down Level (Gray +)**

**Highlight** A29

**Press** (↵) twice

## Row **5**

**Cumulative cash flow before loans** is carried down. The formula on this row will refer to the cumulative cash flows before loans row on the Cash Budget frame.

**Highlight** A5

**Press** **Edit Formula** (**F2**)
(↑)
**Up Level (Gray −)**
(↑)
**Down Level (Gray +)**

**Highlight** A30

**Press** (↵) twice

## Row 6

**Cumulative cash flow after loans** is carried down. The formula on this row will refer to the cumulative cash flows after loans row on the Cash Budget frame.

**Highlight** A6

**Press** **Edit Formula** (**F2**)
↑
**Up Level (Gray −)**
↑
**Down Level (Gray +)**

**Highlight** A33

**Press** ↵ twice

## Copy the Formulas

Now the formulas can be copied across the spreadsheet to carry the headings and key line item values in each of the cash budget columns to this spreadsheet.

*To select the cells to be copied:*

**Highlight** A1

**Press** **Extend Select** (**F6**)
**PgDn** to highlight cells A1 through A7
↵

*To copy the cells:*

**Press** **Copy** (**F8**)

**Highlight** column B

**Press** **Extend Select** (**F6**)
**End** to highlight columns B through M
↵ twice
← and ↑ to shrink the cursor

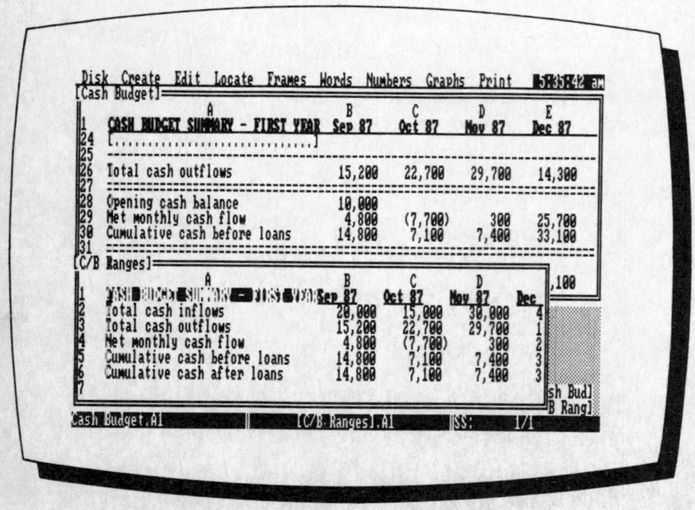


## Tips Protecting Frames

Frames are protected by highlighting the frame border and using the Protect from Editing command on the Edit menu. A protected frame cannot be edited or deleted.

To unprotect a frame, use the Allow Editing command on the Edit menu.

Sections of a frame can be unprotected so that entries can be made in a frame only where you would like them. This is done by highlighting the section and using the Allow Editing command on the Edit menu.

If you try to delete or edit a protected frame, the computer will beep and the message Frame is protected: use Edit: Allow Editing to proceed will appear on the message line.

A frame can be hidden so that it is not seen on the desktop but stays in memory by entering the function @Hide(<frame name>) on the frame border (or on the border of another frame on the desktop). To see the frame again, enter the function @Unhide(<frame name>) on another frame border.

## Tips Frame Formulas

Frame formulas are entered on frame borders behind the frame label. You highlight the frame border and press **Edit Formula (F2)** to enter or edit frame formulas. Frame formulas can be used for several different purposes, including:

- ☐ Setting page formats (like line spacing, footers and headers, etc.).
- ☐ Establishing criteria in a database to extract only those records that match the criteria.
- ☐ Controlling the way currency is formatted.

If you need to enter a frame formula on more than one line, use the **Zoom (F9)** key to make the border full-screen. This is done by highlighting the frame border, presing **Edit Formula (F2)**, and then pressing **Zoom (F9)**. When you're finished, press **Recalc (F5)** instead of ↵. ↵ will break the line instead of entering the formula—just like in a word frame.)

**Result** Your values on this spreadsheet should exactly match those shown on the same rows of the cash budget spreadsheet.

## Align Text

As we noted, the formats from the Numbers menu do not carry over from one spreadsheet to another. Therefore, if we want the labels in row 1 aligned in the middle of their cells, we will have to format them.

*To select the cells whose contents you want to align:*

**Highlight** B1
**Press** **Extend Select (F6)**
**End**
↵
**Ins**
**Highlight** Numbers
Middle
**Press** ↵
← to shrink the cursor

## Protect the Spreadsheet

At this point, we would like to protect this spreadsheet from accidental changes or deletions. The entire spreadsheet can be protected from any sort of editing.

*To protect the entire frame:*

**Highlight** the frame border
**Press** **Ins**
**Highlight** Edit
Protect from Editing
**Press** ↵

**Result** Changes cannot be made in this spreadsheet frame unless **Allow Editing** is turned on when highlighting the frame border.

## Recalculate Automatically

When two linked frames are on the desktop, changes made in one won't be reflected in the other until they are both recalculated. One way to recalculate after a change is made in one frame is to highlight the other frame and press the **Recalc (F5)** key. However, this requires you to leave the first spreadsheet and move to the linked frame before you can see the effects of the change. You can shorten this procedure by adding a formula "behind" the label on the frame where the change is going to be made. The formula is simply the @ symbol followed by the name of the other spreadsheet.

*To move the highlight to the Cash Budget frame border:*

**Press** **Up Level (Gray −)** to highlight the C/B Ranges frame border if it isn't already
↑ to move the highlight to the Cash Budget frame border

*To enter a formula behind the frame label:*

**Press** **Edit Formula (F2)**
**Type** @
**Press** ↑ to begin cursor pointing
↓ to highlight the C/B Ranges frame border
↵ twice
**Message** RECALCULATING

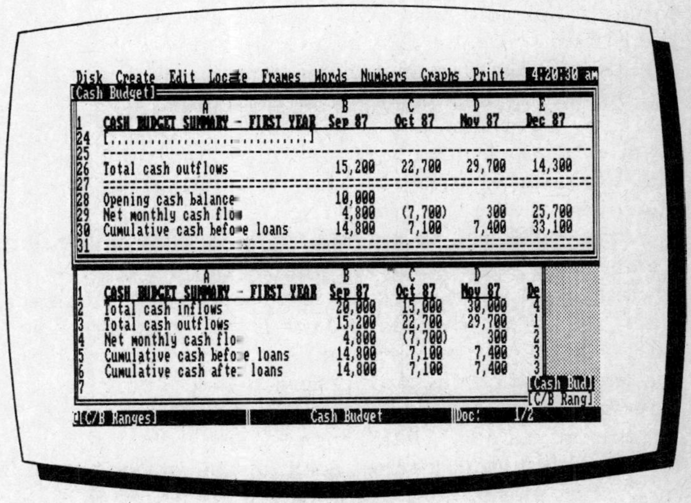


**Result** The highlight will return to the Cash Budget frame border after the spreadsheets are finished recalculating. The formula cannot be seen on the frame border since it is behind the label, but when the frame border is highlighted, as it is now, the formula can be seen in the left section of the status panel.

## Step 4 Create a Containing Frame

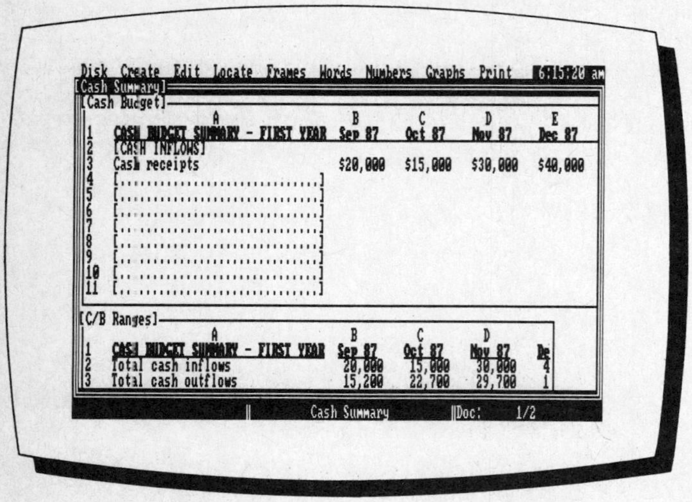


Now that you have two related frames, you can put them together into a *containing frame* so they can be saved and loaded together. If you were to keep these in separate frames you would have to save, retrieve, and print them separately. Putting related spreadsheet frames together in a containing frame is much like keeping printouts of the same sections together in a file folder; it saves time and makes things easier when you want to save, retrieve, and print material. (You could also use outlines to keep materials together, but we will show you how to use containing frames here.)

Framework uses empty word frames to contain other frames, called "subframes." Frames that are used only to contain other frames have to be empty, since frames can't contain both words and other frames at the same time. When you use containing frames (or outlines) you are working with "nested" frames. The containing frames into which other frames are moved are called "document frames," which means they are not contained within other frames. Such frames are identified by double lines around the frame. When you save the frame, regardless of where the cursor is positioned, everything up to this level is saved. Frames contained in the desktop level frame are called "subframes" or "insert" frames, which means they are contained within other frames; they can be identified by the single lines for the frame border.

## Create and Label an Empty Frame

Containing frames are nothing more than empty frames into which other frames can be moved. Word frames and empty frames are identical when first created, but they can be used for only one of the two purposes for which they are designed (to hold text or other frames); they cannot be used for both.

*To create the containing frame:*

**Highlight** either frame border

**Press** **Ins**

**Highlight** Create
Empty / Word Frame

**Press** ↵

*To label the frame:*

**Highlight** the frame border

**Type** **Cash Summary**

**Press** ↵

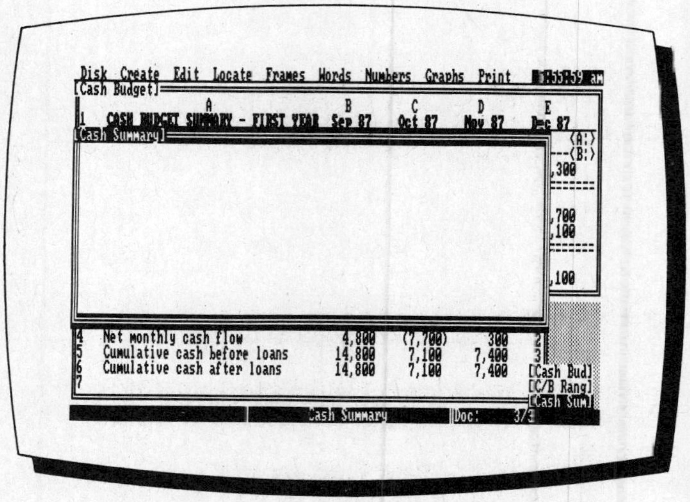


**Result** An empty word frame labeled "Cash Summary" should now be on the desktop.

## Select and Move Frames

Frames can be moved into the containing frame one at a time or in groups. The frames to be moved can be either open on the desktop or closed into their trays when they are selected.

*To select the frames to be moved:*

**Highlight** Cash Budget frame border (use the arrow keys)

**Press** **Extend Select (F6)**
↓ to highlight both spreadsheet frames
↵

**Result** The two frame trays (Cash Bud and C/B Rang) and the frames (Cash Budget and C/B Ranges) are highlighted.

*To move the frames:*

**Press** **Move** (**F7**) to begin moving the highlighted frames

(↓) or (↑) to highlight the containing frame border

**Down Level (Gray +)** to move the cursor into the frame

(↵)

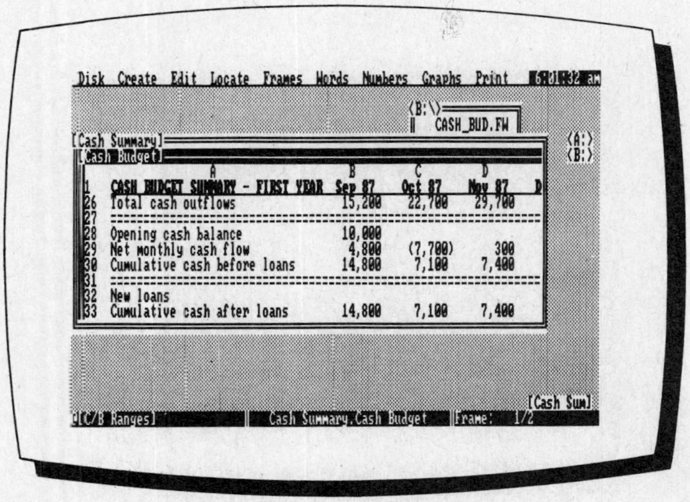


**Result** The highlighted frames are moved into the containing frame. They, and their trays, disappear from the desktop since they are no longer separate frames. You may not be able to see both frames at once now, but if you use the arrow keys to toggle between them you will see that they're still there.

## Size the Containing Frame

The containing frame, or any other frame on the desktop, can be sized to fill the screen.

**Press** **Up Level (Gray −)** to highlight the Cash Summary frame border

**Size** (**F4**) twice

(↵)

**Result** The frame border immediately expands to fill the screen and more of the subframe inside the containing frame can be seen.

## Put Frames into a Column

If the frames you moved into the containing frame were dragged around the desktop before you moved them, they may now be randomly arranged within the containing frame. If you'd rather align them, follow these instructions.

*To align your frames in a column if they are not already aligned:*

**Highlight** either of the spreadsheet frames inside the containing frame

**Press** **Ins**

**Highlight** Frames
Put into Column

**Press** (↵)

**Result** If the frames were not in a column before the command was used, they now will be.

## Tips Copying and Moving Frames

The difference between the Move and Copy commands is that moving deletes the original version from the old location; copying creates a duplicate of the original in a new location.

Use the Copy command to make a duplicate of a graph that you are using for analysis. After changing the related spreadsheet, you can redraw one graph and leave the other unchanged.

When a frame is moved or copied, all frames contained within it are also moved or copied.

If you find it confusing moving and copying frames within a containing frame, try using Outline View.

A subframe contained within another frame can be moved or copied from its containing frame directly to its own file on a disk. First, highlight the frame you want to move and press **Move (F7)** or **Copy (F8)**. Then, move into the directory frame or disk drive for the disk you want to move the frame into by pressing **Scroll Lock** and then **Down Level (Gray +)**. To complete the process, press (↵).

# Exploring the Cash Budget with Graphs

Now that you've entered the cash budget spreadsheet and linked it to the ranges spreadsheet, the fun begins! You have a working model, ready to be used to explore alternatives for your own business.

In this section we'll create and name three graphs of the cash budget that show net monthly cash flow (bar graph), the cumulative cash balance over the twelve-month period (line graph), and cash inflows and outflows by month (pie chart). Then we'll explore "What If" questions to find out how the cash budget is affected by changes in the business — for instance, what happens if cash inflows increase? What if cash outflows increase? Each "What If" will be explored graphically, so you will be able to see instantly the impact of the scenario on the overall cash position of the firm. Graphs are ideal for this kind of "What If" analysis, since they show at a glance how key areas of a business perform over time. Instead of looking for trends in a row or column of numbers, you can see immediately where the general trends are heading.

We'll explore two different "What Ifs" in this chapter, but we encourage you to consider them as just a starting point. Ask your own "What If" questions, and you'll be amazed at how fast you can learn things you never knew about how your business works.

One of Framework's most remarkable features is its ability to instantly create graphs from the numbers on any spreadsheet. With a few keystrokes, you can view your data as any one of six graph types, with a variety of titles, legends, and styling features. And — surprise! — it's easy. If you follow the steps in this section, you'll be creating Framework graphs in ten or fifteen minutes.

## Introduction to Framework Graphs

You can use graphs to find and illustrate trends and relationships of data. In Framework, you must first have a spreadsheet or database on the desktop before you can create a graph. Six types of graphs are available: line graphs, bar graphs, stacked bar graphs, pie charts, marked-point graphs, and X-Y graphs. You can add overlays of one graph type over another.

When you draw a graph, Framework creates a frame for it automatically. Or, you can place a graph in any empty frame you've already created. Graph frames are like other frames — you can size them, drag them, enlarge or reduce them, and move or copy them. If you change the size of a graph frame, Framework automatically adjusts the graph inside to fit the new frame. Framework's graphs are drawn in color; if you have a color display monitor, you can see the color by zooming the graph with the **Zoom** (**F9**) key. If you don't have a color monitor, the graph is displayed in black and white.

One feature of Framework's graphs that you should remember is that you can plot two or more rows or columns of data *only if they are next to each other* on the spreadsheet or database you're working from. You must use graph overlays to plot non-adjacent rows and columns.

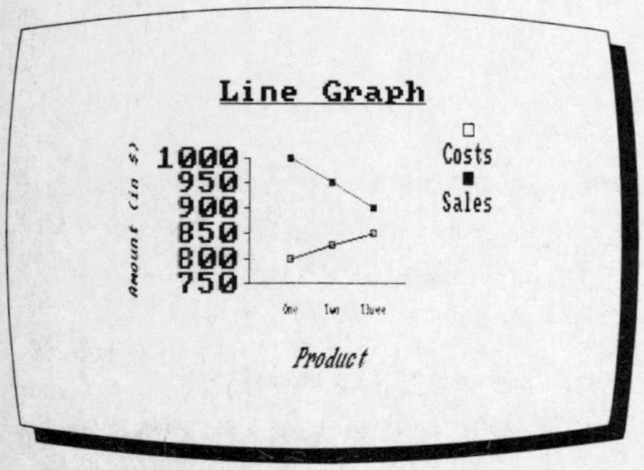

**Line graph**

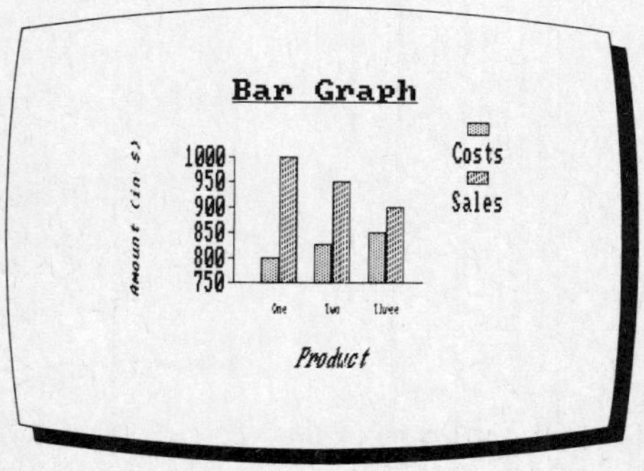

**Bar graph**

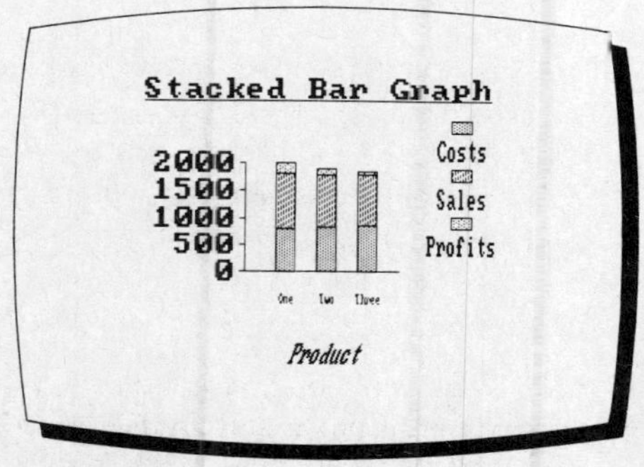

**Stacked bar graph**

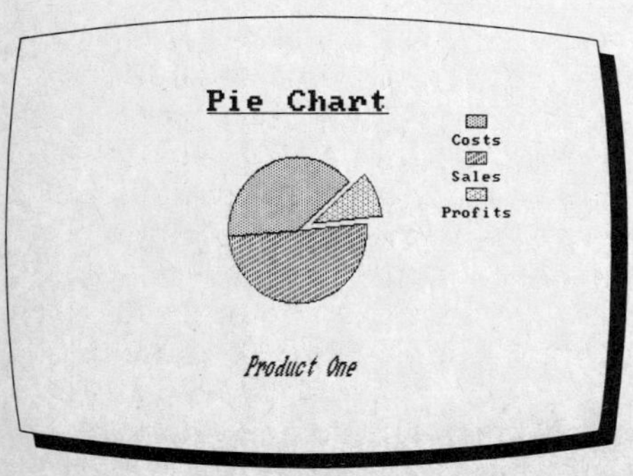

**Pie chart**

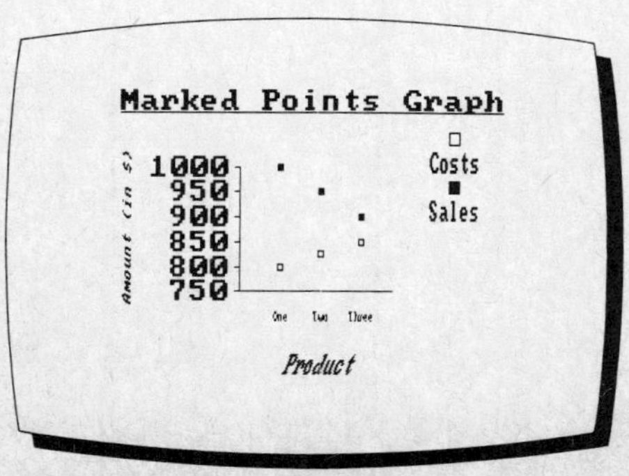

**Marked-points graph**

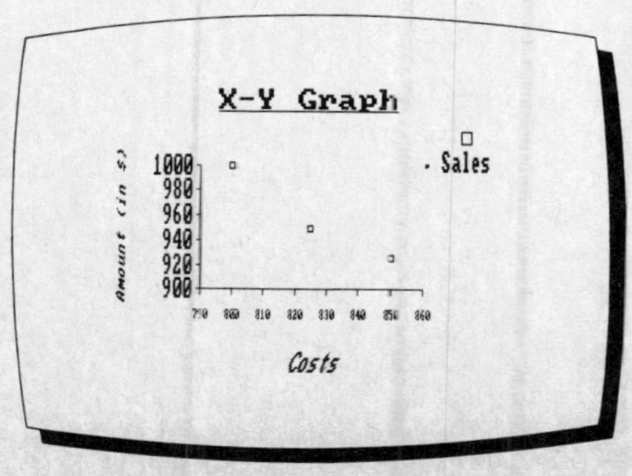

**X-Y graph**

Here are the six types of graphs Framework offers:

**Line graphs** display data ranges as positive or negative lines connecting points against the horizontal X-axis. Line graphs can display trends or relationships between more than one set of values — between sales and costs, for example.

**Bar graphs** display quantities as vertical bars — all on the X-axis. Positive quantities appear as bars above the X-axis, negative quantities as bars below it. Bar graphs can be used just like line graphs to display trends or relationships between more than one set of values, for instance, between sales and costs.

**Stacked bar graphs** can show parts of a whole; each bar is stacked on top of another, and all bars add up to a total. You can easily see the relationship of one part to another and to the whole with a stacked bar graph. For example, a stacked bar graph of costs and profits should equal sales when stacked on top of one another. If your costs were $800, and your profits are $200, your sales have to be $1,000. Stacked bar graphs cannot be used to plot ranges containing negative values.

**Pie charts,** like stacked bar graphs, show parts of a whole. The whole is represented by a circle, and each part is a wedge within it — a "piece of the pie." You cannot plot negative values on a pie chart. And, unlike bar graphs and line graphs, you can plot only one set of values at a time. To show trends or comparisons you would have to use two or more pie charts side by side. Key pieces of a pie chart can be exploded to highlight them on or near the chart.

**Marked-points graphs** (or scattergrams) are like line graphs except that values are plotted with points, and these points are not connected by lines. You can plot negative values on marked-point graphs.

**X-Y graphs** are the only graphs on which the X-axis consists of values, not labels. X-Y graphs plot the values on the two axes against each other.

You can add *overlays* to your graphs in order to highlight key items against a background of related data. For instance, you might overlay a line graph of costs on a bar graph of profits to highlight the profits.

Here are the steps you'll follow to build the Cash Budget graphs:

**Step 1** Getting ready
**Step 2** Create a bar graph
**Step 3** Create a line graph
**Step 4** Create a pie chart
**Step 5** Recalculate automatically
**Step 6** Save your work

## Step 1 Getting Ready

### Retrieve the Containing Frame

If the Cash Summary containing frame you created in the last section isn't on the desktop, you need to retrieve it. The frame will appear on the desktop exactly as it was when last saved.

*To retrieve the Cash Summary frame:*

**Press** **Scroll Lock** to move the cursor to the disk drive

**Highlight** <B:> (or the disk you saved the file on)

**Press** **Down Level (Gray +)** to open the drive frame and move the cursor into it

**Highlight** CASH_SUM.FW

**Press** ⏎

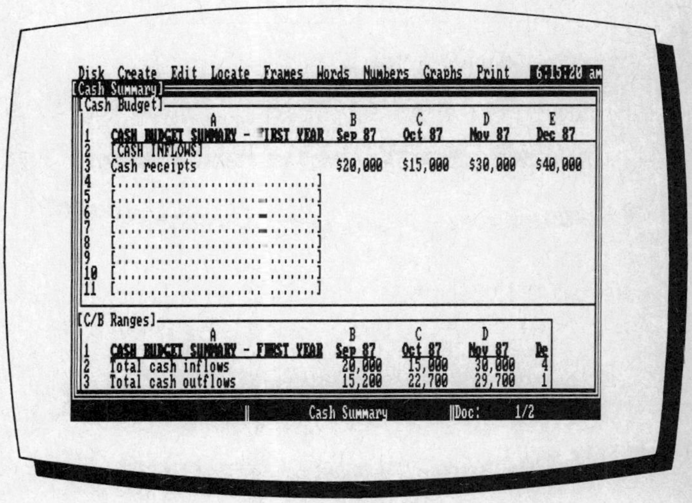


**Result** The drive spins and in a few moments the Cash Summary frame appears on the desktop exactly as it was when last saved. If the file was closed in its tray when it was saved, that is the way it will be retrieved. To open the file, highlight the tray and press ⏎. If the frames are displayed in Outline View, you can change them to Frames View by pressing the **View** (**F10**) key.

## Close the Cash Budget Frame

Let's close the Cash Budget frame so it takes up less room in the containing frame. Later, when we explore "What Ifs," we will open the frame.

*To close the Cash Budget frame:*

**Highlight** the Cash Summary frame border

**Press** **Down Level (Gray +)** to highlight the Cash Budget frame border
↵

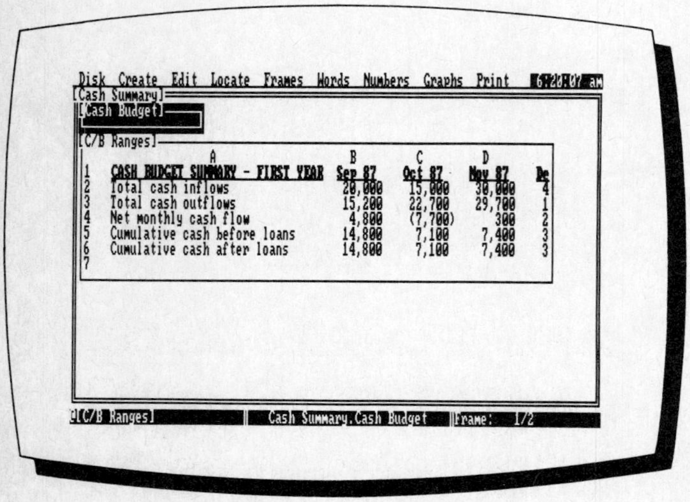


**Result** The Cash Budget frame closes up into a small frame. Try reopening it by pressing ↵ again, but make sure it's closed before you proceed further.

## Tips Selecting Graph Orientation

Pie charts do not have an X-axis, but you still have to select an orientation. The labels that would normally appear on the X-axis are used as legends.

If you are plotting a row of values, you should select Row Has X-axis Labels; if you are plotting a column of values, you should select Column Has X-axis Values. If you are plotting two or more adjacent rows or columns , you can select either.

When graphing a database, the normal orientation is Column Has X-axis Labels—the field names will be the legends on the graph.

## Tips Scaling Graphs

Graphs are scaled automatically unless otherwise specified on the Graphs menu. If manual scaling is selected, you must also select the Lowest Y-axis Value, the Highest Y-axis Value, and the Scale in Increments (all on the Options submenu).

**The Options Submenu on the Graphs Menu**

| MENU COMMAND | DESCRIPTION |
|---|---|
| **X-axis Title** | Allows you to enter a title for the X-axis. |
| **Y-axis Title** | Allows you to enter a title for the Y-axis. |
| **Manual Y-axis Scaling** | Turns on manual scaling. If manual scaling is selected, the next three values must also be entered. |
| **Lowest Y-axis Value** | Indicates the graph's lowest Y-axis value. This must be the same as or greater than the lowest value in the range being plotted. |
| **Highest Y-axis Value** | Indicates the graph's highest Y-axis value. This must be equal to or higher than the largest value in the range being plotted. |
| **Scale in Increments of** | Sets the increment between Y-axis values. |
| **Explode Pie Slice** | Separates a slice or slices from the pie chart. |

Don't use such small increments that there isn't sufficient room for the Y-axis labels or they will not be displayed on the screen.

If you enter high and low settings that do not include the high and low values in the range, Framework will return to automatic scaling.

To leave the Options submenu after scaling press the → or **Up Level (Gray −)** key to return to the main Graphs menu or **Esc** to return to the desktop.

If you will be comparing several graphs, it is usually easier if they are all scaled the same. To create a series of graphs with the same scale, scale the graph with the largest scale automatically and then manually scale the others with the same high and low points.

## Step 2 Create a Bar Graph

Before creating a graph there are two things you must do: highlight the graph ranges and indicate whether the graph's X-axis labels are on the top row of the spreadsheet or in the left-most column. These steps will give you a graph based on Framework's default settings — a bar graph with legends but no titles to identify the X-axis and Y-axis values. You can, however, use the options on the Graphs menu to create different graphs and to add details to them. Here we will start by creating a bar graph; we will take you through all the steps even though we will be "selecting" the default settings in some cases.

### Select Ranges

Begin by selecting the ranges on the spreadsheet to be plotted, the rows for total cash inflows, total cash outflows, and net monthly cash flow.

*To select ranges:*

**Highlight** C/B Ranges frame border
**Press** **Down Level (Gray +)** to enter the frame
**Highlight** B2
**Press** **Extend Select (F6)**
**Highlight** rows 2, 3, and 4 out to column M (using the ↓ and **End** keys)
**Press** ↵

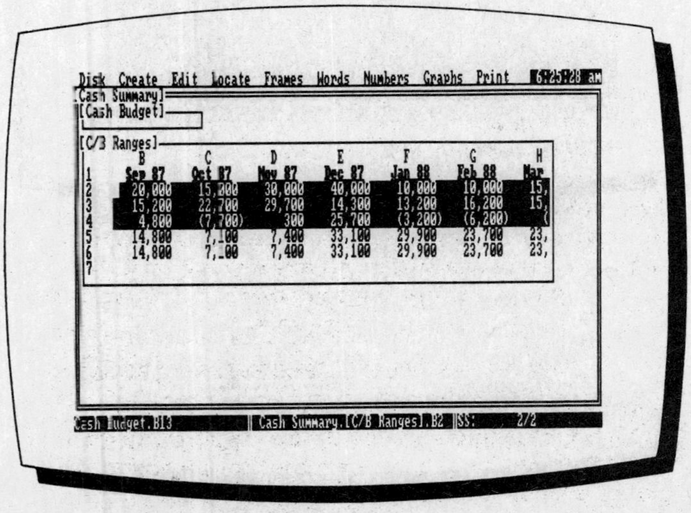

**Result** The highlight covers rows 2, 3, and 4, from column B to column M.

### Select Graph Type

The type of graph you want to create must be selected before you create it. It can be changed later only by redrawing the graph or editing the graph formula. The default setting is for a bar graph, but you could select any of the five other graph types on the Graphs menu. Only one graph type can be on at the same time.

*To select the graph type (in this case, the default setting is used):*

**Press** **Ins**
**Highlight** Graphs
Bar
**Press** ↵

**Result** The Bar selection on the Graphs menu is turned on.

### Select Graph Orientation

Your graph's orientation depends on whether you specify that the left-most column or the top row contains the labels to be used on the graph's X-axis. Your selection determines what the ranges will be plotted against.

*To select the graph orientation (in this case, the default setting is used):*

**Highlight** Row Has X-axis Labels
**Press** ↵

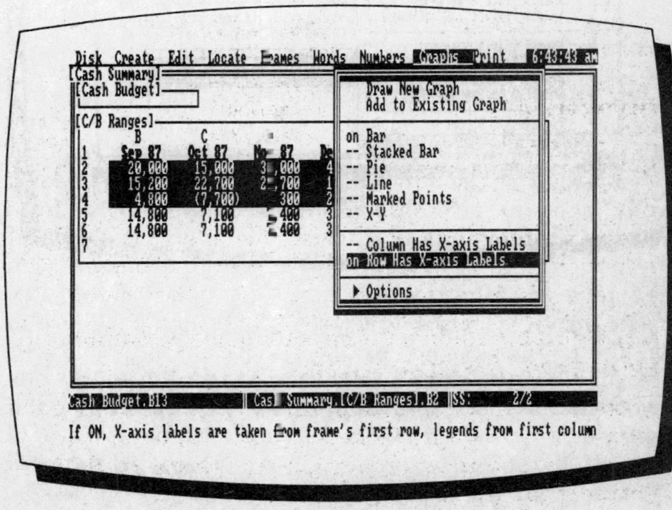


**Result** The row setting is turned on.

## Step 3 Create a Line Graph

Once you have graphed net monthly cash flow, creating a line graph of the cumulative cash balance is a snap. In fact, all of the steps along the way are the same, except that you have to change the range to be plotted and the type of graph to be displayed.

### Select Ranges

In this case, we'll be plotting the ranges from rows 5 and 6, Cumulative cash before loans and Cumulative cash after loans. (First, close the bar graph frame by pressing ⏎.)

*To select ranges:*

**Highlight** C/B Ranges frame border

**Press** **Down Level (Gray +)** to enter the frame

**Highlight** B5

**Press** **Extend Select** (**F6**)

**Highlight** rows 5 and 6 out to column M (using the ↓ and **End** keys)

**Press** ⏎

**Result** The highlight covers rows 5 and 6, from column B out to column M.

### Select Graph Type

The type of graph you want to create must be selected before you create it. In this case the type of graph you want is a line graph.

**Press** **Ins**

**Highlight** Graphs
Line

**Press** ⏎

**Result** The Line selection on the Graphs menu is turned on.

### Add Titles

For this graph, the X-axis title from the last graph will be the same, but we will change the Y-axis title.

**Highlight** Options on the Graphs menu

**Press** ⏎

*To add a Y-axis title:*

**Highlight** Y-axis Title

**Press** ⏎

**Type** **Cash balances**

**Press** ⏎
**Up Level (Gray −)** to leave the submenu

**Result** The new title appears on the submenu in the curly braces next to the Y-axis title.

### Draw the Graph

Now let's draw the new graph.

**Highlight** Draw New Graph

**Press** ⏎

**Message** Press RETURN to draw graph here, or select desired frame and Press RETURN

**Press** ⏎

**Result** The message DRAWING appears on the message line. In a few moments the graph appears in its own frame on the desktop.

### Label the Frame and Graph

The frame label is used to label a graph with a main title; it can be styled for boldface, italics, or underlining.

**Highlight** graph frame border

**Type** **Cumulative Cash Flow**

**Press** ⏎
**Recalc** (**F5**) to title the graph

**Result** The label entered on the frame border appears as the main title at the top of the graph when the **Recalc** (**F5**) key is pressed.

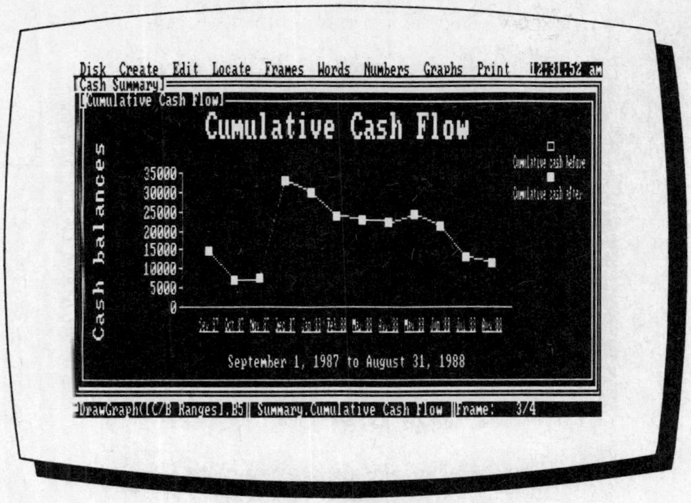


## Analyzing the Graph

The month-to-month relationship is illustrated in this graph showing cumulative cash flows. This graph would show the months in which you really have to worry about covering, from outside sources, a negative cash flow. You might wonder why there is only one line on the graph when you plotted two rows on the spreadsheet. This is because the two rows both have the same values, so the lines overlap. Had a loan been entered on the cash budget (as it will be later), the two lines would separate and you could see the difference between the cumulative cash flow before and after the loan.

## Tips Adding Overlays to Graphs

Only line and marked-point graphs can be used as overlay graphs. You cannot use overlays with pie charts or X-Y graphs.

To overlay a graph onto an existing graph, first select the range, select Add to Existing Graph on the Graphs menu, and then point to the graph to be overlaid.

Use overlays when you want to plot ranges on a spreadsheet that are not adjacent.

Overlaying graphs is a good way to emphasize specific data ranges. For example, overlaying profits as a line graph on top of a bar graph showing sales will emphasize the profits.

When overlays are added to a graph, a new @Drawgraph formula is added to the existing one.

When adding overlays to graphs created from database records, you must turn on Column Has X-axis Labels on the Graphs menu.

## Step 4 Create a Pie Chart

Now let's draw a pie chart that will compare cash inflows and outflows for one month. Remember, pie charts can display only one set of data at a time.

### Select Range

Highlight any pair of monthly net cash inflow and outflow figures.

**Highlight** C/B Ranges frame border

**Press** **Down Level (Gray +)** to enter the frame

**Highlight** a *pair* of cells in rows 2 and 3 in any monthly column using the **Extend Select** (**F6**) key

**Press** (↵)

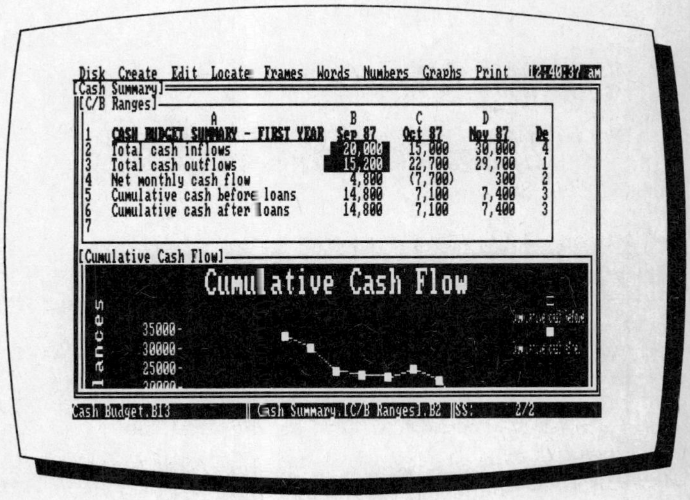


### Enter Pie Chart Settings

To create a pie chart you have to select the type on the Graphs menu. You can choose to explode one or more of the pie shape wedges in a pie chart. The number you enter indicates the row or column in the range you selected. Pie slices appear on the graph numbered counterclockwise from the twelve o'clock position. When it is set to 0, no slices are exploded. When it is set to −1, all of them are exploded.

*To enter pie chart settings:*

**Press** **Ins**

**Highlight** Graphs
Pie

**Press** ↵

**Highlight** Options

**Press** ↵

**Highlight** X-axis Title

**Type** [the month you've chosen, e.g., September]

**Press** ↵

**Highlight** Y-axis Title

**Press** ↵

**Type** **Cash inflows & outflows**

**Press** ↵

**Highlight** Explode Pie Slice

**Press** ↵

**Type** **1**

**Press** ↵
**Up Level (Gray −)** to return to Graphs menu

## Draw and Label the Graph

You can now draw the pie chart. We will let Framework create a new frame for it automatically.

*To draw the pie chart:*

**Highlight** Draw New Graph

**Press** ↵

**Message** Press RETURN to draw graph here, or select desired frame and Press RETURN

**Press** ↵

**Type** **Inflows & outflows:** [month]

**Press** ↵
**Recalc** (**F5**)

**Result** You now have a pie chart, with one "slice" exploded.

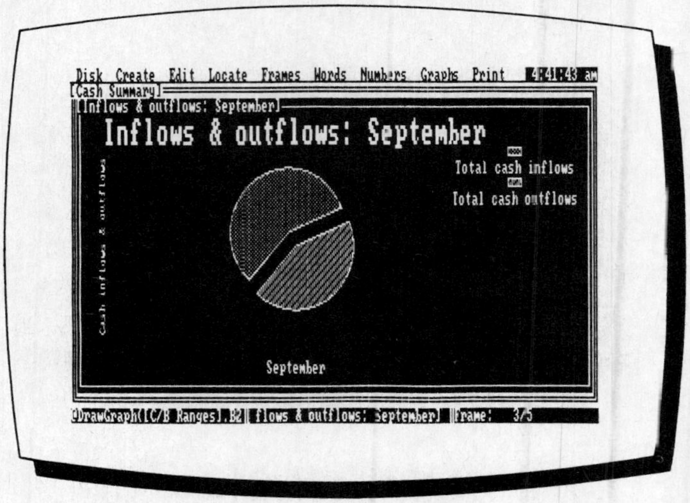


## Step 5 Recalculate Automatically

Just as you could make linked spreadsheets recalculate automatically, you can also make graphs recalculate automatically; the reference is entered in the last cell on the spreadsheet instead of on the frame border (as you did for linked spreadsheets).

*To allow editing in C/B Ranges frame:*

**Highlight** C/B Ranges frame border

**Press** **Ins**

**Highlight** Edit
Allow Editing

**Press** ↵

*To make the pie chart recalculate automatically:*

**Press** **Down Level (Gray +)**

**Highlight** K7

**Type** @

**Press** ↑ to begin cursor pointing
**Up Level (Gray −)**
↓ to highlight the pie chart
↵ twice

*To make the cumulative cash flow graph recalculate automatically:*

**Highlight** L7

**Type** @

**Press** [↑]
**Up Level (Gray −)**
[↓] to highlight the line graph
[↵] twice

*To make the net monthly cash flow graph recalculate automatically:*

**Highlight** M7

**Type** @

**Press** [↑]
**Up Level (Gray −)**
[↓] to highlight the bar graph
[↵] twice

**Result** As each graph reference is entered, the graph is redrawn and the reference #GRAPH appears in the cells of the spreadsheet where they have been entered. Now when the C/B Ranges spreadsheet is recalculated, all of the graphs will be automatically redrawn to reflect the changes.

## Step 6 Save Your Work

Graphs are saved like any other frame. When they are in a containing frame (as they are here), they are saved along with all the other frames as long as the cursor is on the containing frame border or somewhere within the containing frame. Again, since the saved frame will reappear on the desktop exactly as it was when saved, you might want to move the cursor to the frame border or close the frame.

*To save the Cash Summary frame containing the graphs:*

**Press** Ctrl-[↵]

**Message** SAVING
Document saved

**Result** The containing frame, including the graphs, will be saved under the same name (CASH_SUM) as when you last saved the spreadsheets.

## The Net Cash Flow Graph

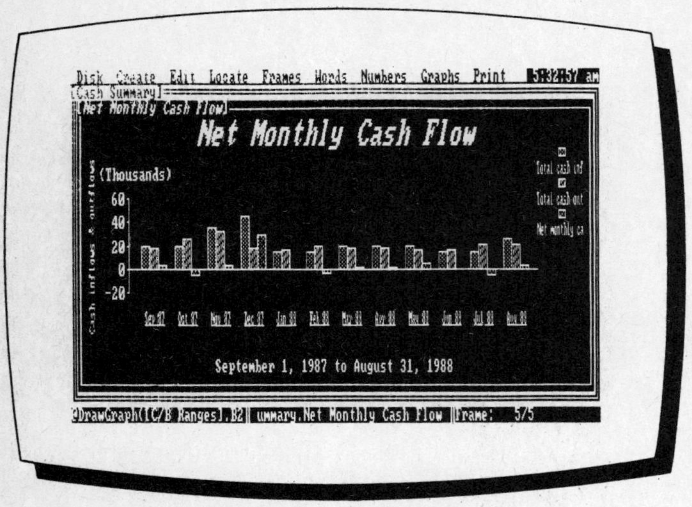


To view the graph showing net monthly cash flow, highlight any frame border inside the containing frame and use the arrow keys to move to the Net Monthly Cash Flow graph. If you want you can zoom it by pressing the **Zoom** (**F9**) key.

There are now fewer months with negative cash flows, and fewer of the monthly variations that we saw in the original example. This is because the increased sales volume is helping to cover the operating expenses of the business.

## The Cumulative Cash Flow Graph

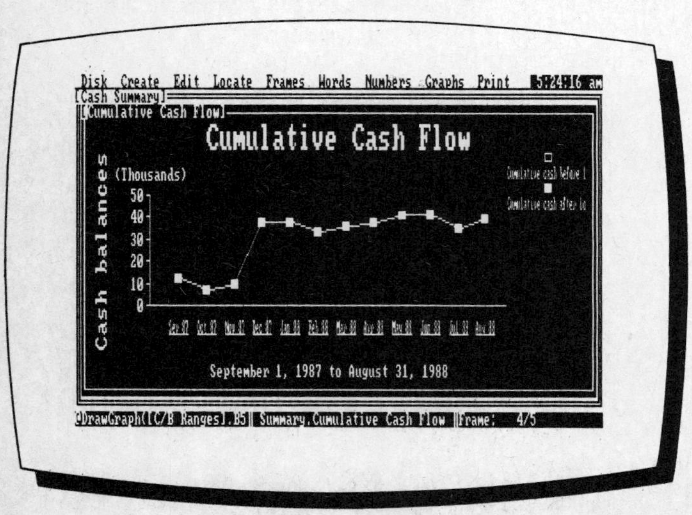


To view the graph showing cumulative cash flow, highlight any frame border inside the containing frame and use the arrow keys to move to the Cumulative Cash Flow graph. If you want you can zoom it by pressing the **Zoom** (**F9**) key.

Even more important than monthly net cash flow is the cumulative cash balance generated by the business. By year-end (August), we have a cash balance of $36,700 — more than three-and-a-half times the opening balance of $10,000. If we were planning to take our profits from the business only after operations are covered, we can now rest easy.

## What If 2 Cash Outflows Increase

First, keeping with our one-change-at-a-time philosophy, we will restore sales to their original level and then explore a new possibility — a looming disaster. Let's assume that one of our suppliers has just announced an 8% across-the-board price increase for all goods that we purchase. The supplier is willing, however, to let us buy on the same one-month-in-advance basis. The net result of the price increases will be increases in monthly inventory purchases, and a new loan, which we'll need to cover our negative cash flows.

## Change the Spreadsheet

Before we explore this "What If," we'll have to restore the original cash receipts changed in the previous "What If" so we aren't exploring the results of two changes simultaneously. Change the values on row 3 back to their original "case study" numbers.

**Highlight** Cash Budget frame border

**Press** **Down Level (Gray +)**

**Highlight** B3 and type **20000** (⇥)
At C3 type **15000** (⇥)
At D3 type **30000** (⇥)
At E3 type **40000** (⇥)
At F3 type **10000** (⇥)
At G3 type **10000** (⇥)
At H3 type **15000** (⇥)
At I3 type **15000** (⇥)
At J3 type **15000** (⇥)
At K3 type **10000** (⇥)
At L3 type **10000** (⇥)
At M3 type **20000** (↵)

Now make changes on rows 16 and 32. To enter changes in inventory purchases on row 16 that reflect the price increases, we'll enter numbers into cells that currently contain formulas, but these formulas won't be needed any longer.

*To increase inventory purchases:*

**Highlight** B16 and type **8100** ⇥
At C16 type **16200** ⇥
At D16 type **21600** ⇥
At E16 type **5400** ⇥
At F16 type **5400** ⇥
At G16 type **8100** ⇥
At H16 type **8100** ⇥
At I16 type **8100** ⇥
At J16 type **5400** ⇥
At K16 type **5400** ⇥
At L16 type **10800** ⇥
At M16 type **13500** ↵

*To increase values for new loans on row 32:*

**Highlight** C32 and type **6000** ⇥
At D32 type **−1040** ⇥
At E32 type **−1040** ⇥
At F32 type **−1040** ⇥
At G32 type **−1040** ⇥
At H32 type **−1040** ⇥
At I32 type **−1040** ↵

*To recalculate the spreadsheet and redraw the graphs:*

**Press** **Recalc (F5)**
**Up Level (Gray −)**

**Result** Your spreadsheet should match the one shown in the illustration on page 89.

## The Net Cash Flow Graph

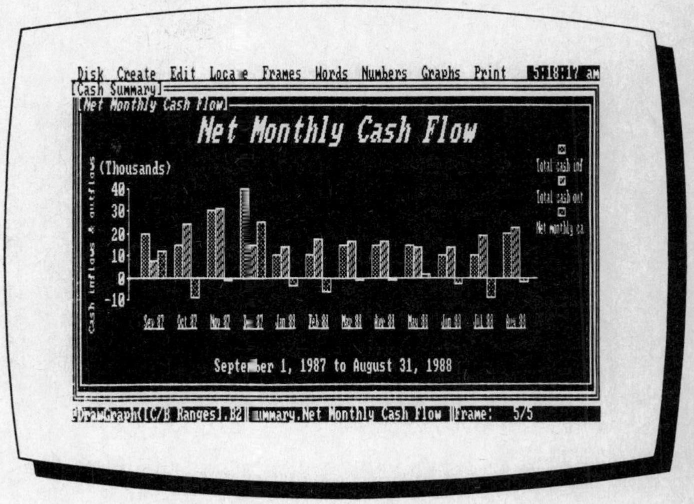


To view the graph showing the net monthly cash flow, highlight any frame border inside the containing frame and use the arrow keys to move to the Net Monthly Cash Flow graph. If you want, you can zoom it by pressing the **Zoom (F9)** key.

As you can see, this company is suddenly awash in negative cash flows. Nine of the twelve months shown have negative balances. As we said earlier, if the positive ones outweigh the negatives over the course of the year, there might be some hope. But as you can see in the next graph (or, as you could see by looking at cell N32 in the Cash Budget spreadsheet), the negatives outweigh the positives. The loan that the proprietor has tested here merely staves off the inevitable. Another year of this kind of cash erosion will put the company out of the game. Something will have to be changed in operations if this company is to survive.

## The Cumulative Cash Flow Graph

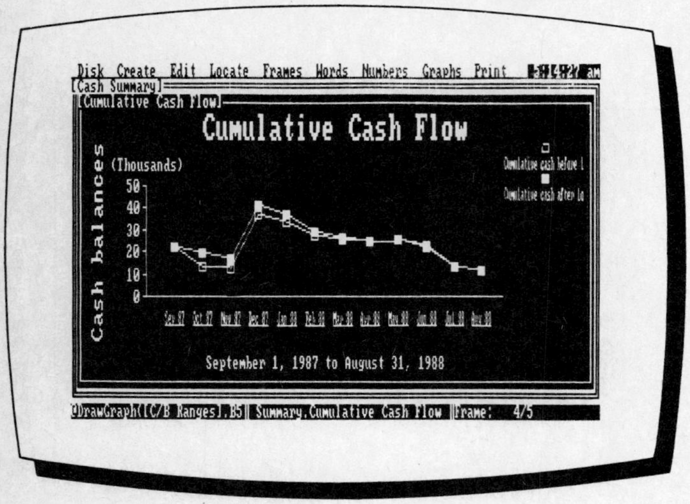


To view the graph showing cumulative cash flow, highlight any frame border inside the containing frame and use the arrow keys to move to the Cumulative Cash Flow graph. If you want, you can zoom it by pressing the **Zoom** (**F9**) key.

This graph shows a real problem. Not only is the company not generating any new cash, it has managed to lose about $7,000 of its opening cash balance by the end of the year, and there is only a little less than $3,000 left at the end of the last month. (Graphs only show numbers approximately — for accurate numbers, refer to the spreadsheet.) The loan in the second month helped for awhile, but as you can see, the cumulative cash balance falls below the danger level once again in August.

Clearly, this is a bad deal. We will have to do something if we intend to make the business work. Our options include the kind of increased volume approach we explored in the first "What If," or we can increase our inflows by raising prices (we even have the excuse of our supplier's price increase). We can also try to decrease our other cash outflows (perhaps making do with a smaller staff) or we could change our product line and try to sell higher-margin products.

Before you move on to the next chapter you might want to explore some of these changes yourself, trying numbers you think might work and immediately seeing their effects. You might be surprised at how quickly you get a feeling for the dynamic relationships involved and how sensitive they are to changes.

## Clear the Sample Data

When you have finished exploring "What Ifs," you should clear the spreadsheet for the entry of your own data by copying blank label entry spaces to the cells containing sample line item labels, and by placing zeros in the cells with sample numbers.

*To copy blank label spaces to cells containing sample line items:*

**Copy from** A15

**Copy to** A8 through A14

*To fill the cells containing dates with a dummy date.*

**Copy from** B15

**Copy to** B8 through B14
D8 through D14

*To fill the cells containing sample numbers with zeros:*

**Copy from** C15

**Copy to** C8 through C14
E8 through E14

**Result** All the sample numbers you entered on the spreadsheet will be replaced by zeros, and the formulas should recalculate to show zero as well. Your spreadsheet should look like the illustration on page 164.

## Save Your Work

Now that you've cleared the spreadsheet of the sample data, be sure to save it again so that it won't be lost if the power fails or if you accidentally hit the wrong key. Use the file name E Outflows for the frame containing the blank spreadsheet so it won't overwrite and erase the version with the sample numbers (Outflows). Remember to make a backup copy of the disk on which the file was saved.

*To name the frame containing the blank spreadsheet:*

**Highlight** the frame border

**Press** **Space Bar** to get the name **Outflows** on the edit line

**Type** **E** (SP)

**Press** (↵)

*To save the frame labeled E Outflows:*

**Press** **Ctrl-**(↵)

**Result** The new frame, E Outflows, will be saved to the disk along with the old frame, Outflows.

# 4 Forecasting and Tracking Cash Inflows

## Introduction

We began this book with a discussion of the cash budget summary spreadsheet so that you could see its many and varied uses. Frankly, we hoped you'd see its usefulness as a business tool right away so that you could begin to profit from it immediately. But to really get the most value out of cash budgeting, you will need more detailed information than you would want in your cash budget summary. So we have provided three detailed spreadsheets: a *cash inflow supplement* which you will enter in this chapter, and two *cash outflow supplements* (which you will enter in Chapter 5 and Chapter 7).These are the spreadsheets that will help you get and maintain control of your business' cash situation. This chapter focuses on cash inflow.

Suppose, for a moment, that the cash inflows shown on your summary cash budget are running behind projections. Using the summary spreadsheet, you might see that cash from skyhooks sales were your problem. The "cash from sales of widgets" line, however, was right on track. In short, the summary will help you pinpoint your problem area. If you want to find out *why* cash from sales of skyhooks is low compared with the projection, however, you will need a level of detail that would merely be confusing if used on the cash budget summary.

The two parts of the cash inflow supplement are designed to facilitate whatever level of detail you believe will be necessary. The upper part of the spreadsheet, the sales budget, is designed to permit you to list individual customers, if you wish. The lower part of the spreadsheet, the cash receipts section, permits you to break down inflows in aggregates—by customer group, by product group, or by total sales.

## Defining the Problem: A Case in Point

In most businesses, defining the problem is the hard part. Once you have the nature of the problem defined, there are usually a number of fairly standard ways to solve it. The trick then becomes performing the analyses to ensure that you choose the best of the possible solutions for your specific problem. If you are looking at the wrong set of potential solutions, however, you may well work yourself into deeper trouble.

Consider the case of a consulting company owner who kept finding herself out of cash and having trouble paying her bills. She immediately called a meeting of her best salespeople/consultants and gave a rousing "go forth and sell" speech. Her assumption—that the problem was too little in sales—is a common response of the small business owner to almost any problem.

In fact, her problem has little to do with sales volume. Had she been a devotee of cash budgeting, her inflow supplement would have saved her a great deal of trouble. Her sales budget would have showed that sales were right on target. What *did* differ from projections was the mix of her customers and their promptness (or lack thereof) in paying for services.

So her problem was tied to the *timing* of inflows from sales, rather than to the sales themselves. If her ace salespeople had gone forth and sold still more to the slow payers, the cash shortages would probably have gotten worse instead of better. (It is very easy to sell merchandise or services to people if they don't really have to pay for them.)

The point here is that *targeting the wrong problem* can be more destructive than doing nothing. The cash budgeting system that we advocate in this book (and for which we provide the tools) is geared to helping you target the right (real) problem—and to defining and testing the best solutions.

## Looking at Cash Inflows

Obviously, determining cash inflows involves figuring out what you are likely to sell in your forecasting period. It often helps to start by looking at what you have sold in the past—assuming that your business has a past.

If you have usable history, now is one of the times to pull it out. Your records should provide all the necessary information. You need to know:

- ☐ the category of merchandise or service sold
- ☐ the volume sold
- ☐ the customer
- ☐ the total price
- ☐ the price paid (these may be different, if your credit policy permits discounts)
- ☐ the date(s) of payment

You then categorize the sales by month and look at what you have. A table something like the one below can help structure your information.

| *Customer* | *Sale Date* | *Item* | *Price* | *Amount Paid* | *Pay Date(s)* |
|---|---|---|---|---|---|
| Acme Co. | 2/01 | 100 Hats | $1,000 | $1,000 | 3/15 |
| Green, Inc. | 2/10 | 10 Caps | 6,000 | 6,000 | 4/10 |

You are looking for patterns. Does Green always take 60 days to pay? Do some customers in the same business as Green pay more promptly? Are larger orders usually paid for more or less quickly than small ones? Are discounted sales paid more quickly? Most important for your cash forecasting process: What is the overall inflow rate of your cash from sales? If you sell $10,000 worth of services or merchandise in one month, how much actual cash will you collect by the end of the month? Within thirty days? Sixty days? Try a table like the one shown. But do *not forget to keep track of the amounts of money that you never collect*—your bad debts. Lots of bad debt can ruin your cash flow.

| *February Sales Collected in:* | *February* | *March* | *April* | *May* |
|---|---|---|---|---|
| $10,000<br>100% | $2,000<br>20% | $5,000<br>50% | $2,000<br>20% | $1,000<br>10% |

Only after you have developed whatever history you have should you begin to project the inflows you expect in the future. Of course, if you have no history, you will have to work with your best estimates of sales and with your best understanding of how the terms of trade actually work in your industry. You can often find help with these in industry-average financial ratio data or simply from talking with people in your industry and reading the industry press.

## Forecasting

Your next step is to forecast next year's sales. I know that this is far easier to say than to do. But go ahead. Make a projection, write it down on a piece of paper, and really commit to it as your best estimate.

It may help to know two things. First, you are not really expected to be right all the time. (In fact, if you consistently hit at plus or minus 5%, give us a call.) This is especially true if you are just beginning a business and have no history to use as a basis for projecting.

Second, you should know that as you do more forecasts, you tend to get better at it. Not only do you grow less fearful of committing to the numbers you develop, but you somehow begin to temper your natural tendencies to either optimism or pessimism. It seems to happen all by itself. You don't have to worry about it. Just start doing your best projections.

Once you have your sales projections by month, you can then apply your company's past rates of cash payment (or industry-average rates) to the sales numbers. If you are using industry-average rates, please pause for a moment or two before you commit to them. Consider whether you really expect your business to operate as the industry in general does. If so, go ahead and use those rates. If not, consider how your particular operational differences are likely to affect your collections. Then modify the results of the industry-average policies to fit your specific circumstances. In short, recognize that the industry averages are a guideline, not a straightjacket.

This process will give you a forecast of your cash inflows for the forecast year. If you deal (or expect to deal) with only a few customers, in volume, you might consider figuring your cash forecasts by customer. For example, if Green does always take 60 days to pay up, you might separate Green's purchases into a separate category each month and figure that those payments will appear 60 days later.

The trick is to achieve the greatest accuracy possible. After all, this is the best any of us can do. But, since most of us are painfully aware that the best is not always good enough, you might try a technique called *bracketing* for your most critical estimates. Sales, for example, is generally a fairly critical estimate.

## Bracketing

Bracketing your best estimates is an approach designed to give you comfort while permitting you to plan effectively. It *assumes* that your estimates are unlikely to be precisely accurate. It lets you see how much margin you have for error. Thus, you can say to yourself, "Even if I'm off by 10%, I'll be O.K." The ability to say this (and really believe it) really helps. It also shows your banker, or anyone else who might care, that you are a true planner—that you do not believe that you are infallible and that you are actively considering how to deal with situations other than those you expect. Not a bad result for completing a simple exercise!

Bracketing requires you to consider how far off you might be in your best estimate for some essential item (in this case, sales). You then develop a complete separate forecast for that amount above and below your best estimate—a "best case" and a "worst case." Using Framework makes this easy. All *you* really have to do is consider how the differences in sales estimates will affect the other items in your statements. You will already have considered these linkages in developing your best, or most likely, estimate.

Once you get your set of three forecasts, you can decide how to deal with the situation presented by each. If you were right on, you can continue as planned. If your less optimistic case seems to be materializing, you will have predetermined contingency plans for correcting the difficulties and/or coping with the situation. If, lo and behold, your sales exceed your wildest estimates, you will already have ways of using the extra funds wisely and productively. You will not be losing any time —either in identifying the situation or in addressing the central issues. You will have done it all beforehand.

## Working with Your Cash Inflow Projections

As we have already noted, cash today is always better for you than cash tomorrow. The issue for you is twofold:

**1** Whether getting all your cash immediately upon sale is enough, and

**2** What getting that cash on that schedule is going to cost you.

You can use your inflow detail to address both issues.

The underlying issue raised in the first part is whether the problem is sales or collections. Both pieces of this question can be considered through playing with your cash inflow detail. Assume, for the moment, that you have developed your best estimate of next year's sales and collections. You have fed this data into your cash budget summary worksheet, and you definitely do not like the results. In a number of months you see that you are likely to have negative cumulative cash balances. Your question is "Why?"

Your next step should be to consider the terms of trade you are offering and the terms of trade that the industry offers. Try two "What Ifs": What if all your accounts actually paid exactly when they were supposed to? If your terms are more liberal than those of your competitors, what if you tightened up *and* if all accounts paid as "required"? If those revised collection patterns—essentially "cash today"—still show you unacceptable results, your problem may well be a sales volume that is too low to support the level of operations you are at, or are considering.

To test this hypothesis, you might try to find a sales level that will afford you acceptable cash inflows. Try successively higher sales estimates in conjunction with your best estimate of your collection rates. When you get a sales level that gives acceptable results, take a good, long look at it. Ask yourself whether this is a reasonable and feasible level for your company to attain *next year*. If your number is half the total potential market in your effective market area, and you have ten competitors and a 5% market share, for example, you can probably label that level unfeasible *for next year*. If, in your judgment, however, the required level *is* feasible for next year, consider making that level your "best case" estimate. Begin to figure out how to get the company from here to there.

If the problem seems to be collections rather than sales, your cumulative cash figures will look better when your collection period is shortened. The issue for you then is basically a marketing issue. If you tighten your credit terms or enforce those you actually have, how much will you lose in sales? (You might also consider how much a sale is worth to you if you don't see the money for six months.) Suppose you tried a carrot-and-stick approach to your customers—offered a small discount for early payment and charged interest for late payments?

You might also consider your bad debt policies. How much in sales do you actually never see in collections? When do you normally assume that you might have a real problem collecting a receivable? What would happen, do you think, if you began to take notice sooner? Suppose your credit people began calling sooner? Suppose you actually turned accounts over to a collection agency after some specified period of time?

You can use the inflow supplement to test out all of these approaches. When you try out an idea, however, do not neglect to make all the other changes that your initial change requires. If, for example, you want to test the collection agency possibility, do not forget that they take a percentage of the actual amount they collect. Adjust your data before you make a judgment.

And, in case we haven't been absolutely clear about this already, please understand that the numbers you are pushing around are only as good as the judgments you make about them. They are there to aid you in your decision making, to enhance your ability to see what is happening. In and of themselves, the numbers that you are generating will not tell you what to do nor how to do it. You remain in control of your business. Your judgment makes the thing work.

## Longer-Term Approaches to Maximizing Inflows

The solutions that we have been looking at are "tightening up" approaches to cash inflow shortages. Tightening up is often all that is needed to make a business run better and more in tune with your objectives. However, as you look over your most likely and best case estimates, you might think that the business could be made to produce even better. Your cash inflow supplement will also facilitate your consideration of some kinds of structural changes to the business.

Go back, for example, to the patterns you discerned when you first listed your historical sales and collections. (Or, go back to the data and look for patterns.) Pull out the sales that were paid for in the shortest periods of time. Do the same with the sales that became bad debts and with those which required months of dunning before you ever saw a nickel. (The database management portion of Framework can help you here if your numbers of sales are too large to work with by hand and calculator.)

What you want to consider is: do the good payers have anything in common? And, do the slow payers (and the nonpayers) have anything in common? In this sort of analysis, you just have to listen to what the data is telling you. If the only thing that the fast payers have in common is that you and their presidents know each other personally, for example, you might make it a high business priority to develop personal relationships with your other major customers.

Actually, this is unlikely. You are more likely to find that the item purchased or the volume purchased over time or the size of the order tends to differentiate the speed of payment. It might also be the case that only a few specific customers create the bulk of your slow- or no-payment problems. It is quite likely that the size of the customer company is the differentiating factor. Although we cannot predict what your specific search for common factors will produce, we would be willing to bet that you find some. And these common factors provide you with the information you need to improve your long-term cash inflow situation.

Consider what your business would be like if all your customers paid as fast as the best payers you have now. You can make this happen—not tomorrow, but over a period of time. But you can only do it if you know the characteristics of the "good guys." You simply redirect your salesforce's energies into companies with the right characteristics. Obviously, you do not drop everything else and expect instantaneous change in customer mix, but working with your cash inflows will have helped you define the goal—a customer list composed of only the probable good guys.

Alternatively, consider the possibility that the size of the order seems to be the differentiating factor. You might consider restructuring your pricing schedule to encourage larger orders (assuming they are the ones that get paid for fast) and to discourage small orders. Again, analysis of your cash inflows will have helped define a goal.

Obviously, such goal-setting needs to have some basis in the reality of the market in which you operate. If, in your judgment, change of this magnitude—even over the long term—is not feasible for your company, you might simply have to grit your teeth and make do with the shorter-term, tightening-up approaches. But consider carefully.

## Using the Cash Inflow Supplement in Business Situations

While the cash inflow supplement is built to feed into your overall cash position analysis, it is a useful worksheet in and of itself. Some situations in which you might work with your inflow detail are discussed in this section. In some cases, the vignettes are similar to, or seeds of, more detailed situations described elsewhere in this book. We include them here simply to demonstrate that your cash inflow detail is usable and useful in everyday business decision making.

### Situation 1 Offering a Discount

Your company manufactures novelty items for the business promotions trade. In general, you tend to deal with a relatively small number of separate customers, but you do a sizable volume with each customer in the course of a year. Their volume of promotions planning contracts is growing rapidly. Their businesses generally operate on a billing basis. They contract for and provide goods and services to a company. Then they bill the company. The company then pays them for their goods and services.

As a supplier to this industry, you are at least indirectly dependent for your cash payments on the speed with which your customers' customers pay them. Except for one or two of your more affluent customers, this means that it is likely to take a long time for you to collect most of your receivables. You are working through at least two standard, 30-day payment cycles.

Since your suppliers are not direct links in this industry chain, they want their payments on more standard terms—within 30 days. This leaves you in the unfortunate position of having to supplement your cash flow by drawing frequently on your line of credit. This approach is expensive. You wonder whether there is any way of reducing your reliance on credit by inducing your customers to send money faster.

You are really dealing with two separate questions here. First, you want to know about how many customers you need to convince to ease your problem significantly. Second, you want to know whether what you would have to give up is worth it to you. A cash inflow worksheet can help you evaluate both issues.

Your first move is to estimate how many of your customers (what proportion of your volume) might go for a discount for early payment. Obviously, this will vary with the size of the discount. Plug the revised cash inflow estimates into your cash inflow supplement and see whether it helps. If not, try a larger discount. (Do not forget to reduce the inflow from sales by the amounts of the discounts you expect to be taken.)

At the point at which you expect to have enough discount takers to make a dent in your borrowing needs, consider the tradeoff cost to you of borrowing as opposed to giving that level of discount. You can do this by feeding your revised inflow data into your cash budget summary and playing with the New Loans section. (We have also provided a spreadsheet for figuring tradeoffs in taking trade discounts; see the Trade Discounts spreadsheet in Chapter 7. You will have to reverse the structure, but it can be used for this purpose.)

## Situation 2 Targeting New Customers

You know that the kinds of novelties you manufacture are used in many fields other than the business promotions field, where you make most of your sales. You wonder whether you might do better on cash flow by choosing your customers more carefully and/or tightening your credit terms. The structure of your cash inflow supplement is ideal for considering this kind of issue.

As we mentioned in the text of the inflow section, you can consider your client base in categories defined in any way that illuminates your business. In considering this kind of question, you might want to categorize by customer's business and, perhaps, by customer size. You want to ascertain payment patterns that may be related to these characteristics.

To consider what would happen to your cash inflows if you could convert all your business into business with the type of customer with the best payment record, simply recast your payment proportions to fit your prospective new clientele. If you like what you see, figure out how to shift your client base to the new type(s) of customers. If, on the other hand, such a shift would make only a marginal difference in your cash position, you will have saved yourself a lot of hassle by testing the potential results by using your computer before actually trying to make such a change.

## Situation 3 Changing Pricing Structure

Perhaps the simplest use of a cash inflow supplement is to test the effect of a change in price on the level of cash in your business. You can adjust the sales for both the increased unit price and for any potential losses of sales due to the price hike. If you make sure to consider whether the changes made will affect the pattern of inflows, your cash inflow supplement will immediately calculate your new projected cash numbers. Keep in mind that if you are pricing some customers out of your market, you do not want to eliminate your good payers. If you are likely to do that, and if you make the appropriate changes in your percentage inflow expectations, you will see fairly quickly why you probably do not want to make the change. Or, if you do, you will probably want to increase the price hike somewhat to compensate for the extra delays in actually getting usable cash through the door.

The checklist below lists cash inflows by various categories. This list method should help you group your inflows in ways that facilitate your later analysis. You might consider using one or more of these categories depending, obviously, on your particular business. It is important that you group by "Type of Payment," either alone or in conjunction with another categorization. This will make it easier for you to see what kinds of sales, which market or region, or which sales method produces cash for you most rapidly. Clearly, in your planning, these will be the types of sales you want to encourage.

## ✓ Checklist Cash Inflows

### By market:

☐ Retail

☐ Wholesale

☐ Direct mail—catalog

☐ Direct mail—space ads

☐ Telephone sales

☐ Export

☐ Domestic

☐ Government

☐ Distributor—special

### By sales organization:

☐ Sales staff—commission

☐ Sales staff—house

☐ Distributor

### By geographic region

A special disk to accompany **Cash Flow Management with Framework** is available. Although the disk is not essential, it will save you time and energy because it contains all the spreadsheets used in this book so you won't have to enter them yourself. If you did not purchase the disk edition of this book, and you want to order the disk, use the Disk Order Form on the last page of the book.

# Our Approach

In the following section, we'll show you how to create a cash inflow supplement covering the same 12-month period as the cash budget summary. You will use the supplement to break down net sales by category and by collection period. The spreadsheet will automatically calculate your cash inflow for each month. Net sales can be broken down by customer, market, territory, or any other category; although the spreadsheet has only seven lines for your sales breakdown, you can easily expand this section to accommodate your own needs (see Tips on "Inserting and Deleting Rows and Columns").

Sales are then broken down by collection period: you enter the percentage of sales paid for in cash, and due within 30 days, 60 days, 90 days, and so on. Formulas on each row then calculate the amounts that will be collected during each month, taking into account the lag between sales and collections. If you don't know what your collection periods are, you can use the aging accounts receivables spreadsheet to calculate them. Collections due from sales made in the period prior to the one covered by this spreadsheet are entered as dollar amounts, and bad debts are entered as a percentage of total sales. Finally, total monthly cash inflows are calculated, and can be transferred to the cash budget summary.

In the process of building the spreadsheets in this book, you will find that we have asked you to "zero-fill" many of the cells along the way. This is a necessary step in the Framework program, because the formulas would calculate out incompletely otherwise, and would fill the cells with the message #VALUE! (a disconcerting sight). This should make no difference to the final calculations with sample numbers, or to the calculations with your own numbers.

After each section is completed, we will enter sample numbers from a typical business situation to check that all the formulas have been entered correctly. When you've explored "What Ifs," you'll clear the spreadsheet of the sample numbers and save the blank spreadsheet for use in your own business.

**Important!**

The instructions for creating this spreadsheet have been abbreviated. We assume that you're now familiar with entering text, values, and ruled lines, which you can copy from the illustrations in this chapter. All formulas, however, are described in detail. If you are unfamiliar with Framework, you should take the time to build the cash budget summary spreadsheet described in Chapter 3. Chapter 3 covers everything you need to know to create this spreadsheet and all the other spreadsheets in this book.

## The Cash Inflow Supplement

| | | A | B | C | D | E | F | G | H | I | J | K | L | M | N | O |
|---|---|---|---|---|---|---|---|---|---|---|---|---|---|---|---|---|
| 1 | 1 | CASH INFLOWS SUPPLEMENT | Month: | Sep 87 | Oct 87 | Nov 87 | Dec 87 | Jan 88 | Feb 88 | Mar 88 | Apr 88 | May 88 | [illegible]n 88 | Jul 88 | Aug 88 | Total |
| | 2 | [NET SALES] | | | | | | | | | | | | | | |
| | 3 | Boats - manufactured | | | | | | | $60,000 | $100,000 | $140,000 | $100,000 | [illegible]0,000 | $40,000 | | $520,000 |
| | 4 | Boats - contracted | | | | | | | | | 75,000 | 75,000 | [illegible]0,000 | 30,000 | | 240,000 |
| | 5 | Motors | | | | | | | | 20,000 | 25,000 | 60,000 | [illegible]0,000 | 45,000 | 15,000 | 215,000 |
| | 6 | [......................] | | | | | | | | | | | | | | 0 |
| | 7 | [......................] | | | | | | | | | | | | | | 0 |
| 2 | 8 | [......................] | | | | | | | | | | | | | | 0 |
| | 9 | [......................] | | | | | | | | | | | | | | 0 |
| | 10 | [......................] | | | | | | | | | | | | | | 0 |
| | 11 | [......................] | | | | | | | | | | | | | | 0 |
| | 12 | [......................] | | | | | | | | | | | | | | 0 |
| | 13 | ------------ | | | | | | | | | | | | | | |
| | 14 | Total sales | | 0 | 0 | 0 | 0 | 0 | 60,000 | 120,000 | 240,000 | 235,000 | [illegible]0,000 | 115,000 | 15,000 | 975,000 |
| | 15 | ============ | | | | | | | | | | | | | | |
| | 16 | [CASH INFLOWS] | | | | | | | | | | | | | | |
| | 17 | ============ | | | | | | | | | | | | | | |
| | 18 | Collection | Percent | | | | | | | | | | | | | |
| | 19 | period | of total | Sep 87 | Oct 87 | Nov 87 | Dec 87 | Jan 88 | Feb 88 | Mar 88 | Apr 88 | May 88 | J[illegible]n 88 | Jul 88 | Aug 88 | Total |
| | 20 | ============ | | | | | | | | | | | | | | |
| | 21 | Cash | 0% | 0 | 0 | 0 | 0 | 0 | 0 | 0 | 0 | 0 | 0 | 0 | 0 | 0 |
| | 22 | 30 days | 0% | 0 | 0 | 0 | 0 | 0 | 0 | 0 | 0 | 0 | 0 | 0 | 0 | 0 |
| | 23 | 60 days | 20% | | 0 | 0 | 0 | 0 | 0 | 12,000 | 24,000 | 48,000 | [illegible]7,000 | 38,000 | 23,000 | 192,000 |
| | 24 | 90 days | 40% | | | 0 | 0 | 0 | 0 | 0 | 24,000 | 48,000 | [illegible]6,000 | 94,000 | 76,000 | 338,000 |
| 3 | 25 | 120 days | 20% | | | | 0 | 0 | 0 | 0 | 0 | 12,000 | [illegible]4,000 | 48,000 | 47,000 | 131,000 |
| | 26 | 150 days | 10% | | | | | 0 | 0 | 0 | 0 | 0 | [illegible]6,000 | 12,000 | 24,000 | 42,000 |
| | 27 | Over 150 days | 5% | | | | | | 0 | 0 | 0 | 0 | 0 | 3,000 | 6,000 | 9,000 |
| | 28 | ------------ | | | | | | | | | | | | | | |
| | 29 | Bad debts | 5% | 0 | 0 | 0 | 0 | 0 | 0 | 0 | 0 | 0 | 0 | 3,000 | 6,000 | 9,000 |
| | 30 | ============ | | | | | | | | | | | | | | |
| | 31 | Total cash inflows | 100% | 0 | 0 | 0 | 0 | 0 | 0 | 12,000 | 48,000 | 108,000 | 1[illegible],000 | 192,000 | 170,000 | 703,000 |
| | 32 | ============ | | | | | | | | | | | | | | |
| | 33 | Total uncollected sales | | | | | | | | | | | | | | 263,000 |
| | 34 | ============ | | | | | | | | | | | | | | |

*The cash inflow supplement has three parts: headings **(1)** identify the spreadsheet and the period covered; the net sales section **(2)** breaks down your sales by category: and the cash inflows section **(3)** calculates the actual cash amount from sales during each of the months covered.*

# Entering the Cash Inflow Supplement

The cash inflow supplement will be created in five steps:

**Step 1** Getting ready
**Step 2** Enter headings
**Step 3** Enter net sales
**Step 4** Enter cash inflows
**Step 5** Save your work

## Step 1 Getting Ready

With the Framework desktop display on the screen, create a spreadsheet frame with the specifications given below. When the spreadsheet is finished, you can change any of the column widths to leave room for your own text and numbers, and you can add or delete rows and columns as necessary.

*To create a spreadsheet frame 15 columns wide and 34 rows deep:*

**Press** **Ins**
**Highlight** Create
Width
**Press** ↵
**Type** **15**
**Press** ↵
**Highlight** Height
**Press** ↵
**Type** **34**
**Press** ↵
**Highlight** Spreadsheet
**Press** ↵

*To label the frame:*

**Highlight** the frame border
**Type** **Inflows**
**Press** ↵

*To set the default display of numbers so the spreadsheet will show commas between thousands and no decimal places:*

**Highlight** the frame border
**Press** **Ins**
**Highlight** Numbers
Decimal Places
**Press** ↵
**Type** **0**
**Press** ↵
**Ins**
**Highlight** Numbers
Business
**Press** ↵

*To set recalculation to manual:*

**Press** **Ins**
**Highlight** Options for Recalc on the Numbers menu
**Press** ↵
**Highlight** Manual
**Press** ↵

*To enter the frame and zoom it to fill the screen:*

**Press** **Zoom** (**F9**)

*To size column A to 25 characters wide:*

**Highlight** A1
**Press** **Size** (**F4**)
→ until status panel reads **Size: 25/1**
↵

*To lock the first column and top row in place:*

**Press** **Ins**
**Highlight** Edit
Lock First Column/Row
**Press** ↵

**Result** Your screen should show columns A through G with column A 25 characters wide and all other columns 9 characters wide. Any numbers you enter will be displayed with commas between thousands and no decimal places. When you enter new values, you will have to remember to press the **Recalc** (**F5**) key.

## Step 2 Enter Headings

1

| | A | B | C | D | E | F | G | H | I | J | K | L | M | N | O |
|---|---|---|---|---|---|---|---|---|---|---|---|---|---|---|---|
| 1 | CASH INFLOWS SUPPLEMENT | Month: | Sep 87 | Oct 87 | Nov 87 | Dec 87 | Jan 88 | Feb 88 | Mar 88 | Apr 88 | May 88 | Jun 88 | Jul 88 | Aug 88 | Total |

The first row of the cash inflow supplement identifies the spreadsheet and the period covered. Our supplement covers one year by month, which is the most common approach to the cash budget. If your company is operating on a particularly tight cash flow, however, you might want to revise it to cover, say, three months by week. If you do this, you should first create the spreadsheet as described in the following steps and then make the necessary changes. (You may have a problem adapting the cash inflow section to calculate extended collection periods when the spreadsheet covers only a few weeks.)

To enter the headings and ruled lines for this spreadsheet, use the techniques you learned in Chapter 3. The formulas you *can* use to calculate the dates are described in detail below. As you enter each formula, your results should match those shown in the illustration. Here again, as in Chapter 3, we recommend that you enter the dates as text; we provide the formulas in case you want to use them. Remember to add the currency format to row 3.

**1**

**Enter dates** *either* by typing them in as text *or* by using the @DATE function. (When you customize the spreadsheet for your own business, you can change the date to the beginning of your operating period. Note that the customization will probably take longer in the future if you opt to type in the dates as text now.)

Whether you decide to type in the text or the formulas, make sure you *style* all the headings so they are both underlined and boldfaced.

*To enter the dates using the @DATE function:*

**Highlight** C1 and type **@DATE2(@DATE(87,9,1))** ⇥
At D1 type **@DATE2(@DATE(87,10,1))** ⇥
At E1 type **@DATE2(@DATE(87,11,1))** ⇥
At F1 type **@DATE2(@DATE(87,12,1))** ⇥
At G1 type **@DATE2(@DATE(88,1,1))** ⇥
At H1 type **@DATE2(@DATE(88,2,1))** ⇥
At I1 type **@DATE2(@DATE(88,3,1))** ⇥
At J1 type **@DATE2(@DATE(88,4,1))** ⇥
At K1 type **@DATE2(@DATE(88,5,1))** ⇥
At L1 type **@DATE2(@DATE(88,6,1))** ⇥
At M1 type **@DATE2(@DATE(88,7,1))** ⇥
At N1 type **@DATE2(@DATE(88,8,1))** ↵

## Step 3 Enter Net Sales

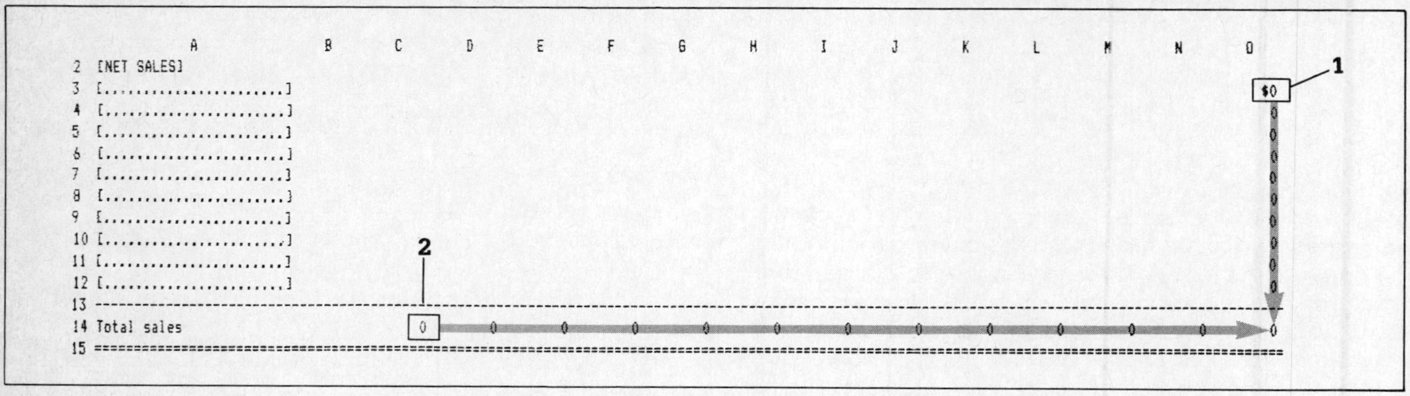


This section is for your sales breakdowns. Most companies break down their sales projections by customer, product, or product category; typical breakdowns by market and sales organization are also given in the cash inflows breakdown on page 100.

However you choose to break down your sales, this section will simply show your best estimate of sales by month. Your expected monthly sales are totaled on row 14 and the annual total for each breakdown category is calculated in column O.

Also, make sure you format the cells on row 3 to display their contents as currency with no decimal places.

**1**

**Enter and copy a formula** that totals the annual sales for each row.

**Highlight** O3 and type @**SUM(C3:N3)** ↵

**Copy to** O4 through O12
O14

**2**

**Enter and copy a formula** that totals monthly sales for each column. (The formula refers to the ruled line on row 13 so you can insert or delete rows later without affecting the formula.)

**Highlight** C14 and type @**SUM(C2:C13)** ↵

**Copy to** D14 through N14

### Check the Formulas

Now that the net sales section of the spreadsheet is finished, let's enter some sample numbers from a typical business case study to see if the formulas are all calculating correctly. The sample numbers entered in this section will also be used later in this chapter to check cash inflows and explore "What Ifs." Enter the numbers exactly as shown in the illustration below.

After recalculation your results should match those in the illustration. If your results are different, check your formulas against the instructions.

| | A | B | C | D | E | F | G | H | I | J | K | L | M | N | O |
|---|---|---|---|---|---|---|---|---|---|---|---|---|---|---|---|
| 2 | [NET SALES] | | | | | | | | | | | | | | |
| 3 | Boats - manufactured | | | | | | | $60,000 | $100,000 | $140,000 | $100,000 | $80,000 | $40,000 | | $520,000 |
| 4 | Boats - contracted | | | | | | | | | 75,000 | 75,000 | 60,000 | 30,000 | | 240,000 |
| 5 | Motors | | | | | | | | 20,000 | 25,000 | 60,000 | 50,000 | 45,000 | 15,000 | 215,000 |
| 6 | [......................] | | | | | | | | | | | | | | 0 |
| 7 | [......................] | | | | | | | | | | | | | | 0 |
| 8 | [......................] | | | | | | | | | | | | | | 0 |
| 9 | [......................] | | | | | | | | | | | | | | 0 |
| 10 | [......................] | | | | | | | | | | | | | | 0 |
| 11 | [......................] | | | | | | | | | | | | | | 0 |
| 12 | [......................] | | | | | | | | | | | | | | 0 |
| 13 | ------------------------ | | | | | | | | | | | | | | |
| 14 | Total sales | | 0 | 0 | 0 | 0 | 0 | 60,000 | 120,000 | 240,000 | 235,000 | 190,000 | 115,000 | 15,000 | 975,000 |
| 15 | ======================== | | | | | | | | | | | | | | |

## Case Study

For this case study, we have chosen the kind of business that often has cash flow difficulties. We'll exaggerate the case of Harrison Marine a bit by making it a start-up company. The problem is essentially the same as that faced by Anderson in Chapter 2: Harrison Marine is also a highly seasonal business, and because the company was started in September, Harrison has to have enough start-up cash to cover a lengthy period of outflows before he sees any cash coming in the door.

As you can see, Harrison expects sales to come from three types of operations. He sells boats he has manufactured himself, he sells boats for which he has contracted, and he sells motors. Since transportation costs in the boat-building business are very high, he plans to keep his business close to home. For a small, start-up operation with a limited market, he expects healthy sales. He expects some boat show sales in February and March, and by April and May, he will probably be stocking dealers' showroom floors (in some cases, this is done at the expense of the boat-maker, under the assumption that having the boat in the showroom will increase sales; this would tend to worsen Harrison's cash position). Not surprisingly, the bulk of Harrison's sales occur in the summer.

## Step 4 Enter Cash Inflows

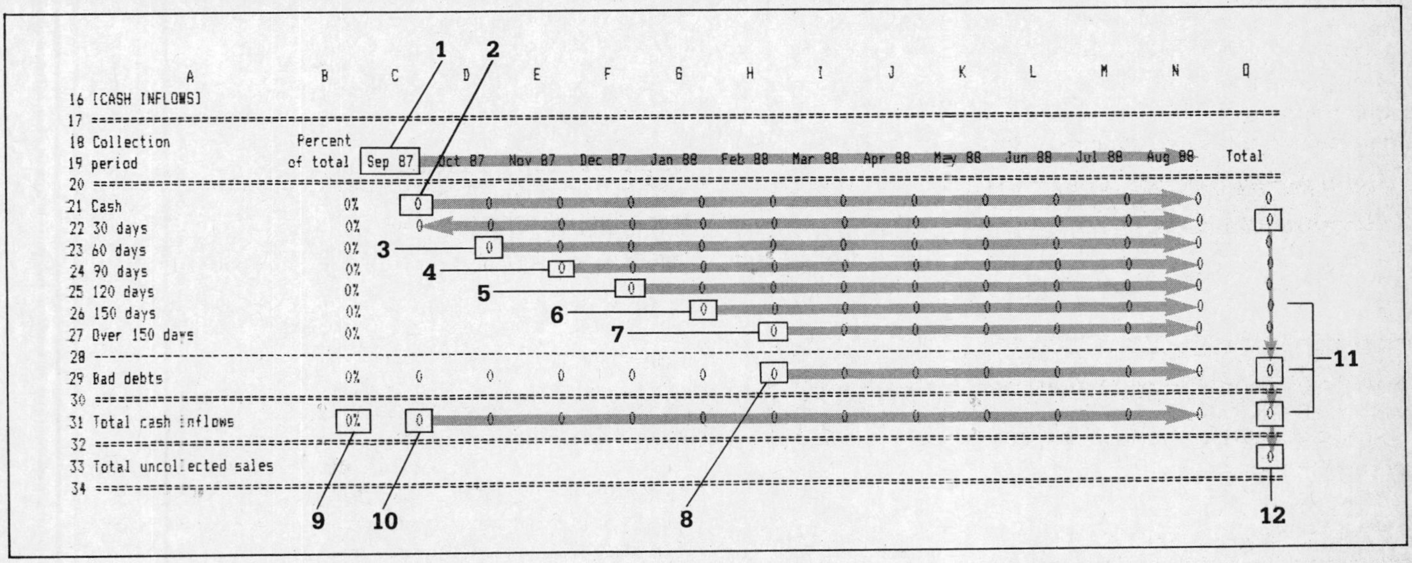


The key to projecting cash inflows is your expected collection pattern. If your company has a sales history, you can simply base your projections on that. (We will show you a spreadsheet later on that will help you find your collection pattern by aging your accounts receivable.) If the historical approach won't work for you, you can base your estimate on your terms of trade and credit policies, modified by your judgment about when your customers are likely to actually pay up. You could also refer to Robert Morris Associates or Dow Jones publications that give average collection patterns for various industries.

However you get there, the key figure is the percentage of sales revenue that is actually collected (received as cash) during each period. The formulas in this section of the spreadsheet simply spread your projected sales over the 12-month period using the percentages you enter.

We have included, and you should not neglect, a line for bad debts (row 29). Our assumption is that a certain percentage of debts will be considered "bad," and spread equally over the 12 months. In real life, they would tend to be written off at specific times and not spread out over the year as they are here.

The total cash inflows line (row 31) shows the actual cash receipts that will come into the company from sales during each month. You can combine the values from this row with your cash budget summary, and if you wish to budget in categories, you can develop separate inflow supplements for each category on your cash budget summary.

Before you enter the formulas for this part of the spreadsheet, enter the headings, the ruled lines, the zeros, and the data entry spaces shown in the illustration. Also, format the appropriate cells in column B to display their contents as percentages with no decimal places.

## What If 2 Collections Are Slower

In this "What If," let's suppose that economists predict a recession for Harrison's projection year—not a terrible recession, but definitely severe enough to worry buyers of small pleasure boats. Harrison should take the prudent step of seeing what would happen to his business if his buyers began to hoard their cash by slowing down their payments on his boats.

In real life, he would also take the next step and consider what would happen if his actual sales declined. (Keep in mind that he's been building boats all along that he'll have to sell during the recession year—disaster! Test it yourself.)

What we'll do is decrease the percentage of payments that is collected between 60 and 90 days, and stretch out the payments over a longer period of time. Although collections are unlikely to remain constant given the circumstances we described, we'll leave the bad debts percentage alone to simplify our comparison.

As you will see, any credit line-type loan that Harrison may have is probably in trouble (unless he expects a massive gross margin on his boats). Obviously, he would have to feed this new inflow data into the cash budget summary to be sure, but note that more of this year's sales will be collected next year, making this year's loan payments harder (but possibly making next year's operations less dependent on new, higher debt). The trick for Harrison will be to get through this year; he might try offering trade discounts based on the new payment expectation.

(Incidentally, this scenario really demonstrates the need—particularly for new companies—to project their cash position for more than one year at a time. Many bankers advocate, and some require, a three-year cash budget for a start-up venture before they will even talk seriously.)

## Change the Worksheet

*To enter changes in the collection pattern:*

**Highlight** the cells that have been changed in the illustration below and enter the new numbers shown

**Press** **Recalc** (**F5**)

**Result** The new numbers should match those shown in the illustration.

| | A | B | C | D | E | F | G | H | I | J | K | L | M | N | O |
|---|---|---|---|---|---|---|---|---|---|---|---|---|---|---|---|
| 1 | CASH INFLOWS SUPPLEMENT | Month: | Sep 87 | Oct 87 | Nov 87 | Dec 87 | Jan 88 | Feb 88 | Mar 88 | Apr 88 | May 88 | Jun 88 | Jul 88 | Aug 88 | Total |
| 2 | [NET SALES] | | | | | | | | | | | | | | |
| 3 | Boats - manufactured | | | | | | | $60,000 | $100,000 | $140,000 | $100,000 | $80,000 | $40,000 | | $520,000 |
| 4 | Boats - contracted | | | | | | | | | 75,000 | 75,000 | 60,000 | 30,000 | | 240,000 |
| 5 | Motors | | | | | | | | 20,000 | 25,000 | 60,000 | 50,000 | 45,000 | 15,000 | 215,000 |
| 6 | [......................] | | | | | | | | | | | | | | 0 |
| 7 | [......................] | | | | | | | | | | | | | | 0 |
| 8 | [......................] | | | | | | | | | | | | | | 0 |
| 9 | [......................] | | | | | | | | | | | | | | 0 |
| 10 | [......................] | | | | | | | | | | | | | | 0 |
| 11 | [......................] | | | | | | | | | | | | | | 0 |
| 12 | [......................] | | | | | | | | | | | | | | 0 |
| 13 | ---------- | | | | | | | | | | | | | | |
| 14 | Total sales | | 0 | 0 | 0 | 0 | 0 | 60,000 | 120,000 | 240,000 | 235,000 | 190,000 | 115,000 | 15,000 | 975,000 |
| 15 | ========== | | | | | | | | | | | | | | |
| 16 | [CASH INFLOWS] | | | | | | | | | | | | | | |
| 17 | ========== | | | | | | | | | | | | | | |
| 18 | Collection | Percent | | | | | | | | | | | | | |
| 19 | period | of total | Sep 87 | Oct 87 | Nov 87 | Dec 87 | Jan 88 | Feb 88 | Mar 88 | Apr 88 | May 88 | Jun 88 | Jul 88 | Aug 88 | Total |
| 20 | ========== | | | | | | | | | | | | | | |
| 21 | Cash | 0% | 0 | 0 | 0 | 0 | 0 | 0 | 0 | 0 | 0 | 0 | 0 | 0 | 0 |
| 22 | 30 days | 0% | 0 | 0 | 0 | 0 | 0 | 0 | 0 | 0 | 0 | 0 | 0 | 0 | 0 |
| 23 | 60 days | 5% | | 0 | 0 | 0 | 0 | 0 | 3,000 | 6,000 | 12,000 | 11,750 | 9,500 | 5,750 | 48,000 |
| 24 | 90 days | 10% | | | 0 | 0 | 0 | 0 | 0 | 6,000 | 12,000 | 24,000 | 23,500 | 19,000 | 84,500 |
| 25 | 120 days | 30% | | | | 0 | 0 | 0 | 0 | 0 | 18,000 | 36,000 | 72,000 | 70,500 | 196,500 |
| 26 | 150 days | 25% | | | | | 0 | 0 | 0 | 0 | 0 | 15,000 | 30,000 | 60,000 | 105,000 |
| 27 | Over 150 days | 25% | | | | | | 0 | 0 | 0 | 0 | 0 | 15,000 | 30,000 | 45,000 |
| 28 | ---------- | | | | | | | | | | | | | | |
| 29 | Bad debts | 5% | 0 | 0 | 0 | 0 | 0 | 0 | 0 | 0 | 0 | 0 | 3,000 | 6,000 | 9,000 |
| 30 | ========== | | | | | | | | | | | | | | |
| 31 | Total cash inflows | 100% | 0 | 0 | 0 | 0 | 0 | 0 | 3,000 | 12,000 | 42,000 | 86,750 | 147,000 | 179,250 | 470,000 |
| 32 | ========== | | | | | | | | | | | | | | |
| 33 | Total uncollected sales | | | | | | | | | | | | | | 496,000 |
| 34 | ========== | | | | | | | | | | | | | | |

## Clear the Sample Data

When you have finished exploring "What Ifs," you should clear the spreadsheet for the entry of your own data by copying blank label entry spaces to the cells containing sample line item labels, and by placing zeros in the cells with sample numbers.

*To copy blank label spaces to cells containing sample line items:*

**Copy from** A6

**Copy to** A3 through A5

*To fill the cells containing sample numbers with zeros:*

**Copy from** G3 through G12

**Copy to** H3 through N3

**Copy from** B22

**Copy to** B23 through B27
B29

**Copy from** H21 through H27

**Copy to** I21 through N21

**Result** All the sample numbers you entered on the spreadsheet will be replaced by zeros, and the formulas should recalculate to show zero as well. Your spreadsheet should look like the illustration on page 164.

## Save Your Work

Now that you've cleared the spreadsheet of the sample data, be sure to save it again so that it won't be lost if the power fails or if you accidentally hit the wrong key. Use the file name E Inflows for the frame containing the blank spreadsheet so it won't overwrite and erase the version with the sample numbers (Inflows). Remember to make a backup copy of the disk on which the file was saved.

*To name the frame containing the blank spreadsheet:*

**Highlight** the frame border

**Press** **Space Bar** to get the name **Inflows** on the edit line

**Type** **E** (SP)

**Press** (↵)

*To save the frame labeled E Inflows:*

**Press** **Ctrl**-(↵)

**Result** The new frame, E Inflows, will be saved to the disk along with the old frame, Inflows.

# 5 Working with Your Pattern of Cash Outflow

## Introduction

As was true of your cash inflows, there are two important perspectives on cash outflows: the underlying cost, and how that cost is handled in your business. Again, the challenges are to figure out where to concentrate your effort and to develop an appropriate set of options for action.

To some degree, working with your outflows is easier than working with your inflows. This is because your estimates in the expense/outflow area are likely to be more accurate. You know what your rent or mortgage is going to cost, for example, and you know when the payments will be due. You know how much raw material it takes to make your products. In short, there are fairly clear limits to your estimates.

It also seems easier to project outflows because you do not commit to them in the same way as you commit to inflow projections. When you commit to a sales or a collections amount, you are, in effect, promising to produce a result through your own effort. Projecting outflows, on the other hand, merely involves having a reasonably good sense of the realities of your business.

This does not mean, however, that projecting your cash outflows is unimportant. In fact, partly because outflows are more fixed, they are often easier to manipulate to your advantage. Since you are the payer, you have some of the options that you detest as a seller. You can, for example, change (or threaten to change) suppliers. You can choose to take prompt payment discounts or not. Presumably, you would not go so far as to defer payment of your payables indefinitely (unless dire circumstances strike), nor would you actually refuse to pay a supplier without an appropriate reason—such as an abysmally shoddy product. The point about outflows, however, is that you *could* control them in any of these ways. Your flexibility is much greater on this side of the ledger.

One of the reasons, then, for working with your cash outflows (aside from the obvious need to use them to figure your total cash position) is to see where and when exercising some of this flexibility is warranted or desirable. This section moves through the "how-to project" issue while concentrating on how to make decisions on the timing of your outflows based on your total cash position.

## Making Cash Outflow Projections

**Collecting your data.** For this exercise in collecting your outflow data, you will need the same kinds of records you used when developing your inflow history. Get it all out again and start listing. Here, too, if you have no usable history, you can only work with your expectations and your contractual arrangements. They are certainly enough for a start.

As you list your cash payments (along with the payee, the order date, amount, volume, and item), categorize each by month of payment, by category of purchase (space costs, for example), and by order date, if any. Your standard, regular payments, such as rent or loan payments, will have no order dates, of course. Note the terms of trade for each item as you go so that you can see how well you are using the time you are granted or how consistently you are taking advantage of trade discounts. Also, include the delivery date so that you can use this listing to consider lead times in your business flow.

As you did when you developed your inflow data, you should look for patterns. This time, however, you are seeking patterns in *your* activities that could give you clues to operating less expensively or more efficiently. Suppose, for example, that you noticed when you put all the outflows together, that you actually ordered essentially the same item from two different sources and that you placed (and paid for) a large number of relatively small orders. Right after you finish this exercise, go out and call each of those suppliers. Find out what would happen to your unit cost if you were to consolidate your purchases with one of the two suppliers and were to order less frequently and in larger quantity.

Unless you originally had some specific reason(s) that still hold for keeping two suppliers of this item, you will find that you can probably save money by asking them both to bid on all your business and choosing one or the other. If you still believe you need two suppliers after you have seen how much it is costing you, you will probably find that you can save some money by making larger purchases less frequently to take advantage of their price break points. The real point is that the exercise of grouping your information and really looking at it can, in and of itself, be a useful and profitable activity.

## Projecting Outflows for Most Items

Even beyond this initial effort, you will use the data you have arrayed and considered as the basis on which to project your expected outflows for next year. The same approach you used to consider inflows should be used again. Start by asking what is likely to stay the same (or roughly the same) next year. Then add your projections of the highly predictable cost increases you expect—your labor costs, for example. Next, tackle the only difficult part—the items related to your sales projections, such as inventory and raw materials costs and sales and marketing costs.

Sales and marketing costs are relatively straightforward. If you are in the kind of business in which advertising costs are fairly directly related to the volume of sales, you would use the figure you intend to sell to determine how much you will spend in advertising and marketing costs. If possible, relate the timing of your advertising expenditures to the production of sales.

Your experience, or the experience of others in the industry, should tell you about the lag between the appearance of your raw material and its effect on your sales figures. Your suppliers and your experience should inform you about the space between the order and its delivery, and between the order and the requirement that you pay for it. Using delivery/invoice dates, work out the pay dates and enter them in your outflow detail schedule.

Commissions are, obviously, directly related to sales. The nice thing about them is that you do not pay them until your customer has paid you. Outflows to commissions, then, will follow inflows from sales, rather than the sales themselves. (As a side note: If you pay your salespeople on the basis of orders, they have little interest in the collection or credit authorization process. Since it is easier to sell on easy terms, this approach to commissions tends to exacerbate any collections problems you might have. Consider paying commissions based on *paid* orders. The interest in collections and credit worthiness of customers will rise rapidly. We also expect that your collection pattern will improve.)

## Outflows for Inventory Purchases

Purchases for inventory generally present the most difficult outflow forecasting problem. Start with your best estimate of sales (your "most probable" case estimate) and work backwards to:

1 How much of what kinds of materials or merchandise you will need, and

2 When you will need it

Total your requirements for the year by item.

**Economic order quantity.** Your next step is to figure out when to order and how much to order each time. Happily, there is a standard approach to determining your *economic order quantity* (EOQ). We have provided a spreadsheet for you to use in Chapter 7. The general idea is simple. It assumes that there is a cost (to you) of carrying excess inventory. It also considers the extra costs incurred by processing and shipping a larger number of smaller orders. The formula entered into the spreadsheet makes these tradeoffs for you and shows the best amount to purchase at any one time.

Use caution when working with this formula, though. First, although unlikely, it is possible that the flow of your business is uneven enough throughout the year to significantly alter the EOQ. If, for example, you really will use half the total amount of materials required in a two-month period, you will want to adjust the formula to reflect this unbalance. Second, the formula does not automatically account for delays and/or speedups in production or sales. Given that it is certainly possible that there will be foul-ups in delivery or increased production needs, you probably want to consider maintaining some minimum level of extra stock—just in case. That level should depend on past history of delays and "speedups" in conjunction with your normal production requirememts for that particular item.

Once you know how much you are ordering (and how often over the course of the year), you will have to work backwards to determine when you will have to place the order to get what you need when you need it. You will then have to figure out when, given the trade terms of your supplier, you will actually have to come up with the cash. Your listing of previous purchases from that supplier should provide you with answers here.

Obviously, there are limits to the use of the EOQ approach to stocking your business. For many small businesses, one major limitation is the cost of purchasing the "proper" amounts of merchandise or materials at one time. Your cash budget can help you here by letting you test payment approaches and consider options before performing the actual operations. We will discuss this further later in this section.

**Trade discounts.** There is still one potential money-saver to consider—the use of legitimate discounts offered by your suppliers to induce you to pay faster. Essentially, most companies are very much like yours in that they would like to get their cash payments as soon as possible. Not only does it improve company flexibility and reduce borrowing costs to those in cash binds, it also reduces the worry associated with lengthening receivables. Thus, most of your suppliers are doing what we recommended that you consider in the chapter on cash inflows. They offer a small percentage off the total price if you will pay earlier than you absolutely have to.

As a purchaser, your question is whether this discount is possible and worthwhile for you to take. The answer depends partly on such items as the size of the discount offered and the amount of additional time for which you have to give up the cash. For example, if the terms are 2/10, net 30 (that is, 2% off if you pay within 10 days, and otherwise the full amount is due within 30 days), you would be giving up your cash for 20 days to gain 2% of the purchase price. We have included a trade discount spreadsheet in Chapter 7 to help you develop and clarify your tradeoff costs.

## How to Use Your Cash Budget to Make Outflow Decisions

Obviously, however, your answers to many of the issues raised in the previous sections revolve around whether you have or can raise the cash. This is where your cash budget comes in.

Suppose you own a small manufacturing company that makes one product using purchased raw materials. Assume that most of your cash tends to appear during the month following the sale. Your suppliers want their money within 30 days of purchase. The first few months of your cash budget (summarized) might look like the table that follows. To simplify and clarify the main points, we have assumed that this is a new company and that it will produce and sell more or less evenly throughout the year.

| *Item* | *Jan.* | *Feb.* | *March* | *April* | *May* |
|---|---|---|---|---|---|
| Cash inflows | | | $10,000 | $10,000 | $10,000 |
| Cash outflows | | | | | |
| Materials | | $6,000 | 6,000 | 6,000 | 6,000 |
| Other items | $2,000 | 3,000 | 3,000 | 3,000 | 3,000 |
| Beginning cash | 10,000 | | | | |
| Net monthly cash | (2,000) | (9,000) | 1,000 | 1,000 | 1,000 |
| Cumulative cash | 8,000 | (1,000) | 0 | 1,000 | 2,000 |
| Loan | | 1,000 | (341) | (341) | (341) |
| Revised cumulative | | 0 | 659 | 1,318 | 1,977 |

You started with a cash balance of $10,000. Your cash budget shows that you would need a loan of at least $1,000, so, let's assume that you already made arrangements to obtain it. Let's see what an EOQ and trade discount analysis might do to your plans.

Assume your EOQ analysis shows that you should order six times a year, rather than twelve times. You can get a 10% discount at that volume level. Your cash budget looks like this.

| *Item* | *Jan.* | *Feb.* | *March* | *April* | *May* |
|---|---|---|---|---|---|
| Cash inflows | | | $10,000 | $10,000 | $10,000 |
| Cash outflows | | | | | |
| Materials | | $10,800 | — | 10,800 | — |
| Other items | $3,000 | 3,000 | 3,000 | 3,000 | 3,000 |
| Beginning cash | 10,000 | | | | |
| Net monthly cash | (2,000) | (13,800) | 7,000 | (3,800) | 7,000 |
| Cumulative cash | 8,000 | (5,800) | 1,200 | (2,600) | 4,400 |
| Loan | | 6,500 | (2,213) | (2,213) | (2,213) |
| Revised cumulative | 700 | 5,487 | (526) | 4,261 | |

While these figures are rough, and we did not run them for the full year, you can see what has occurred. You now have an option (assuming that you have the short-term borrowing capacity) of taking a larger loan for a purpose. Your interest cost for the three-month period will be $139 as opposed to $23 (a 3-month credit line, 13%). But, in the second case, your action would have won you the discount of 10%—$2,400 for the period shown and $7,200 for the year. Not a bad investment...

Now, let's see if we can reduce that loan. Suppose that all your suppliers offer 2/10, net 30. You believe that if you were to offer the same terms to your customers, half of them would take you up on it. We reworked the numbers below to reflect both sets of discounts.

| *Item* | *Jan.* | *Feb.* | *March* | *April* | *May* |
|---|---|---|---|---|---|
| Cash inflows | | $4,900 | $9,900 | $9,900 | $9,900 |
| Cash outflows | | | | | |
| Materials | | $10,584 | — | 10,584 | — |
| Other items | $3,000 | 3,000 | 3,000 | 3,000 | 3,000 |
| Beginning cash | 10,000 | | | | |
| Net monthly cash | (2,000) | (8,684) | 6,900 | (3,684) | 6,900 |
| Cumulative cash | 8,000 | (684) | 6,216 | 2,532 | 9,432 |
| Loan | | 1,000 | (341) | (341) | (341) |
| Revised cumulative | | 316 | 6,875 | 2,850 | 9,409 |

Note that the key item in this part of the analysis was shifting your cash inflows by offering to take less money in payment. (As we said earlier, inflow analysis—getting cash *today*—is a critical function of business planning.) Here, you gave up 2% on half your sales ($100 a month, $1,200 a year) to gain 2% on your purchases (an additional $1,300 for the year). More to the point, you also saved almost $120 in extra interest charges.

The real point of putting you through all of these numbers is to demonstrate an approach to problem solving and planning using these cash budgeting methods. As you can see, each version of the cash budget considers a different set of outflow variables. One considers an inflow variation as well. You have developed a series of options for your company—significantly increasing its flexibility.

In the end, however, *you* are the one who has to choose among the options. In the set of circumstances just mentioned, for example, do you want to increase your debt to the bank (increasing your exposure to outside pressures) to save amounts shown? Do you like the additional flexibility offered by the increased cash balances, which will come with the two alternative cash budgets shown? Do you like it well enough to take the small added risk that you will not sell as well as you expected, and you will not be able to cover the loan as you plan? Or do you view that risk as a *large* risk?

If the level of risk concerns you, you could perform further analyses with this data and your cash budget to determine the margin for error that exists in these estimates. You would simply vary the key estimates to see how far you could go before you ran into cash shortfalls. In this example, those key estimates would include: sales, the proportion of customers who would use your discount structure, and, of course, the discount structures of your suppliers.

If you really want to see how these things interact for this example, enter the numbers in the cash budget summary spreadsheet on your disk and simply play with them. You can run the string for the entire year by following out the assumptions as originally stated.

Please note that more of the key variables are on the inflow side. For the same reason that it is easier to commit to outflow estimates, it is less critical in the overall operation of most small businesses. (The exceptions tend to be those in fields in which expense control is the main basis for competitive survival.) You, theoretically, can sell more. You can control, to some degree, the terms you offer to your customers. You can determine to whom you will and will not sell. Thus, as usual, the scary part is likely to be the most important part—the part within your control.

But the flexibility of your cash budget, and its ease of operation using this book and Framework, should go a long way toward reducing any anxiety. After all, you are minimizing the unknown by previewing it. Whatever your personal attitude toward even slight increases in risk, your cash budget can help by letting you see in advance the level of risk you are incurring or adding. If for no other reason, your cash budget will probably become one of your most valuable tools.

## How to Use the Outflow Spreadsheets

As noted earlier, the outflows in your cash budget can be broken into two distinct categories. The first category includes those outflows that are irregular and tied to the purchases of inventory, supplies, and services for the business. The second category includes those outflows that are highly regular, if not monthly or weekly. Items that would appear in this category include insurance premiums, rent and lease payments, loan repayments, and similar items.

The placement of some outflow items will depend on how your particular business works. Payroll, for example, *can* be a nice, steady outflow—if your work force is stable and salaried. If your workers are largely part-time and/or paid by the hour for irregular schedules, you might find it most useful to categorize the irregular part of your payroll outflow with the "purchased services" and the rest with the regular outflows.

Because of this division in types of outflows, we have provided two separate spreadsheets for you to use in developing your cash budget: a cash outflow supplement *with* leads and lags which you will enter in this chapter, and a cash outflow supplement *without* leads and lags which you will enter in Chapter 7.

The supplement with leads and lags provides an easy way for you to keep track of those outflows that are tied to other people's invoices (or to your own labor needs), since it calculates the lags between invoicing and payment based on your supplier's terms of trade. You'll list each supplier, enter their payment period in days, and then enter the invoice dates of each of your purchases. The spreadsheet calculates the actual outflows for each month.

Because suppliers quote terms in days (while you work in months), the spreadsheet has two additional features. First, it calculates the last day of each month in the supplement as well as the first day; and second, it shows you the last payment date for each supplier before your payment becomes overdue. This feature in particular will help insure a good credit standing with your suppliers—assuming, of course, that you actually pay when you are supposed to. Framework doesn't write out the check, but it won't let you forget.

We recommend that you use the outflow supplement without leads and lags for your regular outflows. It provides spaces in which to list your regular monthly outflows, and sums the outflows by month and by category. You should create several copies of this spreadsheet, one for each major category of outflow. You might, for example, create one for space-related costs, including your rent, heat, electricity, and whatever else you consider as part of this category. You could use the category totals in your cash budget summary, while maintaining the detailed data for control purposes.

Together, these two outflow spreadsheets provide the numbers required for the outflow portion of your cash budget summary. You will want to transfer the monthly total row from the supplement with leads and lags as well as the totals from each of your supplements without leads and lags to the cash budget summary spreadsheet.

## Breaking Down Your Cash Outflows

The cash outflow checklist on the following pages lists many possible uses for your business cash. When you are thinking about your business in global terms, it is very easy to miss one particular use of cash. This list will help prevent such omissions. The list is not intended to be exhaustive; it is, rather, a way of jogging your memory. Scan it. Although we doubt that you will have forgotten a significant outflow of cash, several little items can add up quickly, throwing all your projections into disarray. We hope that this list will, at least, confirm for you that all outflows have been included in your planning process.

## ✓ Checklist Cash Outflows

### Cash Disbursements

**Inventory**

- ☐ Inventory purchases
- ☐ Raw materials purchases
- ☐ Freight-in
- ☐ Packing materials
- ☐ Insurance
- ☐ Royalties

**Payroll and Other Employee Outflows**

- ☐ Regular wages
- ☐ Holiday wages
- ☐ Overtime
- ☐ Vacation pay
- ☐ Full-time employees
- ☐ Part-time employees
- ☐ Bonuses
- ☐ Payroll insurance
- ☐ Disability insurance
- ☐ Health insurance
- ☐ Major medical
- ☐ Dental insurance
- ☐ Workman's compensation
- ☐ Life insurance
- ☐ Bonding
- ☐ Retirement benefits
- ☐ Taxes—FICA
- ☐ Taxes—FUTA
- ☐ State income taxes
- ☐ City income taxes
- ☐ State employment taxes
- ☐ State franchise taxes
- ☐ Training expenses
- ☐ Laundry and dry cleaning
- ☐ Uniform rentals

**Occupancy Expenses**

- ☐ Rent
- ☐ Cleaning (routine)
- ☐ Decorating
- ☐ Remodeling
- ☐ Electricity
- ☐ Water
- ☐ Gas
- ☐ Oil
- ☐ Security staff
- ☐ Alarm systems
- ☐ Staff
- ☐ Maintenance (routine)
- ☐ Repairs
- ☐ Management expenses
- ☐ Air conditioning
- ☐ Heating
- ☐ Insulation
- ☐ Storm doors and windows
- ☐ Designer fees
- ☐ Security deposits
- ☐ Moving expenses

**Office Supplies**

- ☐ Invoices
- ☐ Sales orders
- ☐ Pendaflex folders
- ☐ File folders
- ☐ Boxes
- ☐ Christmas cards
- ☐ Calendars
- ☐ Stationery
- ☐ Envelopes
- ☐ Packing materials
- ☐ Paper clips
- ☐ Staplers and staples
- ☐ Pens and pencils
- ☐ Typewriter ribbons
- ☐ Computer supplies
- ☐ Art supplies

**Office Equipment**

- ☐ Desks
- ☐ Typewriters
- ☐ Filing cabinets
- ☐ Chairs
- ☐ Safe
- ☐ Computers
- ☐ Printers
- ☐ Copy machine
- ☐ Air conditioners
- ☐ Fans
- ☐ Heaters
- ☐ Plants
- ☐ Lighting
- ☐ Packing equipment

**Store/Plant Equipment and Fixtures**

- ☐ Storage cabinets
- ☐ Counters and display cases
- ☐ Safe
- ☐ Lighting fixtures
- ☐ Outside signs
- ☐ Window displays
- ☐ Workbenches
- ☐ Power tools
- ☐ Hand tools

**Postage**

- ☐ Stamps
- ☐ Postage meter
- ☐ UPS/Courier services

**Communications**

- ☐ Telephone
- ☐ Deposit
- ☐ Monthly charge
- ☐ Local calls
- ☐ Long distance service
- ☐ Computer line rental
- ☐ Modems
- ☐ Telegraph
- ☐ Telex

**Dues, Subscriptions, and Memberships**

- ☐ Professional organizations
- ☐ Social organizations
- ☐ Chamber of Commerce
- ☐ Magazine subscriptions
- ☐ Training seminars

**Travel and Entertainment**

- ☐ Hotel/motel
- ☐ Airline
- ☐ Car rental
- ☐ Railroad
- ☐ Bus
- ☐ Meals
- ☐ Entertainment
- ☐ Tips
- ☐ Supplies
- ☐ Taxis
- ☐ Dry cleaning

**Miscellaneous**

- ☐ Franchise fees
- ☐ Loan repayment
- ☐ Bank charges
- ☐ Contributions
- ☐ Auto expenses

**Professional Fees**

- ☐ Collection expenses
- ☐ Organization expenses
- ☐ Accounting services
- ☐ Bookkeeping
- ☐ Consultants
- ☐ Public relations
- ☐ Computer support

**Insurance**

- ☐ Fire and property
- ☐ Personal injury
- ☐ Product liability
- ☐ Vehicles
- ☐ Liability
- ☐ Business continuation

**Taxes**

- ☐ Federal income
- ☐ State and city
- ☐ Real estate
- ☐ Assessments
- ☐ Self-employment
- ☐ Value added

**Permits and Licenses**

- ☐ Building
- ☐ Health department
- ☐ Fire clearance
- ☐ Occupancy
- ☐ Signs
- ☐ Electric
- ☐ Plumbing

**Leasehold Improvements**

- ☐ Electrical
- ☐ Plumbing
- ☐ Carpentry
- ☐ Designer fees
- ☐ Architect fees
- ☐ Painting

**Storage and Shipment**

- ☐ Warehouse costs
- ☐ Freight-out
- ☐ Insurance

**Selling Expenses**

- ☐ Newspaper advertising
- ☐ Magazine advertising
- ☐ Television advertising
- ☐ Radio advertising
- ☐ Direct mail
- ☐ Catalogs
- ☐ Brochures/flyers
- ☐ Logo design
- ☐ Signs
- ☐ Directory listings
- ☐ Advertising agency fees
- ☐ Yellow Pages listing
- ☐ Trade shows and conventions
- ☐ Letter house costs
- ☐ Sales commissions and bonuses
- ☐ Premiums and incentives

## Other expenses

- ☐ ____________________
- ☐ ____________________
- ☐ ____________________
- ☐ ____________________

# Our Approach

In the following steps we'll show you how to create a cash outflow supplement with leads and lags for breaking down cash purchases where a variety of payment terms are offered (for instance, where items are paid for in cash or with 30-day, 60-day, 90-day, or longer credit payment terms).

This spreadsheet will help you track payments and see the effects of the terms of trade offered you on the timing of your cash outflows. It essentially spreads your purchase costs over the months when payments will be due. All you have to do is enter the name of the supplier, the date of the invoice, the payment terms, and the total amount due. The spreadsheet will then automatically calculate the date payment is due and display the amount in the appropriate month on the spreadsheet. The spreadsheet also calculates the payments due before, during, and after the period covered, so you'll always know what payments fall outside of the period. Changing the dates in cells B2 and C2 on the spreadsheet will change all of the dates in the monthly column headings, and will automatically reschedule the payments in the correct months. This feature allows you to "revolve" the cash outflow supplement, to add new payments and delete old ones as time passes.

The monthly payments calculated on the total line can be transferred to the cash budget summary spreadsheet. In those cases where you have more than one major category of purchases—for example, inventory and equipment—you may want to make two or more copies of this spreadsheet and transfer the total lines from both to separate rows on the cash outflow section of the cash budget summary. Although this spreadsheet has only nine separate lines, you can easily expand it to any size you need.

We will enter sample numbers from a typical business situation to check the formulas, and when you've finished exploring "What Ifs," you'll clear the spreadsheet of the sample numbers and save the blank spreadsheet for use in your own business.

## The Cash Outflow Supplement (With Leads and Lags)

| | A | B | C | D (1) | E | F (2) | G | H | I | J | K | L | M | N | O | P | Q | R (3) |
|---|---|---|---|---|---|---|---|---|---|---|---|---|---|---|---|---|---|---|
| 1 | CASH OUTFLOW SUPPLEMENT | Month | Year | | | | | | | | | | | | | | | |
| 2 | WITH LEADS AND LAGS | 9 | 87 | | | | | | | | | | | | | | | |
| 3 | | | | | | | | | | | | | | | | | | |
| 4 | | Supplier | Credit | Date | Total | | | | | | | | | | | | | Total due |
| 5 | | billing | period | payment | amount | | | | | | | | | | | | | in the |
| 6 | Name of supplier: | date | (days) | is due | due | Sep 87 | Oct 87 | Nov 87 | Dec 87 | Jan 88 | Feb 88 | Mar 88 | Apr 88 | May 88 | Jun 88 | Jul 88 | Aug 88 | period |
| 7 | | | | | | | | | | | | | | | | | | |
| 8 | Jarrett Electronics | December 15, 87 | 30 | Jan 14, 88 | $50,000 | $0 | $0 | $0 | $0 | $50,000 | $0 | $0 | $0 | $0 | $0 | $0 | $0 | $50,000 |
| 9 | Jarrett Electronics | July 30, 88 | 30 | Aug 29, 88 | 55,000 | 0 | 0 | 0 | 0 | 0 | 0 | 0 | 0 | 0 | 0 | 0 | 55,000 | 55,000 |
| 10 | Green's Plastics | October 10, 87 | 30 | Nov 9, 87 | 15,000 | 0 | 0 | 15,000 | 0 | 0 | 0 | 0 | 0 | 0 | 0 | 0 | 0 | 15,000 |
| 11 | Green's Plastics | May 10, 88 | 30 | Jun 9, 88 | 15,000 | 0 | 0 | 0 | 0 | 0 | 0 | 0 | 0 | 0 | 15,000 | 0 | 0 | 15,000 |
| 12 | Walton Wire & Cable | March 15, 88 | 30 | Apr 14, 88 | 20,000 | 0 | 0 | 0 | 0 | 0 | 0 | 0 | 20,000 | 0 | 0 | 0 | 0 | 20,000 |
| 13 | Walton Wire & Cable | August 30, 88 | 30 | Sep 29, 88 | 20,000 | 0 | 0 | 0 | 0 | 0 | 0 | 0 | 0 | 0 | 0 | 0 | 0 | 0 |
| 14 | Walton Wire & Cable | October 15, 87 | 30 | Nov 14, 87 | 25,000 | 0 | 0 | 25,000 | 0 | 0 | 0 | 0 | 0 | 0 | 0 | 0 | 0 | 25,000 |
| 15 | [......................] | September 1, 87 | 0 | Sep 1, 87 | 0 | 0 | 0 | 0 | 0 | 0 | 0 | 0 | 0 | 0 | 0 | 0 | 0 | 0 |
| 16 | [......................] | September 1, 87 | 0 | Sep 1, 87 | 0 | 0 | 0 | 0 | 0 | 0 | 0 | 0 | 0 | 0 | 0 | 0 | 0 | 0 |
| 17 | [......................] | September 1, 87 | 0 | Sep 1, 87 | 0 | 0 | 0 | 0 | 0 | 0 | 0 | 0 | 0 | 0 | 0 | 0 | 0 | 0 |
| 18 | [......................] | September 1, 87 | 0 | Sep 1, 87 | 0 | 0 | 0 | 0 | 0 | 0 | 0 | 0 | 0 | 0 | 0 | 0 | 0 | 0 |
| 19 | | | | | | | | | | | | | | | | | | |
| 4— 20 | Total cash outflows | | | | 200,000 | 0 | 0 | 40,000 | 0 | 50,000 | 0 | 0 | 20,000 | 0 | 15,000 | 0 | 55,000 | 180,000 |
| 21 | | | | | | | | | | | | | | | | | | |
| 5— 22 | LOOKUP TABLE FOR DATE CALCULATIONS | | | | | | | | | | | | | | | | | |
| 23 | | | | | | | | | | | | | | | | | | |
| 24 | | | | DATE CALCULATIONS | | Sep 87 | Oct 87 | Nov 87 | Dec 87 | Jan 88 | Feb 88 | Mar 88 | Apr 88 | May 88 | Jun 88 | Jul 88 | Aug 88 | |
| 25 | | | | Month | | 9 | 10 | 11 | 12 | 1 | 2 | 3 | 4 | 5 | 6 | 7 | 8 | |
| 26 | | | | Year | | 87 | 87 | 87 | 87 | 88 | 88 | 88 | 88 | 88 | 88 | 88 | 88 | |
| 27 | | | | Days in month | | 30 | 31 | 30 | 31 | 31 | 28 | 31 | 30 | 31 | 30 | 31 | 31 | |
| 28 | | | | | | | | | | | | | | | | | | |
| 29 | | Month | Days | | | | | | | | | | | | | | | |
| 30 | January | 1 | 31 | | | | | | | | | | | | | | | |
| 31 | February | 2 | 28 | | | | | | | | | | | | | | | |
| 32 | March | 3 | 31 | | | | | | | | | | | | | | | |
| 33 | April | 4 | 30 | | | | | | | | | | | | | | | |
| 34 | May | 5 | 31 | | | | | | | | | | | | | | | |
| 35 | June | 6 | 30 | | | | | | | | | | | | | | | |
| 36 | July | 7 | 31 | | | | | | | | | | | | | | | |
| 37 | August | 8 | 31 | | | | | | | | | | | | | | | |
| 38 | September | 9 | 30 | | | | | | | | | | | | | | | |
| 39 | October | 10 | 31 | | | | | | | | | | | | | | | |
| 40 | November | 11 | 30 | | | | | | | | | | | | | | | |
| 41 | December | 12 | 31 | | | | | | | | | | | | | | | |

*The cash outflow supplement with leads and lags is used for irregular outflows such as inventory purchases. You enter the starting date of the supplement, the name of the supplier, billing date, credit period, and amount due, and the worksheet automatically calculates the date payment is due (**1**), the amounts due in each month (**2**), the amounts due before, during, and after the period covered (**3**), and the total cash outflow for each month (**4**). The lookup table (**5**) provides information for Framework to calculate the dates and the amounts.*

# Entering the Cash Outflow Supplement

The cash outflow supplement with leads and lags will be created in six steps:

**Step 1** Getting ready
**Step 2** Enter heading and starting date
**Step 3** Enter lookup table
**Step 4** Enter headings
**Step 5** Enter cash outflows
**Step 6** Save your work

## Step 1 Getting Ready

With the Framework desktop display on the screen, create a spreadsheet frame with the specifications given below. When the spreadsheet is finished, you can change any of the column widths to leave room for your labels and numbers, and you can add or delete rows and columns as necessary.

*To create a spreadsheet frame 18 columns wide and 41 rows deep:*

**Press** **Ins**
**Highlight** Create
Width
**Press** ↵
**Type** **18**
**Press** ↵
**Highlight** Height
**Press** ↵
**Type** **41**
**Press** ↵
**Highlight** Spreadsheet
**Press** ↵

*To label the frame:*

**Highlight** the frame border
**Type** **Outflows**
**Press** ↵

*To set the default display of numbers so the spreadsheet will show commas between thousands and no decimal places:*

**Highlight** the frame border
**Press** **Ins**
**Highlight** Numbers
Decimal Places
**Press** ↵
**Type** **0**
**Press** ↵
**Ins**
**Highlight** Numbers
Business
**Press** ↵

*To set recalculation to manual:*

**Press** **Ins**
**Highlight** Options for Recalc
**Press** ↵
**Highlight** Manual
**Press** ↵

*To enter the frame and zoom it to fill the screen:*

**Press** **Zoom** (**F9**)

*To size all the columns to 10 characters wide:*

**Press** **Extend Select** (**F6**)
**End**
↵
**Size** (**F4**)
→ until status panel reads **Size: 10/1**
↵
← to shrink the cursor

*To size column A to 23 characters wide:*

**Highlight** A1
**Press** **Size** (**F4**)
→ until status panel reads **Size: 23/1**
↵

*To size column B to 15 characters wide:*

**Highlight** B1
**Press** **Size** (**F4**)
→ until status panel reads **Size: 15/1**
↵

*To size column C to 9 characters wide:*

**Highlight** C1
**Press** **Size** (**F4**)
← until status panel reads **Size: 9/1**
↵

*To size column D to 12 characters wide:*

**Highlight** D1

**Press** **Size** (**F4**)

(→) until status panel reads **Size: 12/1**

(↵)

**Result** Your screen should show columns A through F, with column A 23 characters wide, column B 15 characters wide, column C 9 characters wide, column D 12 characters wide, and all other columns 10 characters wide. Any numbers you enter will be displayed with commas between thousands and no decimal places. When you enter new values, you will have to remember to press the **Recalc** (**F5**) key.

## Step 2 Enter Heading and Starting Date

In the first three rows you'll enter the title of the spreadsheet and the starting month and year. The values in cells B2 and C2 are particularly important, as they factor in almost all the formulas in the spreadsheet. Format and style the cells as shown to make them more readable. Cells B1 and C1 are centered.

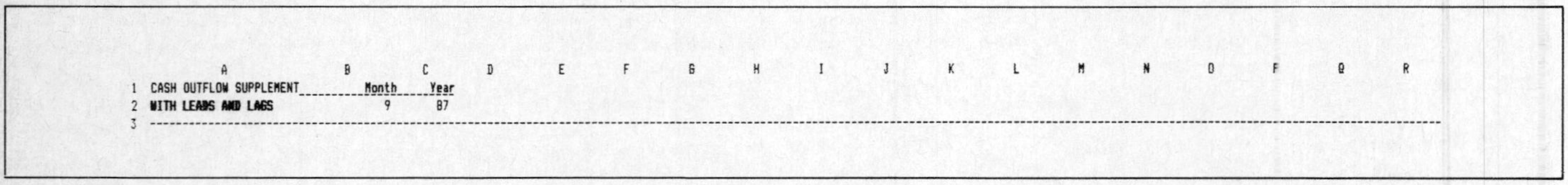


## Step 3 Enter Lookup Table

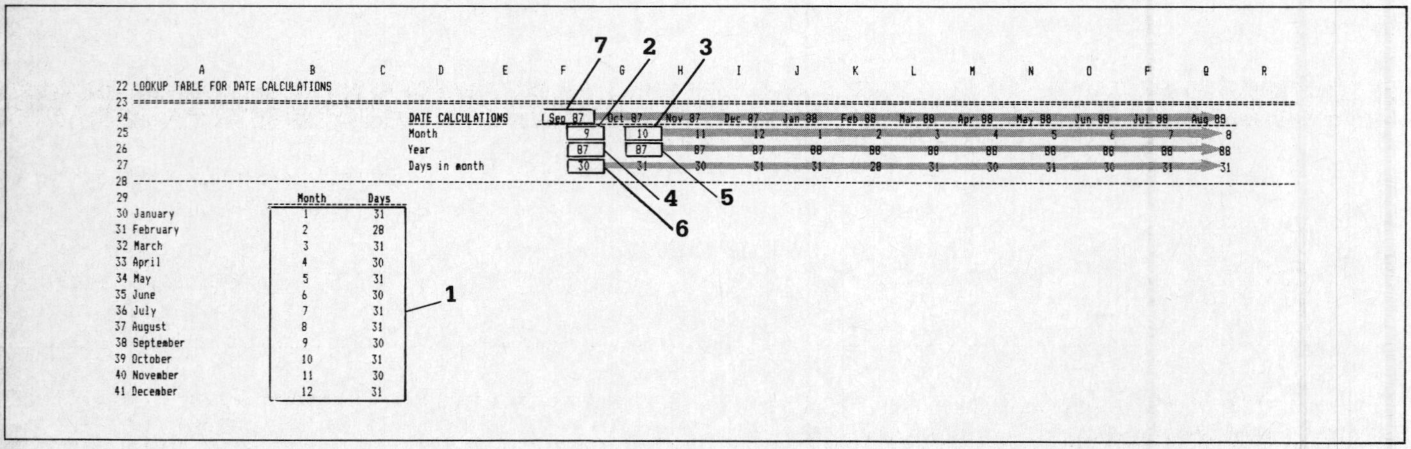


In order to calculate all the dates and amounts in the cash outflow supplement, Framework needs to be able to refer to information about number of days in each month. We will supply that information in this spreadsheet by creating a special lookup table.

The table runs from January to December (rather than September to August) because Framework can only refer to a table with *ascending* numbers. This will not affect the formulas and the results in the supplement itself.

To enter the headings and ruled lines for this spreadsheet, use the techniques you learned in Chapter 3. The formulas are described in detail below. Be careful to format the cells as shown in the illustration so the spreadsheet will be more readable.

**1**

**Enter the months** and the number of days in each. Framework will refer to these when making calculations.

**Highlight** the cells in columns B and C and enter the numbers shown

## 2

**Enter a formula** that calculates the first month of the year. The formula refers to the value entered in cell B2.

**Highlight** F25 and type (EDIT) **B2** (↵)

## 3

**Enter and copy a formula** that adds 1 to the starting month in cell F25. The formula is embedded in an @IF statement so that if the previous month is 12, the next month will be 1.

**Highlight** G25 and type **@IF(F25=12,1,F25+1)** (↵)

**Copy to** H25 through Q25

## 4

**Enter a formula** that calculates the year based on the value entered in cell C2.

**Highlight** F26 and type (EDIT) **C2** (↵)

## 5

**Enter and copy a formula** that carries the year forward. The formula is embedded in an @IF statement so that 1 is added to the year if the previous month is December.

**Highlight** G26 and type **@IF(F25=12,F26+1,F26)** (↵)

**Copy to** H26 through Q26

## 6

**Enter and copy a formula** that looks up the length of the month in the lookup table.

**Highlight** F27 and type **@VLOOKUP(F25,$B$30:$C$41,1)** (↵)

**Copy to** G27 through Q27

## 7

**Enter and copy a formula** that calculates the month and year of each period.

**Highlight** F24 and type **@DATE2(@DATE(F$26,F$25,F$27))** (↵)

**Copy to** G24 through Q24

# Step 4 Enter Headings

1

| | A | B | C | D | E | F | G | H | I | J | K | L | M | N | O | P | Q | R |
|---|---|---|---|---|---|---|---|---|---|---|---|---|---|---|---|---|---|---|
| 4 | | Supplier | Credit | Date | Total | | | | | | | | | | | | | Total due |
| 5 | | billing | period | payment | amount | | | | | | | | | | | | | in the |
| 6 | Name of supplier: | date | (days) | is due | due | Sep 87 | Oct 87 | Nov 87 | Dec 87 | Jan 88 | Feb 88 | Mar 88 | Apr 88 | May 88 | Jun 88 | Jul 88 | Aug 88 | period |
| 7 | ------------ | ------------ | ------------ | ------------ | ------------ | ------------ | ------------ | ------------ | ------------ | ------------ | ------------ | ------------ | ------------ | ------------ | ------------ | ------------ | ------------ | ------------ |

These headings further identify the spreadsheet and also calculate the first and last day of each month covered. To change the starting date for the supplement, simply enter a new month and year in cell B2 and cell C2; all of the dates in the monthly columns will change automatically. (These dates are used by the formulas on rows 8 through 18 to determine if a payment is due in any given month.)

As you enter each formula, your results should match those shown in the illustration. Note that the headings in rows 4, 5, and 6 from column B to column R are in the middle of their cells.

## 1

**Copy the period column headings** to the payment columns.

**Highlight** F24

**Press** **Extend Select (F6)**

(→) to highlight F24 through Q24

(↵)

**Copy to** F6 through Q6

## Step 5 Enter Cash Outflows

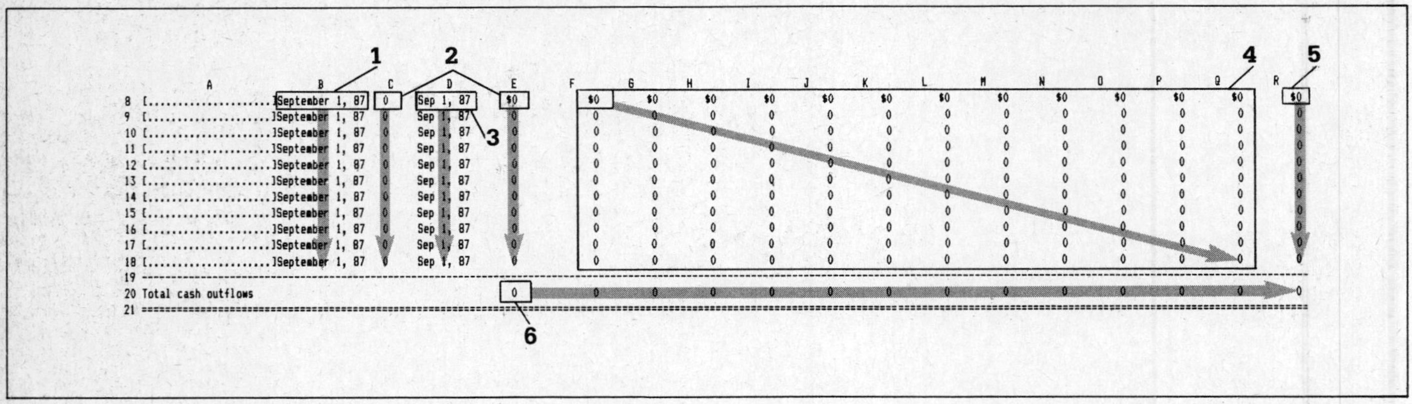

When the names (or invoice numbers) of your suppliers, the billing dates, their credit periods (in days), and the total amounts due are entered in columns A, B, C, and E, several calculations take place. First, the formulas in column D calculate the date payment is due. Next, the formulas in the monthly columns check the date due against the dates on row 6, and if the due date falls within the month, the payment is displayed in that column. Finally, column R calculates the total payments due during the period covered. When the starting date of the spreadsheet is changed in cells B2 and C2, all of the payments will move automatically into the appropriate columns.

Format cells C8 through C18 to display their contents in the middle of the cells; format cells E8 through R8 to display their contents as currency with no decimal places.

**1**

**Enter dummy dates** in column B. Framework needs dummy dates much as it needs dummy numeric values; otherwise the formulas in column D will calculate out incorrectly and display the message #VALUE!

**Highlight** B8 and type **@DATE(87,9,1)** ↵

**Copy to** B9 through B18

**2**

**Enter dummy values** in columns C and E.

**Highlight** C8 and type **0** ↵

**Copy to** C9 through C18
E8 through E18

**3**

**Enter and copy a formula** that calculates the date payment is due by adding the credit period to the billing date.

**Highlight** D8 and type **@DATE1(@SUMDATE(B8,C8))** ↵

**Copy to** D9 through D18

**4**

**Enter and copy a formula** that determines whether a payment is due in each monthly column. In English, this formula means, "If the month and year in the date payment is due column are the same as the month and year in the monthly column, then display the payment; otherwise, display zero." The @MID and @LEN functions are used to compare the relevant pieces of each date. The dollar signs keep the cell references absolute when the formula is copied to the rest of the monthly columns.

**Highlight** F8 and type **@IF(@AND(@MID($D8,1,3)=@MID(F$6,1,3),@MID($D8,@LEN($D8)−1,2)=@MID(F$6,5,2)),$E8,0)** ↵

**Copy to** F8 through Q18

**5**

**Enter and copy a formula** that calculates the payments due within the period covered. This formula sums all of the payments due in each of the monthly columns.

**Highlight** R8 and type **@SUM(F8:Q8)** ↵

**Copy to** R9 through R18

## 6

**Enter and copy a formula** that calculates the total cash outflow by summing the total payments due in each column.

**Highlight** E20 and type **@SUM(E7:E19)** (↵)

**Copy to** F20 through R20

## Check the Formulas

Now that the spreadsheet is finished, let's enter the sample numbers and dates from a typical business case study to see if the formulas are working correctly. The sample numbers will also be used later in this chapter to explore "What Ifs " Enter the numbers exactly as shown in the illustration below; to enter the dates in column B, press (EDIT) and then type in new values.

After recalculation, your results should match those in the illustration. If your results are different, check your formulas against the instructions.

| | A | B | C | D | E | F | G | H | I | J | K | L | M | N | O | P | Q | R |
|---|---|---|---|---|---|---|---|---|---|---|---|---|---|---|---|---|---|---|
| 8 | Jarrett Electronics | December 15, 87 | 30 | Jan 14, 88 | $50,000 | $0 | $0 | $0 | $0 | $50,000 | $0 | $0 | $0 | $0 | $0 | $0 | $0 | $50,000 |
| 9 | Jarrett Electronics | July 30, 88 | 30 | Aug 29, 88 | 55,000 | 0 | 0 | 0 | 0 | 0 | 0 | 0 | 0 | 0 | 0 | 0 | 55,000 | 55,000 |
| 10 | Green's Plastics | October 10, 87 | 30 | Nov 9, 87 | 15,000 | 0 | 0 | 15,000 | 0 | 0 | 0 | 0 | 0 | 0 | 0 | 0 | 0 | 15,000 |
| 11 | Green's Plastics | May 10, 88 | 30 | Jun 9, 88 | 15,000 | 0 | 0 | 0 | 0 | 0 | 0 | 0 | 0 | 0 | 15,000 | 0 | 0 | 15,000 |
| 12 | Walton Wire & Cable | March 15, 88 | 30 | Apr 14, 88 | 20,000 | 0 | 0 | 0 | 0 | 0 | 0 | 0 | 20,000 | 0 | 0 | 0 | 0 | 20,000 |
| 13 | Walton Wire & Cable | August 30, 88 | 30 | Sep 29, 88 | 20,000 | 0 | 0 | 0 | 0 | 0 | 0 | 0 | 0 | 0 | 0 | 0 | 0 | 0 |
| 14 | Walton Wire & Cable | October 15, 87 | 30 | Nov 14, 87 | 25,000 | 0 | 0 | 25,000 | 0 | 0 | 0 | 0 | 0 | 0 | 0 | 0 | 0 | 25,000 |
| 15 | [....................] | September 1, 87 | 0 | Sep 1, 87 | 0 | 0 | 0 | 0 | 0 | 0 | 0 | 0 | 0 | 0 | 0 | 0 | 0 | 0 |
| 16 | [....................] | September 1, 87 | 0 | Sep 1, 87 | 0 | 0 | 0 | 0 | 0 | 0 | 0 | 0 | 0 | 0 | 0 | 0 | 0 | 0 |
| 17 | [....................] | September 1, 87 | 0 | Sep 1, 87 | 0 | 0 | 0 | 0 | 0 | 0 | 0 | 0 | 0 | 0 | 0 | 0 | 0 | 0 |
| 18 | [....................] | September 1, 87 | 0 | Sep 1, 87 | 0 | 0 | 0 | 0 | 0 | 0 | 0 | 0 | 0 | 0 | 0 | 0 | 0 | 0 |
| 19 | ---------- | | | | | | | | | | | | | | | | | |
| 20 | Total cash outflows | | | | 200,000 | 0 | 0 | 40,000 | 0 | 50,000 | 0 | 0 | 20,000 | 0 | 15,000 | 0 | 55,000 | 180,000 |
| 21 | ========== | | | | | | | | | | | | | | | | | |

## Case Study

Jim Hunter's company, Sure Start, manufactures add-on electronic ignitions for lawn mowers. At the outset, he decided that he would try to produce his product on a year-round basis, rather than in the few months before and during his peak selling season (April through September). That way, he figured, he would not be constantly hiring, firing, and training personnel, and he could ensure that his good people would stay with him. He also disliked the notion that he might contribute to a seasonal unemployment pattern.

But this level production strategy often produces cash difficulties for Sure Start. In the upcoming year, Jim expects $400,000 in revenue. His sales are half to retailers, and half to consumers through magazine and television advertising. Consumers send payment with their orders; retailers have thirty days in which to pay. Since the retailers generally order their stock slightly before the peak season, the bulk of his cash comes in between May and August, with a trickle in April and a bit more in September.

Level production demands that he purchase his materials throughout the year, however. Even though he deals with only three major suppliers and tries to purchase in reasonable quantities, he often finds himself short of cash. He is also always seeking to reduce his costs.

One of the more obvious ways of doing this would be to invest his excess cash—whenever it is feasible to do so. At present, he is considering two options. The first is to use cash to pay off his largest supplier early, since this supplier is offering a 2% discount to customers who pay within 10 days rather than the usual 30 days. The second option (and the reason for the supplier's discount) is to take his business to a new competitor in the market. Emmett Resistors can supply Jim with the same components, and is luring potential customers with an offer of extended trade credit—60 days rather than the usual 30. Jim knows that he could invest the excess cash for an extra month at a 9.5% annual rate.

Jim's solution is to get out his cash outflow supplement, which he has used to time the bulk of his purchases during months when there is likely to be some cash around. His major difficulty, he knows from his cash budget summary, is likely to be his $50,000 December purchase of electronic components. His $20,000 March purchase of wire and cable could have been even more difficult, except that the amount is so much smaller. Whether he will have to take a short-term loan really depends on how accurate his forecast of this year's sales is; his summer inflows must be enough to cover the outflows.

## Step 4 Save Your Work

Now that the cash outflow supplement is finished, save your work. Make sure that your data disk is in drive B, and don't forget to make a backup copy of the spreadsheet on another disk.

*To save the frame containing the spreadsheet to the disk:*

| | |
|---|---|
| **Highlight** | A1 or the frame border |
| **Press** | **Ctrl** - ↵ |
| **Message** | SAVING<br>Document saved |

# Exploring "What Ifs"

## What If 1 Supplier's Discount Is Taken

In his first "What If," Jim Hunter assumes that he will stay with Jarrett and take the 2% discount, paying within 10 days. There are, of course, inherent attractions to this course for a man who likes stability; Jarrett is a known quantity, and might be even more grateful and flexible to an old customer who does not bolt to the competition at the first opportunity. On the whole, Jim rather hopes that the analysis will show this to be the prudent course.

To enter the 2% discount on the spreadsheet, we will multiply the total amounts due by 98%; for instance, **50,000*.98**.

## Change the Worksheet

*To enter changes in the credit period and the total amount due to Jarrett:*

**Highlight** the cells that have been changed in the illustration below and enter the new numbers shown

**Press** **Recalc (F5)**

**Result** After recalculation, your new numbers should match those in the illustration.

| | A | B | C | D | E | F | G | H | I | J | K | L | M | N | O | P | Q | R |
|---|---|---|---|---|---|---|---|---|---|---|---|---|---|---|---|---|---|---|
| 1 | CASH OUTFLOW SUPPLEMENT | Month | Year | | | | | | | | | | | | | | | |
| 2 | WITH LEADS AND LAGS | 9 | 87 | | | | | | | | | | | | | | | |
| 3 | ----------- | | | | | | | | | | | | | | | | | |
| 4 | | Supplier | Credit | Date | Total | | | | | | | | | | | | | Total due |
| 5 | | billing | period | payment | amount | | | | | | | | | | | | | in the |
| 6 | Name of supplier: | date | (days) | is due | due | Sep 87 | Oct 87 | Nov 87 | Dec 87 | Jan 88 | Feb 88 | Mar 88 | Apr 88 | May 88 | Jun 88 | Jul 88 | Aug 88 | period |
| 7 | ----------- | | | | | | | | | | | | | | | | | |
| 8 | Jarrett Electronics | December 15, 87 | 30 | Jan 14, 88 | $49,000 | $0 | $0 | $0 | $0 | $49,000 | $0 | $ | $0 | $0 | $0 | $0 | $0 | $49,000 |
| 9 | Jarrett Electronics | July 30, 88 | 30 | Aug 29, 88 | 53,900 | 0 | 0 | 0 | 0 | 0 | 0 | | 0 | 0 | 0 | 0 | 53,900 | 53,900 |
| 10 | Green's Plastics | October 10, 87 | 30 | Nov 9, 87 | 15,000 | 0 | 0 | 15,000 | 0 | 0 | 0 | | 0 | 0 | 0 | 0 | 0 | 15,000 |
| 11 | Green's Plastics | May 10, 88 | 30 | Jun 9, 88 | 15,000 | 0 | 0 | 0 | 0 | 0 | 0 | | 0 | 0 | 15,000 | 0 | 0 | 15,000 |
| 12 | Walton Wire & Cable | March 15, 88 | 30 | Apr 14, 88 | 20,000 | 0 | 0 | 0 | 0 | 0 | 0 | | 20,000 | 0 | 0 | 0 | 0 | 20,000 |
| 13 | Walton Wire & Cable | August 30, 88 | 30 | Sep 29, 88 | 20,000 | 0 | 0 | 0 | 0 | 0 | 0 | | 0 | 0 | 0 | 0 | 0 | 0 |
| 14 | Walton Wire & Cable | October 15, 87 | 30 | Nov 14, 87 | 25,000 | 0 | 0 | 25,000 | 0 | 0 | 0 | | 0 | 0 | 0 | 0 | 0 | 25,000 |
| 15 | [....................] | September 1, 87 | 0 | Sep 1, 87 | 0 | 0 | 0 | 0 | 0 | 0 | 0 | | 0 | 0 | 0 | 0 | 0 | 0 |
| 16 | [....................] | September 1, 87 | 0 | Sep 1, 87 | 0 | 0 | 0 | 0 | 0 | 0 | 0 | | 0 | 0 | 0 | 0 | 0 | 0 |
| 17 | [....................] | September 1, 87 | 0 | Sep 1, 87 | 0 | 0 | 0 | 0 | 0 | 0 | 0 | | 0 | 0 | 0 | 0 | 0 | 0 |
| 18 | [....................] | September 1, 87 | 0 | Sep 1, 87 | 0 | 0 | 0 | 0 | 0 | 0 | 0 | | 0 | 0 | 0 | 0 | 0 | 0 |
| 19 | ----------- | | | | | | | | | | | | | | | | | |
| 20 | Total cash outflows | | | | 197,900 | 0 | 0 | 40,000 | 0 | 49,000 | 0 | | 20,000 | 0 | 15,000 | 0 | 53,900 | 177,900 |
| 21 | =========== | | | | | | | | | | | | | | | | | |
| 22 | LOOKUP TABLE FOR DATE CA[illegible] | | | | | | | | | | | | | | | | | |

## Analysis

The most obvious result is the absolute reduction of Jim's inventory cost by $2,100. Assuming that his sales estimate for the year was correct, this would represent .5% of his sales. Not bad. He would, however, lose the use of his cash for 20 days following each of his two payments to Jarrett. For the December order, this was of little consequence, but it was a factor for the July order: he would lose the use of $53,900 for 20 days. At his expected investment rate, that would be a loss of almost $300. He smiles to himself and says, "No contest!"

But what if he had to borrow to meet the December payment (and the April one)? He assumes that he would have no trouble getting a 7-month loan. He also knows that he reduces his loan by $1,000 if he stays with Jarrett. If he stays and takes the discount, his interest cost would be $2,787 on a $69,000 loan. If, on the other hand, he does not take the discount, he would probably need to borrow $70,000, but he would need it for only six months. The interest cost would be $2,470. The scoreboard reads as follows:

| | |
|---|---|
| No loan | minus $300 (lost interest) |
| | plus $2,100 (lower payments) |
| With loan | minus $320 (extra loan interest) |
| Net—with loan | plus $1,480 |
| Net—no loan | plus $1,800 |

He smiles again. His gut feeling had probably been right. Inertia wins. But he decides to continue with his analysis—just in case.

## What If 2 Change in Suppliers

Jim now assumes that he will change to Emmett to see the effect of a new supplier on his cash outflows.

### Change the Worksheet

*To enter changes in the supplier, the credit period, and the total amounts due:*

**Highlight** the cells that have been changed in the illustration below and enter the new numbers shown

**Press** **Recalc** (**F5**)

**Result** After recalculation, your new numbers should match those in the illustration.

| | A | B | C | D | E | F | G | H | I | J | K | L | M | N | O | P | Q | R |
|---|---|---|---|---|---|---|---|---|---|---|---|---|---|---|---|---|---|---|
| 1 | CASH OUTFLOW SUPPLEMENT | Month | Year | | | | | | | | | | | | | | | |
| 2 | WITH LEADS AND LAGS | 9 | 87 | | | | | | | | | | | | | | | |
| 3 | | | | | | | | | | | | | | | | | | |
| 4 | | Supplier | Credit | Date | Total | | | | | | | | | | | | | Total due |
| 5 | | billing | period | payment | amount | | | | | | | | | | | | | in the |
| 6 | Name of supplier: | date | (days) | is due | due | Sep 87 | Oct 87 | Nov 87 | Dec 87 | Jan 88 | Feb 88 | Mar 88 | Apr 88 | May 88 | Jun 88 | Jul 88 | Aug 88 | period |
| 7 | | | | | | | | | | | | | | | | | | |
| 8 | Emmett Resistors | December 15, 87 | 60 | Feb 13, 88 | $50,000 | $0 | $0 | $0 | $0 | $0 | $50,000 | $0 | $0 | $0 | $0 | $0 | $0 | $50,000 |
| 9 | Emmett Resistors | July 30, 88 | 60 | Sep 28, 88 | 55,000 | 0 | 0 | 0 | 0 | 0 | 0 | 0 | 0 | 0 | 0 | 0 | 0 | 0 |
| 10 | Green's Plastics | October 10, 87 | 30 | Nov 9, 87 | 15,000 | 0 | 0 | 15,000 | 0 | 0 | 0 | 0 | 0 | 0 | 0 | 0 | 0 | 15,000 |
| 11 | Green's Plastics | May 10, 88 | 30 | Jun 9, 88 | 15,000 | 0 | 0 | 0 | 0 | 0 | 0 | 0 | 0 | 0 | 15,000 | 0 | 0 | 15,000 |
| 12 | Walton Wire & Cable | March 15, 88 | 30 | Apr 14, 88 | 20,000 | 0 | 0 | 0 | 0 | 0 | 0 | 0 | 20,000 | 0 | 0 | 0 | 0 | 20,000 |
| 13 | Walton Wire & Cable | August 30, 88 | 30 | Sep 29, 88 | 20,000 | 0 | 0 | 0 | 0 | 0 | 0 | 0 | 0 | 0 | 0 | 0 | 0 | 0 |
| 14 | Walton Wire & Cable | October 15, 87 | 30 | Nov 14, 87 | 25,000 | 0 | 0 | 25,000 | 0 | 0 | 0 | 0 | 0 | 0 | 0 | 0 | 0 | 25,000 |
| 15 | [......................] | September 1, 87 | 0 | Sep 1, 87 | 0 | 0 | 0 | 0 | 0 | 0 | 0 | 0 | 0 | 0 | 0 | 0 | 0 | 0 |
| 16 | [......................] | September 1, 87 | 0 | Sep 1, 87 | 0 | 0 | 0 | 0 | 0 | 0 | 0 | 0 | 0 | 0 | 0 | 0 | 0 | 0 |
| 17 | [......................] | September 1, 87 | 0 | Sep 1, 87 | 0 | 0 | 0 | 0 | 0 | 0 | 0 | 0 | 0 | 0 | 0 | 0 | 0 | 0 |
| 18 | [......................] | September 1, 87 | 0 | Sep 1, 87 | 0 | 0 | 0 | 0 | 0 | 0 | 0 | 0 | 0 | 0 | 0 | 0 | 0 | 0 |
| 19 | | | | | | | | | | | | | | | | | | |
| 20 | Total cash outflows | | | | 200,000 | 0 | 0 | 40,000 | 0 | 0 | 50,000 | 0 | 20,000 | 0 | 15,000 | 0 | 0 | 125,000 |
| 21 | | | | | | | | | | | | | | | | | | |

### Analysis

The most obvious change brought about by a shift to Emmett is that the July order of components shifted into the "after period" payments category. Jim picks up an additional month's interest here for September, a peak cash month. This would mean an additional $435 —but it would show up in next year's inflows.

The key, however, is that if he has to borrow at all, he could borrow a month later; which means, in effect, for a month less. Assuming that he would borrow the full $70,000, this would save him about $365:

| | |
|---|---|
| Interest on $70,000 @12% for 6 months | $2,470 |
| Interest on $70,000 @12% for 5 months | $2,114 |

The score still favors staying with Jarrett.

Jim Hunter is nothing, however, if not thorough. He is also very serious about saving a buck. As he looks over his analysis, he notices that under either set of circumstances, the bulk of his inflow savings would come with his second order. The main outflow savings has to do with the discount and loan interest.

He considers splitting his orders, but even as he tests this approach, he realizes that nothing could overcome the direct savings of the discount. He grins again. Jarrett has won.

Jim also realizes that he really does not have to decide for a month or two yet. If Emmett were, for example, to match the discount with a 30-day credit period, Jim might be forced to make a change.

In any case, Jim Hunter will be ready: his cash flow statements can evaluate any set circumstances. Most of all, he has not let his fondness for stability and continuity get in the way of his judgment.

## Clear the Sample Data

When you have finished exploring "What Ifs," you should clear the spreadsheet for the entry of your own data by copying blank label spaces to the cells containing sample line item labels, and by placing zeros in the cells with sample numbers. You should also enter dummy dates in column B.

*To copy blank label spaces to cells containing sample line items:*

**Copy from** A15

**Copy to** A8 through A14

*To enter dummy dates in column B (the supplier billing date):*

**Copy from** B15

**Copy to** B8 through B14

*To fill the cells containing sample numbers with zeros:*

**Copy from** C15

**Copy to** C8 through C14

**Highlight** E8 and type **0** (↵)
E9 and type **0** (↵)

**Copy to** E10 through E14

**Press** **Recalc** (**F5**)

**Result** All the numbers you entered on the spreadsheet will be replaced by zeros, and the formulas will recalculate to show zero. Your blank spreadsheet should look like the illustration on page 164.

## Save Your Work

Now that you've cleared the spreadsheet of the sample data, be sure to save it again so that it won't be lost if the power fails or if you accidentally hit the wrong key. Use the file name E Outflows for the blank spreadsheet so it won't overwrite and erase the version with the sample numbers (Outflows).

*To name the frame containing the blank spreadsheet:*

**Highlight** the frame border

**Press** **Space Bar** to get the name **Outflows** on the edit line

**Type** **E** (SP)

**Press** (↵)

*To save the frame labeled E Outflows:*

**Press** **Ctrl**-(↵)

**Result** The new frame will be saved to the disk along with the old frame.

# 6 Keeping Track: Controlling Your Cash

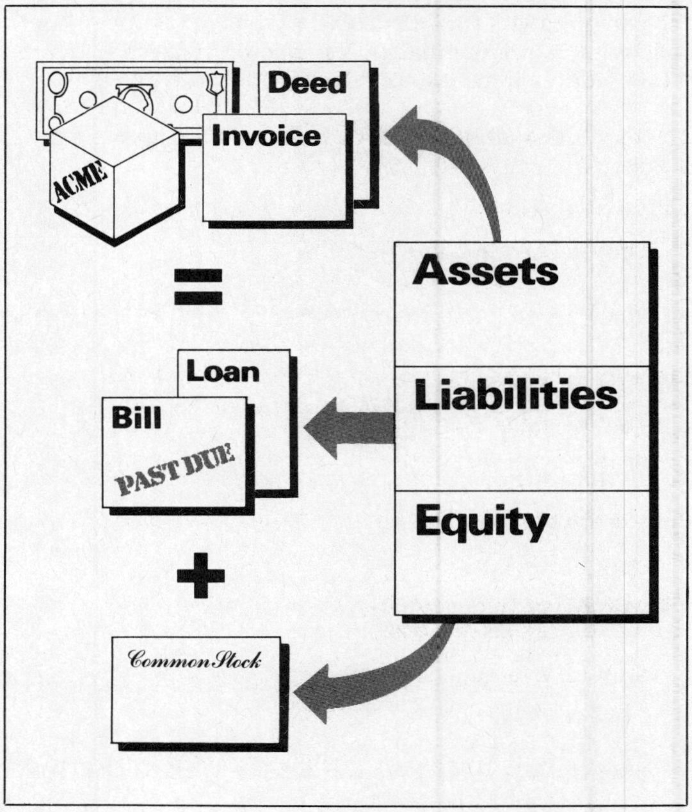


## Introduction

Suppose that you have diligently developed a set of cash budgeting documents. They *have* helped you to foresee some difficulties down the road. You are convinced that the cash budget really works as a planning tool. But, if you use it *only* for planning, you will be wasting half (or more) of the potential value that you have just created. Your cash budget can give you *more*.

Until now, we, too, have been talking about the cash budget as a planning tool. We have shown you how to use it to anticipate cash shortfalls and surpluses. We have shown you how to use it to test alternative solutions to such problems. We have shown you how to use it to make decisions about the future cash inflows and outflows of your company. Amazingly enough, however, this flexible little budget can also provide you with a significant control device for your business. In this section, we will describe how. It is rather simple and, we believe, fun.

## A Plan Is Not Enough

It is unbelievable how many people think that simply by virtue of developing some kind of plan they gain immunity from the business woes that beset the rest of the world. It ain't so. No one ever gains that immunity. But the person who creates a plan and does not monitor it may be in worse shape than those who do nothing. He thinks that he has said the "magic words." The person who has done nothing knows, at least, that he is vulnerable.

Happily, using your cash budget as a talisman is an easy trap to avoid. It is as simple as developing a tracking mechanism and setting aside some time each month for analysis.

Actually, we expect that you will find it fascinating, rather than a chore. You will be testing a number of things at once. And such testing gives you an opportunity to get better at what you do—in particular, better at forecasting. You will also feel, justifiably, more "in control" of your business.

## What Is Really Going on in Your Business

The basic notion underlying the use of your cash budget to control your operation is that a plan is really a step-by-step blueprint for getting something accomplished. If step 1 or step 2 isn't right, odds are that by step 37 you will have a disaster on your hands—or, at least, you will not end up where you had planned. If, however, you catch the problems at steps 1 and 2 when they happen, you may still complete your plan in pretty good shape. The key is to catch problems early enough to give you time to figure out how to solve them.

If you view your cash budget as your plan for next year's cash flows, monitoring is necessary and easy to implement. You need to collect information in the same categories that you used for your cash budget. If, for example, you decided to work your sales budget and inflow detail by product line, then you need to collect information on sales and collections by product line. The way in which you categorized expenses for your outflow statements is the way you should aggregate data as it comes in.

*Note:* You have to collect sales and cost data for Uncle Sam. Your accountant should also be making you track your collections data and age your receivables. All we are recommending is that you add a categorization of your data to match that in your cash budget. If you were working from historical data when you developed your cash budget in the first place, odds are that your data is categorized in this way already. *Voilà!* No additional work.

What you will really need here is a way of comparing budget with actual data as it comes into your company. You are looking, of course, for *deviations* from plan or budget. But all deviations are not equally troubling. Nor will all deviations reflect a problem in operations. As is true of all accounting-based methodologies, tracking reality against your cash budget is intended more to raise questions than to provide "the definitive answer." Deviations from plan are signals. *You* get to figure out what message the signals are sending, and to develop, test, and implement a solution (if one is needed). (That's part of the deal when you own the place.)

## Making the Comparisons

In theory (and in practice, once you get going) the approach is very simple. You compare each month's results (actual cash coming into and going out of your company during each month) with the flows that you had projected for that month. Where they differ significantly, you have a *deviation* or a *variance*. You also want to keep track of the total variance for the year through the current month.

A deviation can be better or worse than your plan. You want to note and analyze *any* deviation—even if you collected, for example, three times as much as you expected in a particular month. You need to see where all this extra cash is coming from. Are you taking in next month's expected collections in the current month? Or are these new and unexpected funds? As you will see, how you deal with the rest of the year will differ based on the answer to this question.

Let's consider an example. Sunburst Bakery, owned by Jennie Holdane, makes breads, cakes, cookies, and pies for the institutional food trade. She sells her products to larger companies that run industrial feeding operations for local factories and office building cafeterias. She has projected only modest growth in her business as she knows that the current fitness craze has caused many potential consumers of her products to diet and to avoid sugars and cream products. On the whole, she figures that if she could do 5% more business this year than last, she would be in fine shape. Her key to additional profitability is to be a strict cost control program in her operation.

Holdane normally pays for her supplies in the month they are used. She is generally paid by her customers in the month of delivery. The first month of this purely hypothetical, projected cash budget for one year looked as follows. (We have omitted the year-to-date data to simplify, and because it is the first projection month of Holdane's year.)

**Budget vs. Actuals—January, 1986**

| | *Budget* | *Actual* | *Variance* |
|---|---|---|---|
| **Cash inflows** | | | |
| Breads and rolls | $5,000 | | |
| Cakes | 3,000 | | |
| Cookies | 6,000 | | |
| Pies | 4,000 | | |
| Total cash inflows | $18,000 | | |
| **Cash outflows** | | | |
| Purchases: | | | |
| Flour | $4,000 | | |
| Yeast | 500 | | |
| Sugar | 2,000 | | |
| Other | 2,000 | | |
| Wages, fringe benefits | 4,000 | | |
| Space | 2,500 | | |
| Insurance & other financial items | 1,000 | | |
| Total cash outflows | $16,000 | | |
| **Net monthly cash** | $2,000 | | |

As you can see, in this purely hypothetical example, Jennie Holdane expects most of her business to be in breads and cookies. She expects the cookies to go during coffee breaks—they are portable and good. She expects relatively little activity in the cake and pie lines. The bulk of her purchases are in flour.

Suppose her first month's actual results are as follows:

**Budget vs. Actuals—January, 1986**

| | *Budget* | *Actual* | *Variance* |
|---|---|---|---|
| **Cash inflows** | | | |
| Breads and rolls | $5,000 | $5,000 | $0 |
| Cakes | 3,000 | 3,000 | 0 |
| Cookies | 6,000 | 6,000 | 0 |
| Pies | 4,000 | 4,000 | $0 |
| Total cash inflows | $18,000 | $18,000 | $0 |
| **Cash outflows** | | | |
| Purchases: | | | |
| Flour | $4,000 | $3,000 | ($1,000) |
| Yeast | 500 | 500 | 0 |
| Sugar | 2,000 | 2,500 | 500 |
| Other | 2,000 | 2,500 | 500 |
| Wages, fringe benefits | 4,000 | 4,000 | 0 |
| Space | 2,500 | 2,500 | 0 |
| Insurance & other financial items | 1,000 | 1,000 | $0 |
| Total cash outflows | $16,000 | $16,000 | $0 |
| **Net monthly cash** | $2,000 | $2,000 | $0 |

# Our Approach

In the following steps we'll show you how to create a spreadsheet that you can use to compare your actual cash flows against your budget on a monthly and year-to-date basis. The left side of the spreadsheet shows the figures for the specific month that you are considering: your budgeted figures, your actual results, and the variance or difference between the two in both dollars and percentages. The right side of the spreadsheet shows the same figures, but for your year to date.

Note that column B on the spreadsheet mirrors the structure of your cash budget summary spreadsheet, showing cash inflows, cash outflows, and net cash flow for the period; there is no cumulative cash row, since net cash flow for the year to date is, in fact, your cumulative cash. Since this spreadsheet shows only one month at a time, you will need to create a new spreadsheet for each month.

The budget vs. actuals spreadsheet is the only spreadsheet in this book that does not permit you to test alternative approaches and solutions. It is here solely to assist you in controlling your business operation and in spotting potential difficulties before they become major disasters.

## The Cash Budget vs. Actuals Spreadsheet

| | | | 3 | | 5 | | 4 | | 5 | |
|---|---|---|---|---|---|---|---|---|---|---|
| | | A | B | C | D | E | F | G | H | I |
| | 1 | **CASH BUDGET VS. ACTUALS** | [---------**This month: September, 1987** | | | ----------][ | -----------**Year-to-date: 1987** | | | ---------------] |
| | 2 | Inflows & Outflows | Budget | Actual | $ variance | % variance | Budget | Actual | $ variance | % variance |
| | 3 | ==================== | | | | | | | | |
| 1 | 4 | [CASH INFLOWS] | | | | | | | | |
| 1 | 5 | From search services | $7,000 | $7,000 | $0 | .0% | $37,000 | $36,000 | ($1,000) | -2.7% |
| 1 | 6 | From consulting services | 15,000 | 13,000 | (2,000) | -13.3% | 90,000 | 85,000 | (5,000) | -5.6% |
| 1 | 7 | From training services | 10,000 | 10,000 | 0 | .0% | 50,000 | 52,000 | 2,000 | 4.0% |
| 1 | 8 | From sales of materials | 9,000 | 11,000 | 2,000 | 22.2% | 36,000 | 40,000 | 4,000 | 11.1% |
| 1 | 9 | [.........................] | 0 | 0 | 0 | .0% | 0 | 0 | 0 | .0% |
| 1 | 10 | [.........................] | 0 | 0 | 0 | .0% | 0 | 0 | 0 | .0% |
| 1 | 11 | [.........................] | 0 | 0 | 0 | .0% | 0 | 0 | 0 | .0% |
| 1 | 12 | [.........................] | 0 | 0 | 0 | .0% | 0 | 0 | 0 | .0% |
| 1 | 13 | [.........................] | 0 | 0 | 0 | .0% | 0 | 0 | 0 | .0% |
| 1 | 14 | -------------------- | | | | | | | | |
| 1 | 15 | Total cash inflows | 41,000 | 41,000 | 0 | .0% | 213,000 | 213,000 | 0 | .0% |
| | 16 | ==================== | | | | | | | | |
| 2 | 17 | [CASH OUTFLOWS] | | | | | | | | |
| 2 | 18 | Business development | 8,000 | 10,000 | 2,000 | 25.0% | 45,000 | 58,000 | 13,000 | 28.9% |
| 2 | 19 | Wages and salaries | 12,000 | 10,000 | (2,000) | -16.7% | 65,000 | 55,000 | (10,000) | -15.4% |
| 2 | 20 | Rent and other space costs | 3,000 | 3,000 | 0 | .0% | 18,000 | 18,000 | 0 | .0% |
| 2 | 21 | Telephone | 6,000 | 8,000 | 2,000 | 33.3% | 38,000 | 45,000 | 7,000 | 18.4% |
| 2 | 22 | Supplies | 1,000 | 1,000 | 0 | .0% | 6,000 | 4,000 | (2,000) | -33.3% |
| 2 | 23 | Other G&A | 10,000 | 8,000 | (2,000) | -20.0% | 34,000 | 26,000 | (8,000) | -23.5% |
| 2 | 24 | [.........................] | 0 | 0 | 0 | .0% | 0 | 0 | 0 | .0% |
| 2 | 25 | [.........................] | 0 | 0 | 0 | .0% | 0 | 0 | 0 | .0% |
| 2 | 26 | [.........................] | 0 | 0 | 0 | .0% | 0 | 0 | 0 | .0% |
| 2 | 27 | -------------------- | | | | | | | | |
| 2 | 28 | Total cash outflows | 40,000 | 40,000 | 0 | .0% | 206,000 | 206,000 | 0 | .0% |
| | 29 | ==================== | | | | | | | | |
| 6 | 30 | Net cash flow | 1,000 | 1,000 | 0 | .0% | 7,000 | 7,000 | 0 | .0% |
| | 31 | ==================== | | | | | | | | |

*Like the cash budget summary, this spreadsheet has a cash inflows section (**1**) and an outflows section (**2**). When the budgeted and actual cash inflows for the current month (**3**) and the year to date (**4**) are entered, the spreadsheet calculates the variance between the budget and actual figures in dollars and percentages (**5**). The net cash flow for the month and year to date is also calculated (**6**).*

# Exploring Scenarios

Since you cannot really play "What If" games with this spreadsheet, we will look at two scenarios instead. Both scenarios represent the Acme Consulting Company, and the *projected* data in both cases is the same. The actual results, however, are assumed to be different, and the analysis will focus on what the variance can tell you (and how you might interpret your own figures). In neither case is Acme in an obvious cash bind; in Scenario 1, the worksheet shows a steady net inflow, and in Scenario 2, it shows a greater, but probably more erratic, net inflow.

## Scenario 1

If you look *only* at the totals—total inflows, total outflows, and net cash flow—Acme is in great shape. Its projections are dead on. There is clearly no cause for cheering, however. Though the predictors got the bottom lines right, they messed up practically everything else they could. The magnitude and the direction of these deviations from the budget are of great value to Acme, as the following analysis will demonstrate.

Let's look at the inflows first. Essentially, the comparison of actual inflows to budgeted inflows tells management (that's you) that sales are not coming from the areas that you expected. While Acme seems to think of itself as a company providing mainly personnel consulting services, the folks out there who are buying Acme's services tend to see Acme as a training and materials development outfit.

Under these circumstances, Acme has two major options. First, it can keep hustling its consulting services. Second, it can take the advice of its buyers and concentrate more on its training and development activities. Obviously, these are not mutually exclusive strategies; they represent either end of a continuum for Acme's services. What the inflow numbers suggest is that some adjustment may have to be made in Acme's position along that continuum.

The outflow numbers might also help Acme to figure out which strategy it should pursue. These figures show that while business development and telephone expenses are significantly above budget, personnel costs, supplies, and G&A are well below budget. Clearly, fewer folks are out there selling, so Acme saves on paper, paper clips, and manpower. (Since fewer training materials are sold than predicted, there is also a savings in paper and printing costs.) If we start with the premise that consulting requires more "development" expense than does the sale of training materials, it would be a fair bet that Acme is out selling what its customers do not particularly want to buy. (In all fairness, it must be noted that the smaller staff is still bringing home the bacon. Their inflows are the same as budgeted, which means improved productivity.)

We can also see from the year-to-date figures that these problems have been around for awhile. Some of the trends seem to be decreasing and others appear to be becoming even greater. The variance in some sales categories, for example, may be moderating, while some cost variances seem to be getting progressively more out of hand.

Assuming that the owners of Acme have been doing their variance analysis homework, and simply waiting a bit to ensure that what they were seeing was not a momentary "blip," they will have the intervening data and will be able to tell for certain. Although they definitely should not jump to conclusions on the basis of a month or two of variances, they should certainly consider revising their forecasts and, perhaps, reconsidering their operating strategy.

The real point here is that the nice, clean total lines for Acme mask potentially really serious problems. What if those four people had not quit three months ago? What if Acme's materials did not almost sell themselves? Using this kind of analysis, the potential problem areas leap out and hit you, and only when you see the problems can you do anything about them.

## Scenario 2

This variance analysis shows a more robust Acme in terms of its net cash flow: inflows from all sources are running well above budget. In fact, the trend in this direction may be accelerating, since the current month's percentages of positive variance exceed those for the year to date. While some cost categories seem to be under better control than under Scenario 1, others seem even more deviant. Cash is being spent more along the lines that the owners planned in their budgets, with the exception of the telephone and business development categories.

One thing to point out is that the extra cash outlays for these items may have something to do with the increased inflows. If a good deal of the extra telephone expense, for example, resulted from a major collections effort, there may be no difficulty here at all. Similarly, training might be a new field for Acme, requiring a greater development expenditure. Just looking at the bare numbers, one cannot tell. As the Music Man said, "You gotta know the territory."

Once you develop your own cash variance analysis worksheet, you will find it invaluable. Not only does it tell you what is going on in your company, where your money is coming from and what it's going out for, but it will also help you to become better at projecting. As you consider why the actuals differ from your projections, you will gain new insights into how your business really works and what drives it. This will help you to concentrate your efforts and energies in new ways.

The real trick is to look at the variances for your own business with the eye of an "outside insider." You want to really see what the numbers are telling you, but you also want to be in tune with why the numbers may be doing what they are doing. You do not want to make excuses for your company as it goes down the tubes, but you also do not want to change things that "look funny" if they really make a great deal of sense. As we have been saying throughout this book, your judgment is the key.

## Clear the Sample Data

Clear the spreadsheet for entry of your own data by copying blank label entry spaces to the cells containing sample line item labels, and by placing zeros in the cells with sample numbers.

*To copy blank label spaces to cells containing sample line items:*

**Copy from** A9

**Copy to** A5 through A8
A18 through A23

*To fill the cells containing sample numbers with zeros:*

**Highlight** B5 and type **0** (↵)
B6 and type **0** (↵)

**Copy to** B7 through B8

**Copy from** B5 through B13

**Copy to** C5
F5 through G5

**Copy from** B24

**Copy to** B18 through C23
F18 through G23

**Press** **Recalc** (**F5**)

**Result** All the numbers you entered on the spreadsheet will be replaced by zeros, and the formulas will recalculate to show zero. Your blank spreadsheet should look like the illustration on page 165.

## Save Your Work

Now that you've cleared the spreadsheet of the sample data, be sure to save it again using the file name E Budget vs. Actuals.

*To name the frame containing the blank spreadsheet:*

**Highlight** the frame border

**Press** **Space Bar** to get the name **Budget vs. Actuals** on the edit line

**Type** **E** (SP)

**Press** (↵)

*To save the frame labeled E Budget vs. Actuals:*

**Press** **Ctrl-**(↵)

**Result** The new frame, E Budget vs. Actuals, will be saved to the disk along with the old frame.

## Scenario 1

| | A | B | C | D | E | F | G | H | I |
|---|---|---|---|---|---|---|---|---|---|
| 1 | **CASH BUDGET VS. ACTUALS** | [--------This month: September, 1987--------- | | | ] | [-----------Year-to-date: 1987 | | | --------------] |
| 2 | Inflows & Outflows | Budget | Actual | $ variance | % variance | Budget | Actual | $ variance | % variance |
| 3 | ========== | | | | | | | | |
| 4 | [CASH INFLOWS] | | | | | | | | |
| 5 | From search services | $7,000 | $7,000 | $0 | .0% | $37,000 | $36,000 | ($1,000) | -2.7% |
| 6 | From consulting services | 15,000 | 13,000 | (2,000) | -13.3% | 90,000 | 85,000 | (5,000) | -5.6% |
| 7 | From training services | 10,000 | 10,000 | 0 | .0% | 50,000 | 52,000 | 2,000 | 4.0% |
| 8 | From sales of materials | 9,000 | 11,000 | 2,000 | 22.2% | 36,000 | 40,000 | 4,000 | 11.1% |
| 9 | [........................] | 0 | 0 | 0 | .0% | 0 | 0 | 0 | .0% |
| 10 | [........................] | 0 | 0 | 0 | .0% | 0 | 0 | 0 | .0% |
| 11 | [........................] | 0 | 0 | 0 | .0% | 0 | 0 | 0 | .0% |
| 12 | [........................] | 0 | 0 | 0 | .0% | 0 | 0 | 0 | .0% |
| 13 | [........................] | 0 | 0 | 0 | .0% | 0 | 0 | 0 | .0% |
| 14 | ---------- | | | | | | | | |
| 15 | Total cash inflows | 41,000 | 41,000 | 0 | .0% | 213,000 | 213,000 | 0 | .0% |
| 16 | ========== | | | | | | | | |
| 17 | [CASH OUTFLOWS] | | | | | | | | |
| 18 | Business development | 8,000 | 10,000 | 2,000 | 25.0% | 45,000 | 58,000 | 13,000 | 28.9% |
| 19 | Wages and salaries | 12,000 | 10,000 | (2,000) | -16.7% | 65,000 | 55,000 | (10,000) | -15.4% |
| 20 | Rent and other space costs | 3,000 | 3,000 | 0 | .0% | 18,000 | 18,000 | 0 | .0% |
| 21 | Telephone | 6,000 | 8,000 | 2,000 | 33.3% | 38,000 | 45,000 | 7,000 | 18.4% |
| 22 | Supplies | 1,000 | 1,000 | 0 | .0% | 6,000 | 4,000 | (2,000) | -33.3% |
| 23 | Other G&A | 10,000 | 8,000 | (2,000) | -20.0% | 34,000 | 26,000 | (8,000) | -23.5% |
| 24 | [........................] | 0 | 0 | 0 | .0% | 0 | 0 | 0 | .0% |
| 25 | [........................] | 0 | 0 | 0 | .0% | 0 | 0 | 0 | .0% |
| 26 | [........................] | 0 | 0 | 0 | .0% | 0 | 0 | 0 | .0% |
| 27 | ---------- | | | | | | | | |
| 28 | Total cash outflows | 40,000 | 40,000 | 0 | .0% | 206,000 | 206,000 | 0 | .0% |
| 29 | ========== | | | | | | | | |
| 30 | Net cash flow | 1,000 | 1,000 | 0 | .0% | 7,000 | 7,000 | 0 | .0% |
| 31 | ========== | | | | | | | | |

## Scenario 2

| | A | B | C | D | E | F | G | H | I |
|---|---|---|---|---|---|---|---|---|---|
| 1 | **CASH BUDGET VS. ACTUALS** | [--------This month: September, 1987--------- | | | ] | [-----------Year-to-date: 1987 | | | --------------] |
| 2 | Inflows & Outflows | Budget | Actual | $ variance | % variance | Budget | Actual | $ variance | % variance |
| 3 | ========== | | | | | | | | |
| 4 | [CASH INFLOWS] | | | | | | | | |
| 5 | From search services | $7,000 | $9,000 | $2,000 | 28.6% | $37,000 | $41,000 | $4,000 | 10.8% |
| 6 | From consulting services | 15,000 | 16,000 | 1,000 | 6.7% | 90,000 | 93,000 | 3,000 | 3.3% |
| 7 | From training services | 10,000 | 12,000 | 2,000 | 20.0% | 50,000 | 56,000 | 6,000 | 12.0% |
| 8 | From sales of materials | 9,000 | 10,000 | 1,000 | 11.1% | 36,000 | 41,000 | 5,000 | 13.9% |
| 9 | [........................] | 0 | 0 | 0 | .0% | 0 | 0 | 0 | .0% |
| 10 | [........................] | 0 | 0 | 0 | .0% | 0 | 0 | 0 | .0% |
| 11 | [........................] | 0 | 0 | 0 | .0% | 0 | 0 | 0 | .0% |
| 12 | [........................] | 0 | 0 | 0 | .0% | 0 | 0 | 0 | .0% |
| 13 | [........................] | 0 | 0 | 0 | .0% | 0 | 0 | 0 | .0% |
| 14 | ---------- | | | | | | | | |
| 15 | Total cash inflows | 41,000 | 47,000 | 6,000 | 14.6% | 213,000 | 231,000 | 18,000 | 8.5% |
| 16 | ========== | | | | | | | | |
| 17 | [CASH OUTFLOWS] | | | | | | | | |
| 18 | Business development | 8,000 | 10,000 | 2,000 | 25.0% | 45,000 | 52,000 | 7,000 | 15.6% |
| 19 | Wages and salaries | 12,000 | 12,000 | 0 | .0% | 65,000 | 61,000 | (4,000) | -6.2% |
| 20 | Rent and other space costs | 3,000 | 3,000 | 0 | .0% | 18,000 | 18,000 | 0 | .0% |
| 21 | Telephone | 6,000 | 8,000 | 2,000 | 33.3% | 38,000 | 44,000 | 6,000 | 15.8% |
| 22 | Supplies | 1,000 | 1,000 | 0 | .0% | 6,000 | 5,000 | (1,000) | -16.7% |
| 23 | Other G&A | 10,000 | 9,000 | (1,000) | -10.0% | 34,000 | 26,000 | (8,000) | -23.5% |
| 24 | [........................] | 0 | 0 | 0 | .0% | 0 | 0 | 0 | .0% |
| 25 | [........................] | 0 | 0 | 0 | .0% | 0 | 0 | 0 | .0% |
| 26 | [........................] | 0 | 0 | 0 | .0% | 0 | 0 | 0 | .0% |
| 27 | ---------- | | | | | | | | |
| 28 | Total cash outflows | 40,000 | 43,000 | 3,000 | 7.5% | 206,000 | 206,000 | 0 | .0% |
| 29 | ========== | | | | | | | | |
| 30 | Net cash flow | 1,000 | 4,000 | 3,000 | 300.0% | 7,000 | 25,000 | 18,000 | 257.1% |
| 31 | ========== | | | | | | | | |

# 7 Supplemental Spreadsheets

In addition to the main spreadsheets discussed in the earlier chapters, we are providing four supplemental spreadsheets for you to use in cash flow planning and management. The first two spreadsheets can be used in conjunction with those already described; the second two are used separately.

**The aging accounts receivables spreadsheet** lets you track your accounts receivables so you can tell who is paying late and then take corrective action. This spreadsheet tells you the average number of days it takes to collect each account and the percentage of total accounts receivables collected in 0, 30, 60, 90, and 120 days. Once you know these percentages, you can forecast cash inflows on the cash inflow supplement.

**The cash outflow supplement without leads and lags** is used to break down regular cash outflows such as rent, salaries, and utilities. The total line on this spreadsheet can then be used on the cash flow summary spreadsheet. (See Chapter 5 for the cash outflow supplement *with* leads and lags.)

**The trade discounts spreadsheet** will tell you how much it will save you (and how much it will cost you in interest) if you take your suppliers' discounts for early payments.

**The economic order quantity spreadsheet** shows you how to keep inventory costs under control by finding the point at which your ordering costs and your carrying costs are minimized.

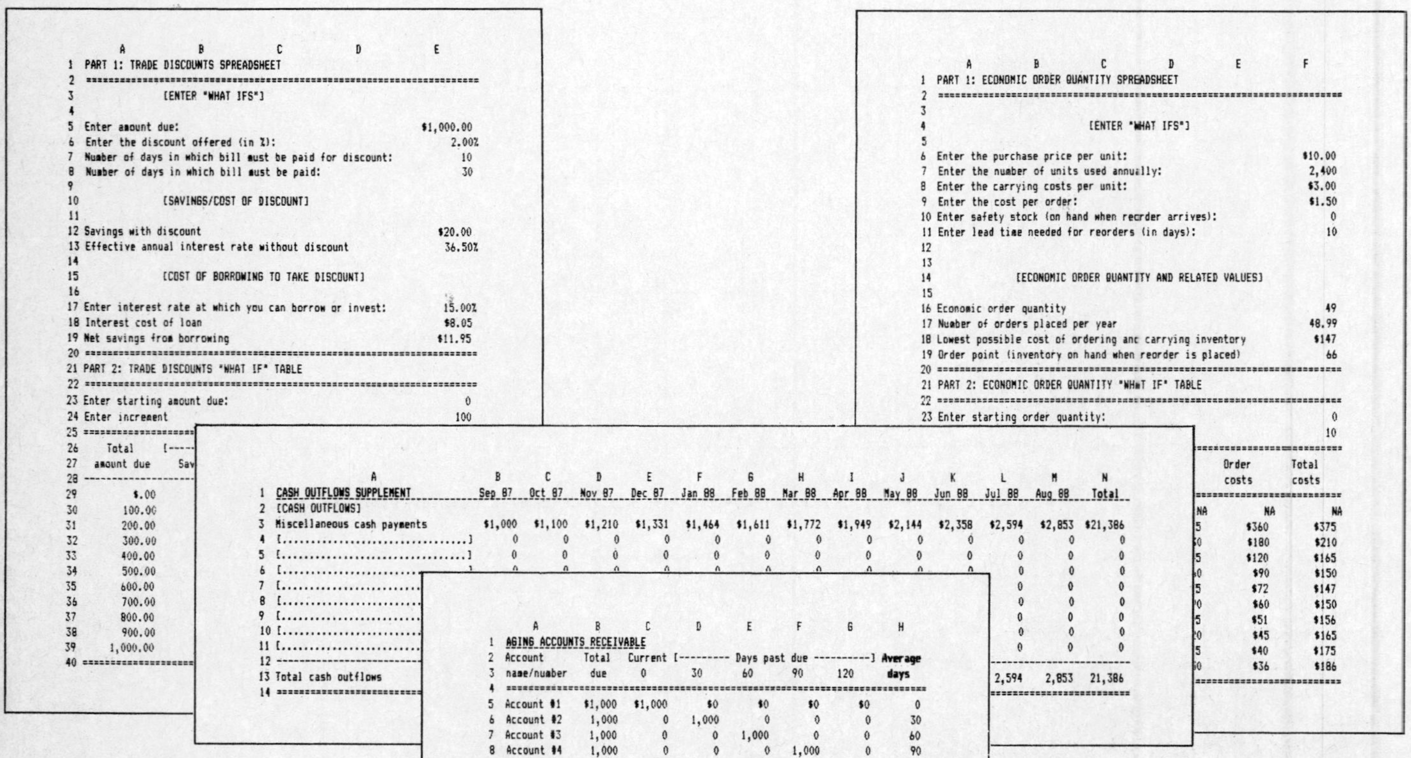

PART 1: TRADE DISCOUNTS SPREADSHEET

[ENTER "WHAT IFS"]

| | |
|---|---|
| Enter amount due: | $1,000.00 |
| Enter the discount offered (in %): | 2.00% |
| Number of days in which bill must be paid for discount: | 10 |
| Number of days in which bill must be paid: | 30 |

[SAVINGS/COST OF DISCOUNT]

| | |
|---|---|
| Savings with discount | $20.00 |
| Effective annual interest rate without discount | 36.50% |

[COST OF BORROWING TO TAKE DISCOUNT]

| | |
|---|---|
| Enter interest rate at which you can borrow or invest: | 15.00% |
| Interest cost of loan | $8.05 |
| Net savings from borrowing | $11.95 |

PART 2: TRADE DISCOUNTS "WHAT IF" TABLE

| | |
|---|---|
| Enter starting amount due: | 0 |
| Enter increment | 100 |

| Total amount due |
|---|
| $.00 |
| 100.00 |
| 200.00 |
| 300.00 |
| 400.00 |
| 500.00 |
| 600.00 |
| 700.00 |
| 800.00 |
| 900.00 |
| 1,000.00 |

PART 1: ECONOMIC ORDER QUANTITY SPREADSHEET

[ENTER "WHAT IFS"]

| | |
|---|---|
| Enter the purchase price per unit: | $10.00 |
| Enter the number of units used annually: | 2,400 |
| Enter the carrying costs per unit: | $3.00 |
| Enter the cost per order: | $1.50 |
| Enter safety stock (on hand when reorder arrives): | 0 |
| Enter lead time needed for reorders (in days): | 10 |

[ECONOMIC ORDER QUANTITY AND RELATED VALUES]

| | |
|---|---|
| Economic order quantity | 49 |
| Number of orders placed per year | 48.99 |
| Lowest possible cost of ordering and carrying inventory | $147 |
| Order point (inventory on hand when reorder is placed) | 66 |

PART 2: ECONOMIC ORDER QUANTITY "WHAT IF" TABLE

| | |
|---|---|
| Enter starting order quantity: | 0 |
| | 10 |

| Order costs | Total costs |
|---|---|
| NA | NA |
| $360 | $375 |
| $180 | $210 |
| $120 | $165 |
| $90 | $150 |
| $72 | $147 |
| $60 | $150 |
| $51 | $156 |
| $45 | $165 |
| $40 | $175 |
| $36 | $186 |

CASH OUTFLOWS SUPPLEMENT

| [CASH OUTFLOWS] | Sep 87 | Oct 87 | Nov 87 | Dec 87 | Jan 88 | Feb 88 | Mar 88 | Apr 88 | May 88 | Jun 88 | Jul 88 | Aug 88 | Total |
|---|---|---|---|---|---|---|---|---|---|---|---|---|---|
| Miscellaneous cash payments | $1,000 | $1,100 | $1,210 | $1,331 | $1,464 | $1,611 | $1,772 | $1,949 | $2,144 | $2,358 | $2,594 | $2,853 | $21,386 |
| Total cash outflows | | | | | | | | | | | 2,594 | 2,853 | 21,386 |

AGING ACCOUNTS RECEIVABLE

| Account name/number | Total due | Current 0 | 30 | 60 | 90 | 120 | Average days |
|---|---|---|---|---|---|---|---|
| Account #1 | $1,000 | $1,000 | $0 | $0 | $0 | $0 | 0 |
| Account #2 | 1,000 | 0 | 1,000 | 0 | 0 | 0 | 30 |
| Account #3 | 1,000 | 0 | 0 | 1,000 | 0 | 0 | 60 |
| Account #4 | 1,000 | 0 | 0 | 0 | 1,000 | 0 | 90 |
| Account #5 | 1,000 | 0 | 0 | 0 | 0 | 1,000 | 120 |
| Account #6 | 1,000 | 500 | 500 | 0 | 0 | 0 | 15 |
| Account #7 | 1,500 | 500 | 500 | 500 | 0 | 0 | 30 |
| Account #8 | 2,000 | 500 | 500 | 500 | 500 | 0 | 45 |
| Account #9 | 2,500 | 500 | 500 | 500 | 500 | 500 | 60 |
| Account #10 | 0 | 0 | 0 | 0 | 0 | 0 | NA |
| Total due | 12,000 | 3,000 | 3,000 | 2,500 | 2,000 | 1,500 | 50 |
| Percentage | 100% | 25% | 25% | 21% | 17% | 13% | |

# The Aging Accounts Receivable Spreadsheet

In the following section we'll show you how to create a spreadsheet that you can use to analyze your accounts receivables. This spreadsheet provides an easy way for you to keep track of who owes you what, and for how long. We recommend that you update this spreadsheet at least monthly, so that you can see what progress, if any, you are making in keeping your collections under control.

The spreadsheet is structured so that all you have to do is enter the account name or number and the amounts outstanding. It is broken into five columns: current amounts, and 30, 60, 90, and 120 days past due. You will need to determine when each outstanding amount is due, and enter it in the appropriate column.

Obviously, if your terms differ from those shown here, you alter the spreadsheet. Note that this spreadsheet is set up so that amounts due within the first 30-day period are considered "current"; any outstanding amounts in the 30-day column, then, are really due between 30 and 60 days.

Once you have entered the amounts, the spreadsheet will calculate the total receivables due by account, the percentage of receivables due within each period, and the average number of days past due for each account and for all your accounts. The percentages due within each period can be used to forecast your cash inflows (see Chapter 4).

## The Aging Accounts Receivable Spreadsheet

| | | | 1 | | | | | | 4 |
|---|---|---|---|---|---|---|---|---|---|
| | | A | B | C | D | E | F | G | H |
| | 1 | AGING ACCOUNTS RECEIVABLE | | | | | | | |
| | 2 | Account | Total | Current | [--------- | Days past due | | ----------] | **Average** |
| | 3 | name/number | due | 0 | 30 | 60 | 90 | 120 | **days** |
| | 4 | ======== | ======== | ======== | ======== | ======== | ======== | ======== | ======== |
| | 5 | Account #1 | $1,000 | $1,000 | $0 | $0 | $0 | $0 | 0 |
| | 6 | Account #2 | 1,000 | 0 | 1,000 | 0 | 0 | 0 | 30 |
| | 7 | Account #3 | 1,000 | 0 | 0 | 1,000 | 0 | 0 | 60 |
| | 8 | Account #4 | 1,000 | 0 | 0 | 0 | 1,000 | 0 | 90 |
| | 9 | Account #5 | 1,000 | 0 | 0 | 0 | 0 | 1,000 | 120 |
| | 10 | Account #6 | 1,000 | 500 | 500 | 0 | 0 | 0 | 15 |
| | 11 | Account #7 | 1,500 | 500 | 500 | 500 | 0 | 0 | 30 |
| | 12 | Account #8 | 2,000 | 500 | 500 | 500 | 500 | 0 | 45 |
| | 13 | Account #9 | 2,500 | 500 | 500 | 500 | 500 | 500 | 60 |
| | 14 | Account #10 | 0 | 0 | 0 | 0 | 0 | 0 | NA |
| | 15 | ======== | ======== | ======== | ======== | ======== | ======== | ======== | ======== |
| 2 | 16 | Total due | 12,000 | 3,000 | 3,000 | 2,500 | 2,000 | 1,500 | 50 |
| | 17 | -------- | -------- | -------- | -------- | -------- | -------- | -------- | -------- |
| 3 | 18 | Percentage | 100% | 25% | 25% | 21% | 17% | 13% | |
| | 19 | ======== | ======== | ======== | ======== | ======== | ======== | ======== | ======== |

*When you enter the individual accounts and the current amounts and amounts due within 30, 60, 90, and 120 days, the aging accounts receivable spreadsheet automatically calculates the totals due by account (**1**), the totals due by period (**2**), the percentage due in each period (**3**), and the average days past due for each account (**4**).*

# Entering the Aging Accounts Receivable Spreadsheet

The aging accounts receivable spreadsheet will be created in five steps:

**Step 1** Getting ready
**Step 2** Enter headings
**Step 3** Enter the aging section
**Step 4** Enter the summary section
**Step 5** Save your work

## Step 1 Getting Ready

With the Framework desktop display on the screen, create a spreadsheet frame with the specifications given below. When the spreadsheet is finished, you can change any of the column widths to leave room for your own labels and numbers, and you can add or delete rows and columns as necessary.

*To create a spreadsheet frame 8 columns wide and 19 rows deep:*

**Press** **Ins**
**Highlight** Create
Width
**Press** ↵
**Type** **8**
**Press** ↵
**Highlight** Height
**Press** ↵
**Type** **19**
**Press** ↵
**Highlight** Spreadsheet
**Press** ↵

*To label the frame:*

**Highlight** the frame border
**Type** **Aging Accounts Receivable**
**Press** ↵

*To set the default display of numbers so the spreadsheet will show commas between thousands and no decimal places:*

**Highlight** the frame border
**Press** **Ins**
**Highlight** Numbers
Decimal Places
**Press** ↵
**Type** **0**
**Press** ↵
**Ins**
**Highlight** Numbers
Business
**Press** ↵

*To set recalculation to manual:*

**Press** **Ins**
**Highlight** Options for Recalc
**Press** ↵
**Highlight** Manual
**Press** ↵

*To enter the frame and zoom it to fill the screen:*

**Press** **Zoom** (**F9**)

*To size column A to 12 characters wide:*

**Highlight** A1
**Press** **Size** (**F4**)
→ until status panel reads **Size: 12/1**
↵

**Result** Your screen should show columns A through H with column A 12 characters wide and all other columns 9 characters wide. Any numbers you enter will be displayed with commas between thousands and no decimal places.

## Step 2 Enter Headings

```
        A             B        C          D          E         F        G         H
1  AGING ACCOUNTS RECEIVABLE
2  Account          Total   Current [--------- Days past due ----------] Average
3  name/number       due       0         30         60        90       120     days
4  =========================================================================
```

The first four lines of the aging accounts receivable spreadsheet identify the collection periods; the numbers 0, 30, 60, 90, and 120 on row 3 must be entered as numbers and not as labels because they will be used by the formulas in column H. Still, you should align them in the middle of their cells to make the spreadsheet more readable.

To enter the headings and ruled lines, use the techniques you learned in Chapter 3. You can make column A wider if you like, so it will accommodate the full names of your accounts. Again, notice the styling of the labels.

## Step 3 Enter the Aging Section

```
                     1                                                 2
        A         B        C        D        E        F        G        H
5  [..........]  [$0]     $0       $0       $0       $0       $0     [NA]
6  [..........]    0       0        0        0        0        0       NA
7  [..........]    0       0        0        0        0        0       NA
8  [..........]    0       0        0        0        0        0       NA
9  [..........]    0       0        0        0        0        0       NA
10 [..........]    0       0        0        0        0        0       NA
11 [..........]    0       0        0        0        0        0       NA
12 [..........]    0       0        0        0        0        0       NA
13 [..........]    0       0        0        0        0        0       NA
14 [..........]    0       0        0        0        0        0       NA
15 ======================================================================
```

This section provides spaces for your account names or numbers in column A, and for the amounts due from each account in columns C through G. Formulas in column B sum up the entries for each account, and formulas in column H calculate the average number of days that each account is overdue in making payments.

You should "zero-fill" the appropriate cells, and be sure to format cells B5 through G5 to display their contents as currency with no decimal places.

**1**

**Enter and copy a formula** that calculates the total amount due for each account.

**Highlight** B5 and type **@SUM(C5:G5)** ↵

**Copy to** B6 through B14

**2**

**Enter and copy a formula** that calculates the average number of days past due for each account. This formula means, "If the total amount due is greater than zero, then multiply each amount in columns C through G by the number of days past due on row 3, and divide the sum of the results by the total amount due. If the total amount due is zero, display NA."

**Highlight** H5 and type **@IF(B5>0,((C5*C$3)+(D5*D$3)+(E5*E$3)+(F5*F$3)+(G5*G$3))/B5,"NA")** ↵

**Copy to** H6 through H14

## Step 4 Enter the Summary Section

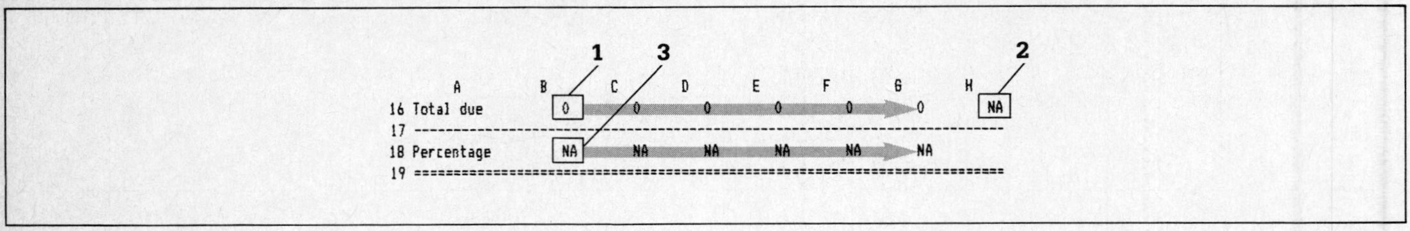


Rows 16 and 18 calculate the total amount and the percentage of the total due in each period. The formula in cell H16 calculates the average number of days past due for all accounts.

### 1

**Enter and copy a formula** that calculates the total amounts due in each period.

**Highlight** B16 and type **@SUM(B4:B15)** ↵

**Copy to** C16 through G16

### 2

**Copy a formula** that calculates the average number of days past due for all accounts from the aging section of the spreadsheet.

**Copy from** H14

**Copy to** H16

### 3

**Enter and copy a formula** that calculates the percentage of the total amount due that falls within each column. Format the cells on row 18 so they will display their contents as percentages with no decimal places.

**Highlight** B18 and type **@IF($B16>0,B16/ $B16,"NA")** ↵

**Copy to** C18 through G18

## Check the Formulas

Now that the spreadsheet is finished, let's enter some sample numbers to see if the formulas are all working correctly. Enter the numbers exactly as shown in the illustration below.

After recalculation, your results should match those shown in the illustration. If your results are different, check your formulas against the instructions.

| | A | B | C | D | E | F | G | H |
|---|---|---|---|---|---|---|---|---|
| 5 | Account #1 | $1,000 | $1,000 | $0 | $0 | $0 | $0 | 0 |
| 6 | Account #2 | 1,000 | 0 | 1,000 | 0 | 0 | 0 | 30 |
| 7 | Account #3 | 1,000 | 0 | 0 | 1,000 | 0 | 0 | 60 |
| 8 | Account #4 | 1,000 | 0 | 0 | 0 | 1,000 | 0 | 90 |
| 9 | Account #5 | 1,000 | 0 | 0 | 0 | 0 | 1,000 | 120 |
| 10 | Account #6 | 1,000 | 500 | 500 | 0 | 0 | 0 | 15 |
| 11 | Account #7 | 1,500 | 500 | 500 | 500 | 0 | 0 | 30 |
| 12 | Account #8 | 2,000 | 500 | 500 | 500 | 500 | 0 | 45 |
| 13 | Account #9 | 2,500 | 500 | 500 | 500 | 500 | 500 | 60 |
| 14 | Account #10 | 0 | 0 | 0 | 0 | 0 | 0 | NA |
| 15 | ======== | | | | | | | |
| 16 | Total due | 12,000 | 3,000 | 3,000 | 2,500 | 2,000 | 1,500 | 50 |
| 17 | -------- | | | | | | | |
| 18 | Percentage | 100% | 25% | 25% | 21% | 17% | 13% | |
| 19 | ======== | | | | | | | |

## Step 5 Save Your Work

Now that the aging accounts receivable spreadsheet is finished, save your work. Make sure that your data disk is in drive B, and don't forget to make a backup copy of the spreadsheet on another disk.

*To save the frame containing the spreadsheet to the disk:*

**Highlight** A1 or the frame border

**Press** **Ctrl-↵**

**Message** SAVING
Document saved

## Clear the Sample Data

Clear the spreadsheet for entry of your own data.

*To enter a blank label space:*

**Highlight** A5

**Type** [.........] ↵

*To copy the blank label space to cells containing sample line items:*

**Copy from** A5

**Copy to** A6 through A14

*To fill the cells containing sample numbers with zeros:*

**Copy from** D5

**Copy to** C5

**Copy from** C6

**Copy to** C6 through G14

**Press** **Recalc** (**F5**)

**Result** All the numbers you entered on the spreadsheet will be replaced by zeros, and the formulas will recalculate to show zero or NA. Your blank spreadsheet should look like the illustration on page 165.

### Save Your Work

Now that you've cleared the spreadsheet of the sample data, be sure to save it again using the file name E Aging Accounts Receivable.

*To name the frame containing the blank spreadsheet:*

**Highlight** the frame border

**Press** **Space Bar** to get the name **Aging Accounts Receivable** on the edit line

**Type** **E** (SP)

**Press** ↵

*To save the frame labeled E Aging Accounts Receivable:*

**Press** **Ctrl-↵**

**Result** The new frame containing the blank spreadsheet will be saved to the disk along with the old frame.

# The Cash Outflow Supplement Without Leads and Lags

In this section we'll show you how to create the companion spreadsheet to the cash outflow supplement with leads and lags that you entered in Chapter 5—a spreadsheet that you can use to break down regular cash outflows. This supplement is simply a handy way of listing all of the expenses that recur on a monthly or quarterly basis; you can make the expense categories as broad or as narrow as you like, although the level of detail you use should reflect the importance of the particular item or category to your business. If you have only a few regular expenses, and if they are all simple, you might choose to skip this spreadsheet and just use your cash budget summary.

You may, however, find this spreadsheet particularly useful if your expenses are rising within a certain category, since you can break the expense category down to its individual components and see which expenses are responsible for the rise.

It can also be useful for businesses with weekly payrolls, especially when the work force fluctuates from month to month. In short, this supplement gives you a level of detail impossible in the cash budget summary.

When the supplement is finished, you can carry the total row to the cash budget summary.

## The Cash Outflow Supplement (Without Leads and Lags)

| | A | B | C | D | E | F | G | H | I | J | K | L | M | N (1) |
|---|---|---|---|---|---|---|---|---|---|---|---|---|---|---|
| 1 | CASH OUTFLOWS SUPPLEMENT | Sep 87 | Oct 87 | Nov 87 | Dec 87 | Jan 88 | Feb 88 | Mar 88 | Apr 88 | May 88 | Jun 88 | Jul 88 | Aug 88 | Total |
| 2 | [CASH OUTFLOWS] | | | | | | | | | | | | | |
| 3 | Miscellaneous cash payments | $1,000 | $1,100 | $1,210 | $1,331 | $1,464 | $1,611 | $1,772 | $1,949 | $2,144 | $2,358 | $2,594 | $2,853 | $21,386 |
| 4 | [................................] | 0 | 0 | 0 | 0 | 0 | 0 | 0 | 0 | 0 | 0 | 0 | 0 | 0 |
| 5 | [................................] | 0 | 0 | 0 | 0 | 0 | 0 | 0 | 0 | 0 | 0 | 0 | 0 | 0 |
| 6 | [................................] | 0 | 0 | 0 | 0 | 0 | 0 | 0 | 0 | 0 | 0 | 0 | 0 | 0 |
| 7 | [................................] | 0 | 0 | 0 | 0 | 0 | 0 | 0 | 0 | 0 | 0 | 0 | 0 | 0 |
| 8 | [................................] | 0 | 0 | 0 | 0 | 0 | 0 | 0 | 0 | 0 | 0 | 0 | 0 | 0 |
| 9 | [................................] | 0 | 0 | 0 | 0 | 0 | 0 | 0 | 0 | 0 | 0 | 0 | 0 | 0 |
| 10 | [................................] | 0 | 0 | 0 | 0 | 0 | 0 | 0 | 0 | 0 | 0 | 0 | 0 | 0 |
| 11 | [................................] | 0 | 0 | 0 | 0 | 0 | 0 | 0 | 0 | 0 | 0 | 0 | 0 | 0 |
| 12 | ---------- | | | | | | | | | | | | | |
| (2) 13 | Total cash outflows | 1,000 | 1,100 | 1,210 | 1,331 | 1,464 | 1,611 | 1,772 | 1,949 | 2,144 | 2,358 | 2,594 | 2,853 | 21,386 |
| 14 | ========== | | | | | | | | | | | | | |

*The cash outflow supplement without leads and lags is used for regular outflows such as rent, salaries, and utilities. You enter the starting date of the supplement, the outflow categories, and the actual outflows for each month, and the spreadsheet calculates the annual totals for each outflow category **(1)** as well as the total outflow for each month **(2)**.*

# Entering the Cash Outflow Supplement

The supplement will be created in four steps:

**Step 1** Getting ready
**Step 2** Enter headings
**Step 3** Enter the cash outflows
**Step 4** Save your work

## Step 1 Getting Ready

With the Framework desktop display on the screen, create a spreadsheet frame with the specifications given below. When the spreadsheet is finished, you can change any of the column widths to leave room for your own labels and numbers, and you can add or delete rows and columns as necessary.

*To create a spreadsheet frame 14 columns wide and 14 rows deep:*

**Press** **Ins**
**Highlight** Create
Width
**Press** ↵
**Type** **14**
**Press** ↵
**Highlight** Height
**Press** ↵
**Type** **14**
**Press** ↵
**Highlight** Spreadsheet
**Press** ↵

*To label the frame:*

**Highlight** the frame border
**Type** **Supplement**
**Press** ↵

*To set the default display of numbers so the spreadsheet will show commas between thousands and no decimal places:*

**Highlight** the frame border
**Press** **Ins**
**Highlight** Numbers
Decimal Places
**Press** ↵
**Type** **0**
**Press** ↵
**Ins**
**Highlight** Numbers
Business
**Press** ↵

*To enter the frame and zoom it to fill the screen:*

**Press** **Zoom** (**F9**)

*To size column A to 35 characters wide:*

**Highlight** A1
**Press** **Size** (**F4**)
→ until status panel reads **Size: 35/1**
↵

*To lock the top row and first column in place:*

**Press** **Ins**
**Highlight** Edit
Lock First Column/Row
**Press** ↵

**Result** Your screen should show columns A through F with column A 35 characters wide and all other columns 9 characters wide. Any numbers you enter will be displayed with commas between thousands and no decimal places.

## Step 2 Enter Headings

| | A | B | C | D | E | F | G | H | I | J | K | L | M | N |
|---|---|---|---|---|---|---|---|---|---|---|---|---|---|---|
| 1 | CASH OUTFLOWS SUPPLEMENT | Sep 87 | Oct 87 | Nov 87 | Dec 87 | Jan 88 | Feb 88 | Mar 88 | Apr 88 | May 88 | Jun 88 | Jul 88 | Aug 88 | Total |

1

**1**

**Enter dates** *either* by typing them in as labels *or* by using the @DATE function. (You can enter your own dates after the spreadsheet is finished. This will be easier if you enter the dates now by using the @DATE function.)

*To enter the dates using the @DATE function:*

**Highlight** B1 and type **@DATE2(@DATE(87,9,1))** →|
At C1 type **@DATE2(@DATE(87,10,1))** →|
At D1 type **@DATE2(@DATE(87,11,1))** →|
At E1 type **@DATE2(@DATE(87,12,1))** →|
At F1 type **@DATE2(@DATE(88,1,1))** →|
At G1 type **@DATE2(@DATE(88,2,1))** →
At H1 type **@DATE2(@DATE(88,3,1))** →|
At I1 type **@DATE2(@DATE(88,4,1))** →|
At J1 type **@DATE2(@DATE(88,5,1))** →|
At K1 type **@DATE2(@DATE(88,6,1))** →|
At L1 type **@DATE2(@DATE(88,7,1))** →|
At M1 type **@DATE2(@DATE(88,8,1))** ↵

## Step 3 Enter the Cash Outflows

| | A | B | C | D | E | F | G | H | I | J | K | L | M | N |
|---|---|---|---|---|---|---|---|---|---|---|---|---|---|---|
| 2 | [CASH OUTFLOWS] | | | | | | | | | | | | | |
| 3 | [................................] | $0 | $0 | $0 | $0 | $0 | $0 | $0 | $0 | $0 | $0 | $0 | $0 | $0 |
| 4 | [................................] | 0 | 0 | 0 | 0 | 0 | 0 | 0 | 0 | 0 | 0 | 0 | 0 | 0 |
| 5 | [................................] | 0 | 0 | 0 | 0 | 0 | 0 | 0 | 0 | 0 | 0 | 0 | 0 | 0 |
| 6 | [................................] | 0 | 0 | 0 | 0 | 0 | 0 | 0 | 0 | 0 | 0 | 0 | 0 | 0 |
| 7 | [................................] | 0 | 0 | 0 | 0 | 0 | 0 | 0 | 0 | 0 | 0 | 0 | 0 | 0 |
| 8 | [................................] | 0 | 0 | 0 | 0 | 0 | 0 | 0 | 0 | 0 | 0 | 0 | 0 | 0 |
| 9 | [................................] | 0 | 0 | 0 | 0 | 0 | 0 | 0 | 0 | 0 | 0 | 0 | 0 | 0 |
| 10 | [................................] | 0 | 0 | 0 | 0 | 0 | 0 | 0 | 0 | 0 | 0 | 0 | 0 | 0 |
| 11 | [................................] | 0 | 0 | 0 | 0 | 0 | 0 | 0 | 0 | 0 | 0 | 0 | 0 | 0 |
| 12 | ------------------------------------ | | | | | | | | | | | | | |
| 13 | Total cash outflows | 0 | 0 | 0 | 0 | 0 | 0 | 0 | 0 | 0 | 0 | 0 | 0 | 0 |
| 14 | ==================================== | | | | | | | | | | | | | |

1

2

When you enter your regular cash outflows in the appropriate monthly columns, annual totals for each line item are calculated automatically in column N and total outflows for each month are calculated on row 13.

Remember to fill the spreadsheet with zeros so the formulas will calculate out to show zero as well. Row 3 should be formatted to display its contents as currency with no decimal places.

**1**

**Enter and copy a formula** that calculates the annual total for each line item.

**Highlight** N3 and type **@SUM(B3:M3)** (↵)

**Copy to** N4 through N11

**2**

**Enter and copy a formula** that calculates the total cash outflow for each month.

**Highlight** B13 and type **@SUM(B2:B12)** (↵)

**Copy to** C13 through N13

## Check the Formulas

Now that the supplement is finished, let's enter some sample numbers in row 3. Enter the numbers exactly as shown in the illustration below.

| | A | B | C | D | E | F | G | H | I | J | K | L | M | N |
|---|---|---|---|---|---|---|---|---|---|---|---|---|---|---|
| 2 | [CASH OUTFLOWS] | | | | | | | | | | | | | |
| 3 | Miscellaneous cash payments | $1,000 | $1,100 | $1,210 | $1,331 | $1,464 | $1,611 | $1,772 | $1,949 | $2,144 | $2,358 | $2,594 | $2,853 | $21,386 |
| 4 | [................................] | 0 | 0 | 0 | 0 | 0 | 0 | 0 | 0 | 0 | 0 | 0 | 0 | 0 |
| 5 | [................................] | 0 | 0 | 0 | 0 | 0 | 0 | 0 | 0 | 0 | 0 | 0 | 0 | 0 |
| 6 | [................................] | 0 | 0 | 0 | 0 | 0 | 0 | 0 | 0 | 0 | 0 | 0 | 0 | 0 |
| 7 | [................................] | 0 | 0 | 0 | 0 | 0 | 0 | 0 | 0 | 0 | 0 | 0 | 0 | 0 |
| 8 | [................................] | 0 | 0 | 0 | 0 | 0 | 0 | 0 | 0 | 0 | 0 | 0 | 0 | 0 |
| 9 | [................................] | 0 | 0 | 0 | 0 | 0 | 0 | 0 | 0 | 0 | 0 | 0 | 0 | 0 |
| 10 | [................................] | 0 | 0 | 0 | 0 | 0 | 0 | 0 | 0 | 0 | 0 | 0 | 0 | 0 |
| 11 | [................................] | 0 | 0 | 0 | 0 | 0 | 0 | 0 | 0 | 0 | 0 | 0 | 0 | 0 |
| 12 | ---------- | ---------- | ---------- | ---------- | ---------- | ---------- | ---------- | ---------- | ---------- | ---------- | ---------- | ---------- | ---------- | ---------- |
| 13 | Total cash outflows | 1,000 | 1,100 | 1,210 | 1,331 | 1,464 | 1,611 | 1,772 | 1,949 | 2,144 | 2,358 | 2,594 | 2,853 | 21,386 |
| 14 | ========== | ========== | ========== | ========== | ========== | ========== | ========== | ========== | ========== | ========== | ========== | ========== | ========== | ========== |

**Result** The formula in cell N3 should calculate $21,386, and the total cash outflows on row 13 should match row 3.

## Step 4 Save Your Work

Now that the cash outflow supplement is finished, save your work. Make sure that your data disk is in drive B, and don't forget to make a backup copy of the spreadsheet on another disk.

*To save the frame containing the spreadsheet to the disk:*

**Highlight** A1 or the frame border

**Press** Ctrl-↵

**Message** SAVING
Document saved

## Clear the Sample Data

Clear the spreadsheet for entry of your own data.

*To copy the blank label space to the cell containing a sample line item:*

**Copy from** A4

**Copy to** A3

*To fill the cells containing sample numbers with zeros:*

**Highlight** B3 and type **0** ↵

**Copy to** C3 through M3

**Result** All the numbers you entered on the spreadsheet will be replaced by zeros, and the formulas will recalculate to show zero. Your blank spreadsheet should look like the illustration on page 165.

## Save Your Work

Now that you've cleared the spreadsheet of the sample data, be sure to save it again using the file name E Supplement.

*To name the frame containing the blank spreadsheet:*

**Highlight** the frame border

**Press** **Space Bar** to get the name Supplement on the edit line

**Type** E (SP)

**Press** ↵

*To save the frame labeled E Supplement:*

**Press** Ctrl-↵

**Result** The new frame containing the blank spreadsheet will be saved to the disk along with the old frame.

# The Trade Discounts Spreadsheet

Next, we'll show you how to create a spreadsheet that you can use to calculate your savings if you take advantage of trade discounts. The first part of this spreadsheet is divided into three sections: The first section asks you for the basic data—the amount due, the discount offered, and the terms of the discount. The sample numbers in our example use a very common 2/10, net/30 discount—that is, if you pay within 10 days, you can take a 2% discount. The total amount is due within 30 days. The second section calculates your savings when you take the discount, and also gives you the effective annual interest rate you would be paying if you failed to take advantage of the discount. (You will generally find this rate to be astronomical, so you should always take the trade discount unless there is a compelling reason not to do so.) The third section considers the fact that you might have to borrow money to take advantage of the discount, and calculates the cost of borrowing the required sum.

Part 2 of this spreadsheet is a table that you'll use to graph your net savings (with and without a loan) over a range of total amounts due.

## The Trade Discounts Spreadsheet

```
           A             B             C             D             E
    1  PART 1: TRADE DISCOUNTS SPREADSHEET
    2  ======================================================================
    3              [ENTER "WHAT IFS"]
    4
    5  Enter amount due:                                           $1,000.00
    6  Enter the discount offered (in %):                              2.00%
    7  Number of days in which bill must be paid for discount:            10
    8  Number of days in which bill must be paid:                         30
    9
1— 10              [SAVINGS/COST OF DISCOUNT]
   11
   12  Savings with discount                                          $20.00
   13  Effective annual interest rate without discount                36.50%
   14
   15              [COST OF BORROWING TO TAKE DISCOUNT]
   16
   17  Enter interest rate at which you can borrow or invest:         15.00%
   18  Interest cost of loan                                           $8.05
   19  Net savings from borrowing                                     $11.95
   20  ======================================================================
   21  PART 2: TRADE DISCOUNTS "WHAT IF" TABLE
   22  ======================================================================
   23  Enter starting amount due:                                          0
   24  Enter increment                                                   100
   25  ======================================================================
   26      Total     [----- With discount ------][- Borrowing for discount -]
   27    amount due     Savings    Amount paid       Cost       Net savings
   28  ----------------------------------------------------------------------
   29          $.00         $.00         $.00         $.00           $.00
2— 30        100.00         2.00        98.00          .81           1.19
   31        200.00         4.00       196.00         1.61           2.39
   32        300.00         6.00       294.00         2.42           3.58
   33        400.00         8.00       392.00         3.22           4.78
   34        500.00        10.00       490.00         4.03           5.97
   35        600.00        12.00       588.00         4.83           7.17
   36        700.00        14.00       686.00         5.64           8.36
   37        800.00        16.00       784.00         6.44           9.56
   38        900.00        18.00       882.00         7.25          10.75
   39      1,000.00        20.00       980.00         8.05          11.95
   40  ======================================================================
```

*The trade discounts spreadsheet consists of two parts. When you enter your invoice credit terms in Part 1 (**1**), the spreadsheet calculates the amount that you'll save if you take the discount and the effective annual rate you're paying if you don't. The amount that you'll save if you borrow money to take advantage of the discount is also calculated. Part 2 of the spreadsheet (**2**) lets you explore the effect of the discount terms on a range of amounts due.*

# Entering the Trade Discounts Spreadsheet

The spreadsheet will be created in four steps:

**Step 1** Getting ready
**Step 2** Enter Part 1
**Step 3** Enter Part 2
**Step 4** Save your work

## Step 1 Getting Ready

With the Framework desktop display on the screen, create a spreadsheet frame with the specifications given below. When the spreadsheet is finished, you can change any of the column widths to leave room for your own labels and numbers, and you can add or delete rows and columns as necessary.

*To create a spreadsheet frame 5 columns wide and 40 rows deep:*

**Press** **Ins**
**Highlight** Create
Width
**Press** ↵
**Type** **5**
**Press** ↵
**Highlight** Height
**Press** ↵
**Type** **40**
**Press** ↵
**Highlight** Spreadsheet
**Press** ↵

*To label the frame:*

**Highlight** the frame border
**Type** **Trade Discounts**
**Press** ↵

*To set the default display of numbers so the spreadsheet will show commas between thousands:*

**Highlight** the frame border
**Press** **Ins**
**Highlight** Numbers
Business
**Press** ↵

*To set recalculation to manual:*

**Press** **Ins**
**Highlight** Options for Recalc
**Press** ↵
**Highlight** Manual
**Press** ↵

*To enter the frame and zoom it to fill the screen:*

**Press** **Zoom** (**F9**)

*To size all the columns to 14 characters wide:*

**Highlight** A1
**Press** **Extend Select** (**F6**)
**End**
↵
**Size** (**F4**)
→ five times (until status panel reads Size: 14/1)
↵
← to shrink the cursor

**Result** Your screen should show columns A through E, with all columns 14 characters wide. Any numbers you enter will be displayed with commas between thousands and no decimal places.

## Step 2 Enter Part 1

```
        A            B            C            D            E
1  PART 1: TRADE DISCOUNTS SPREADSHEET
2  ======================================================================
3                 [ENTER "WHAT IFS"]
4
5  Enter amount due:                                               $.00
6  Enter the discount offered (in %):                              .00%
7  Number of days in which bill must be paid for discount:            0
8  Number of days in which bill must be paid:                         0
9
10                [SAVINGS/COST OF DISCOUNT]
11
12 Savings with discount                                           $.00  — 1
13 Effective annual interest rate without discount                   NA  — 2
14
15                [COST OF BORROWING TO TAKE DISCOUNT]
16
17 Enter interest rate at which you can borrow or invest:          .00%  — 3
18 Interest cost of loan                                             NA
19 Net savings from borrowing                                        NA  — 4
20 ======================================================================
```

Enter the headings and ruled lines in this section, using the techniques you learned in Chapter 3. Begin by entering zeros in the appropriate cells, and by formatting the cells to display their contents as shown above.

### 1

**Enter a formula** that calculates how much you'll save if you take advantage of the discount by multiplying the amount due by the discount offered.

**Highlight** E12 and type (EDIT) **E6*E5** (↵)

**Format** Currency

### 2

**Enter a formula** that calculates the effective annual interest rate that you are paying for the period between the last date the discount can be obtained and the date when the bill is due. One way of judging the value of a trade discount is by assuming that if you *don't* take the discount you are, in effect, borrowing money from your supplier, and paying as interest for this "loan" the amount of the discount that you are not taking. You can then see whether this interest rate is reasonable or not.

This formula "annualizes" the discount offered: it divides the discount by the number of extra days that you get to "keep" the amount due, and then multiplies this daily rate by 365 to give the effective annual interest rate.

**Highlight** E13 and type **@IF(@AND(E6>0,E7>0, E8>0),E6/(E8−E7)*365,"NA")** (↵)

**Format** Percent

### 3

**Enter a formula** that calculates how much a loan will cost you in interest if you borrow money to take advantage of the discount. This formula multiplies the net amount due (after the discount) by the interest rate entered in cell E17, and divides the result by 365 to calculate the daily interest payment. This result is then multiplied by the number of days remaining before the normal due date.

**Highlight** E18 and type **@IF(E17>0,(E17*(E5−E12)/ 365)*(E8−E7),"NA")** (↵)

**Format** Currency

### 4

**Enter a formula** that calculates your net savings if you borrow to take advantage of the discount.

**Highlight** E19 and type **@IF(@AND(E12>0,E18>0), E12−E18,"NA")** (↵)

**Format** Currency

## Check the Formulas

Now that Part 1 of the spreadsheet is finished, let's enter some sample numbers in rows 5 through 8 and in row 17. After recalculation, your results should match those shown in the illustration. If your results are different, check your formulas against the instructions.

```
        A            B            C            D            E
1  PART 1: TRADE DISCOUNTS SPREADSHEET
2  ======================================================================
3                 [ENTER "WHAT IFS"]
4
5  Enter amount due:                                          $1,000.00
6  Enter the discount offered (in %):                             2.00%
7  Number of days in which bill must be paid for discount:           10
8  Number of days in which bill must be paid:                        30
9
10                [SAVINGS/COST OF DISCOUNT]
11
12 Savings with discount                                         $20.00
13 Effective annual interest rate without discount               36.50%
14
15                [COST OF BORROWING TO TAKE DISCOUNT]
16
17 Enter interest rate at which you can borrow or invest:        15.00%
18 Interest cost of loan                                          $8.05
19 Net savings from borrowing                                    $11.95
20 ======================================================================
```

## Step 3 Enter Part 2

```
              A              B             C             D            E
21 PART 2: TRADE DISCOUNTS "WHAT IF" TABLE
22 ======================================================================
23 Enter starting amount due:                                          0
24 Enter increment                                                     0
25 ======================================================================
26    Total      [----- With discount ------][- Borrowing for discount -]
27  amount due     Savings     Amount paid      Cost      Net savings
28 ----------------------------------------------------------------------
29        $.00         $.00         $.00         $.00         $.00
30         .00          .00          .00          .00          .00
31         .00          .00          .00          .00          .00
32         .00          .00          .00          .00          .00
33         .00          .00          .00          .00          .00
34         .00          .00          .00          .00          .00
35         .00          .00          .00          .00          .00
36         .00          .00          .00          .00          .00
37         .00          .00          .00          .00          .00
38         .00          .00          .00          .00          .00
39         .00          .00          .00          .00          .00
40 ======================================================================
```

Begin by entering zeros in cells E23 and E24. Format these cells to display their contents with no decimal places; format row 29 for currency.

### 1

**Enter a formula** that carries down the starting amount due from cell E23.

**Highlight** A29 and type (EDIT) **E23** (↵)

### 2

**Enter and copy a formula** that adds the increment in cell E24 to the starting amount due in cell A29.

**Highlight** A30 and type (EDIT) **A29+E$24** (↵)

**Copy to** A31 through A39

### 3

**Enter and copy a formula** that calculates your savings with the discount by multiplying the discount offered (cell E6) by the total amount due (cell A29).

**Highlight** B29 and type (EDIT) **E$6*A29** (↵)

**Copy to** B30 through B39

### 4

**Enter and copy a formula** that calculates the total amount paid with the discount by subtracting the savings in cell B29 from the total amount due in cell A29.

**Highlight** C29 and type (EDIT) **A29–B29** (↵)

**Copy to** C30 through C39

### 5

**Enter and copy a formula** that calculates the cost of borrowing to take the discount at the interest rate entered in cell E17. This formula first calculates the daily interest rate by dividing cell E17 by 365, and then multiplies this result by the number of days you need to borrow the money for (cell E8 minus cell E7). Finally, this interest rate is multiplied by the total amount due in cell A29.

**Highlight** D29 and type (EDIT) **E$17/365*(E$8-E$7)*C29** (↵)

**Copy to** D30 through D39

### 6

**Enter and copy a formula** that calculates your net savings if you borrow to take advantage of the discount.

**Highlight** E29 and type (EDIT) **B29–D29** (↵)

**Copy to** E30 through E39

## Check the Formulas

Now enter the sample numbers in rows 23 and 24. After recalculation, your results should match those shown in the illustration.

```
              A              B             C             D            E
21 PART 2: TRADE DISCOUNTS "WHAT IF" TABLE
22 ======================================================================
23 Enter starting amount due:                                          0
24 Enter increment                                                   100
25 ======================================================================
26    Total      [----- With discount ------][- Borrowing for discount -]
27  amount due     Savings     Amount paid      Cost      Net savings
28 ----------------------------------------------------------------------
29        $.00         $.00         $.00         $.00         $.00
30      100.00         2.00        98.00          .81         1.19
31      200.00         4.00       196.00         1.61         2.39
32      300.00         6.00       294.00         2.42         3.58
33      400.00         8.00       392.00         3.22         4.78
34      500.00        10.00       490.00         4.03         5.97
35      600.00        12.00       588.00         4.83         7.17
36      700.00        14.00       686.00         5.64         8.36
37      800.00        16.00       784.00         6.44         9.56
38      900.00        18.00       882.00         7.25        10.75
39    1,000.00        20.00       980.00         8.05        11.95
40 ======================================================================
```

## Step 4 Save Your Work

Now that the trade discounts spreadsheet is finished, save your work. Make sure that your data disk is in drive B, and don't forget to make a backup copy of the spreadsheet on another disk.

*To save the frame containing the spreadsheet to the disk:*

**Highlight** A1 or the frame border

**Press** **Ctrl-**↵

**Message** SAVING
Document saved

## Clear the Sample Data

Clear the spreadsheet for entry of your own data.

*To fill the cells containing sample numbers with zeros:*

**Highlight** E5 and type **0** ↵
E6 and type **0** ↵
E7 and type **0** ↵
E8 and type **0** ↵
E17 and type **0** ↵
E24 and type **0** ↵

**Result** All the numbers you entered on the spreadsheet will be replaced zeros, and the formulas will recalculate to show zero or NA. Your blank spreadsheet should look like the illustration on page 165.

## Save Your Work

Now that you've cleared the spreadsheet of the sample data, be sure to save it again using the file name E Trade Discounts.

*To name the frame containing the blank spreadsheet:*

**Highlight** the frame border

**Press** **Space Bar** to get the name **Trade Discounts** on the edit line

**Type** **E** SP

**Press** ↵

*To save the frame labeled E Trade Discounts:*

**Press** **Ctrl-**↵

**Result** The new frame containing the blank spreadsheet will be saved to the disk along with the old frame.

# The Economic Order Quantity Spreadsheet

Finally, we'll show you how to create a spreadsheet that you can use to calculate your most economic order quantities (or EOQ)—the inventory items that will cost you *least* to order. The spreadsheet consists of two parts: the first part uses your purchases price per unit, the number of units you use per year, your carrying costs per unit, and your order costs to calculate the EOQ:

$$\text{EOQ} = \sqrt{\frac{2 \times \text{units used annually} \times \text{costs per order}}{\text{price per unit} \times \text{carrying cost}}}$$

This section also calculates the number of orders you will need to place each year using your most economic order quantity, the cost of ordering and carrying inventory at the EOQ, and your order point—the number of inventory units you will have on hand when you place your order.

Part 2 of the spreadsheet lets you explore your ordering and carrying costs for a variety of order sizes, and see the effects of fixed or minimum order quantities on your costs. It will also show you the benefit of purchasing at, or near, your EOQ.

*Note:* This spreadsheet does *not* account for volume discounts offered by suppliers. If your supplier offers volume discounts, we recommend that you enter two different sets of numbers that reflect your unit prices and volume levels with and without the discount. See whether you save enough with the discount over the course of the year to overcome the cost of exceeding your EOQ. Part 2 in particular will help here.

## The Economic Order Quantity Spreadsheet

```
            A          B          C          D          E          F
     1  PART 1: ECONOMIC ORDER QUANTITY SPREADSHEET
     2  ======================================================================
     3
     4                             [ENTER "WHAT IFS"]
     5
     6  Enter the purchase price per unit:                              $10.00
     7  Enter the number of units used annually:                         2,400
     8  Enter the carrying costs per unit:                               $3.00
     9  Enter the cost per order:                                        $1.50
1—  10  Enter safety stock (on hand when reorder arrives):                   0
    11  Enter lead time needed for reorders (in days):                      10
    12
    13
    14                [ECONOMIC ORDER QUANTITY AND RELATED VALUES]
    15
    16  Economic order quantity                                             49
    17  Number of orders placed per year                                 48.99
    18  Lowest possible cost of ordering and carrying inventory           $147
    19  Order point (inventory on hand when reorder is placed)              66
    20  ======================================================================
    21  PART 2: ECONOMIC ORDER QUANTITY "WHAT IF" TABLE
    22  ======================================================================
    23  Enter starting order quantity:                                       0
    24  Enter increment:                                                    10
    25  ======================================================================
    26    Order      Safety     Average    Carrying    Order      Total
    27     size      stock     inventory    costs      costs      costs
    28  ======================================================================
    29        0         NA         NA         NA         NA         NA
2—  30       10          0          5        $15       $360       $375
    31       20          0         10        $30       $180       $210
    32       30          0         15        $45       $120       $165
    33       40          0         20        $60        $90       $150
    34       50          0         25        $75        $72       $147
    35       60          0         30        $90        $60       $150
    36       70          0         35       $105        $51       $156
    37       80          0         40       $120        $45       $165
    38       90          0         45       $135        $40       $175
    39      100          0         50       $150        $36       $186
    40  ======================================================================
```

*When you enter your inventory costs and ordering information in Part 1 (**1**), the spreadsheet calculates your most economic order quantity, the number of orders you'll place per year, your costs with the EOQ, and how much inventory will be on hand when you reorder. Part 2 (**2**) is used to explore costs and economic order quantities for various order sizes.*

# Entering the Economic Order Quantity Spreadsheet

The EOQ spreadsheet will be created in four steps:

**Step 1** Getting ready
**Step 2** Enter Part 1
**Step 3** Enter Part 2
**Step 4** Save your work

## Step 1 Getting Ready

With the Framework desktop display on the screen, create a spreadsheet frame with the specifications given below. When the spreadsheet is finished, you can change any of the column widths to leave room for your own labels and numbers, and you can add or delete rows and columns as necessary.

*To create a spreadsheet frame 6 columns wide and 40 rows deep:*

**Press** **Ins**
**Highlight** Create
Width
**Press** ↵
**Type** **6**
**Press** ↵
**Highlight** Height
**Press** ↵
**Type** **40**
**Press** ↵
**Highlight** Spreadsheet
**Press** ↵

*To label the frame:*

**Highlight** the frame border
**Type** **EOQ**
**Press** ↵

*To set the default display of numbers so the spreadsheet will show commas between thousands and no decimal places:*

**Highlight** the frame border
**Press** **Ins**
**Highlight** Numbers
Decimal Places
**Press** ↵
**Type** **0**
**Press** ↵
**Ins**
**Highlight** Numbers
Business
**Press** ↵

*To set recalculation to manual:*

**Press** **Ins**
**Highlight** Options for Recalc
**Press** ↵
**Highlight** Manual
**Press** ↵

*To enter the frame and zoom it to fill the screen:*

**Press** **Zoom** (**F9**)

*To size all the columns to 12 characters wide:*

**Highlight** A1
**Press** **Extend Select** (**F6**)
**End**
↵
**Size** (**F4**)
→ three times (until status panel reads Size: 12/1)
↵
← to shrink the cursor

**Result** Your screen should show columns A through F, with all columns 12 characters wide. Any numbers you enter will be displayed with commas between thousands and no decimal places.

## Step 2 Enter Part 1

```
     A        B        C        D        E        F
1  PART 1: ECONOMIC ORDER QUANTITY SPREADSHEET
2  =====================================================================
3
4                        [ENTER "WHAT IFS"]
5
6  Enter the purchase price per unit:                              $.00
7  Enter the number of units used annually:                           0
8  Enter the carrying costs per unit:                              $.00
9  Enter the cost per order:                                       $.00
10 Enter safety stock (on hand when reorder arrives):                 0
11 Enter lead time needed for reorders (in days):                     0
12
13
14            [ECONOMIC ORDER QUANTITY AND RELATED VALUES]
15
16 Economic order quantity                                           NA -1
17 Number of orders placed per year                                  NA -2
18 Lowest possible cost of ordering and carrying inventory           NA -3
19 Order point (inventory on hand when reorder is placed)             0 -4
20 =====================================================================
```

To enter the headings and ruled lines in this section, use the techniques you learned in Chapter 3. Enter zeros in the appropriate cells, and format them as shown in the illustration. We have also formatted cells F16, F17, and F18 so their contents are displayed on the right side of the cells; this won't affect numbers, but it will align the message NA with numbers in other cells.

### 1

**Enter a formula** that calculates the most economic order quantity.

**Highlight** F16 and type **@IF(F11<>0,@SQRT((2*F7*F9)/F8),"NA")** ↵

### 2

**Enter a formula** that calculates the number of orders that will be placed per year if the most economic order quantity is used. This formula divides the total number of units used annually by the economic order quantity.

**Highlight** F17 and type **@IF(F16>0,F7/F16,"NA")** ↵

**Format** Business
2 Decimal Places

### 3

**Enter a formula** that calculates the lowest possible cost of ordering and carrying inventory. This formula adds the total annual ordering costs—the cost per order (cell F9) times the number of orders placed per year (cell F17)—to the total annual carrying costs, the carrying costs per unit (cell F8) times the average inventory on hand (safety stock in cell F10 plus half of the EOQ in cell F16).

**Highlight** F18 and type **@IF(F16>0,(F9*F17)+(F8*(F10+(F16/2))),"NA")** ↵

**Format** Currency

### 4

**Enter a formula** that calculates the order point, the inventory level at which you should place a new order. This formula multiplies the number of items used per day (the number of units used annually in cell F7 divided by 365) by the lead time needed for reorders (cell F11) and adds the result to safety stock (cell F10).

**Highlight** F19 and type **(F7/365*F11)+F10** ↵

## Check the Formulas

Now that Part 1 of the spreadsheet is finished, let's enter some sample numbers in rows 6 through 11.

After recalculating, your results should match those shown in the illustration.

```
     A        B        C        D        E        F
1  PART 1: ECONOMIC ORDER QUANTITY SPREADSHEET
2  =====================================================================
3
4                        [ENTER "WHAT IFS"]
5
6  Enter the purchase price per unit:                            $10.00
7  Enter the number of units used annually:                       2,400
8  Enter the carrying costs per unit:                             $3.00
9  Enter the cost per order:                                      $1.50
10 Enter safety stock (on hand when reorder arrives):                 0
11 Enter lead time needed for reorders (in days):                    10
12
13
14            [ECONOMIC ORDER QUANTITY AND RELATED VALUES]
15
16 Economic order quantity                                           49
17 Number of orders placed per year                               48.99
18 Lowest possible cost of ordering and carrying inventory         $147
19 Order point (inventory on hand when reorder is placed)            66
20 =====================================================================
```

## Case Study

The sample numbers we will enter show an inventory item with high carrying costs and low ordering costs. This makes it advisable to keep a relatively small stock of this item beyond our buffer or safety stock. In fact, if we are going to use the calculated EOQ, we will be placing an order for 49 units of this item every seven days or so. (You might simply have your computer place an order every Friday, which could reduce your ordering costs even further.)

## Step 3 Enter Part 2

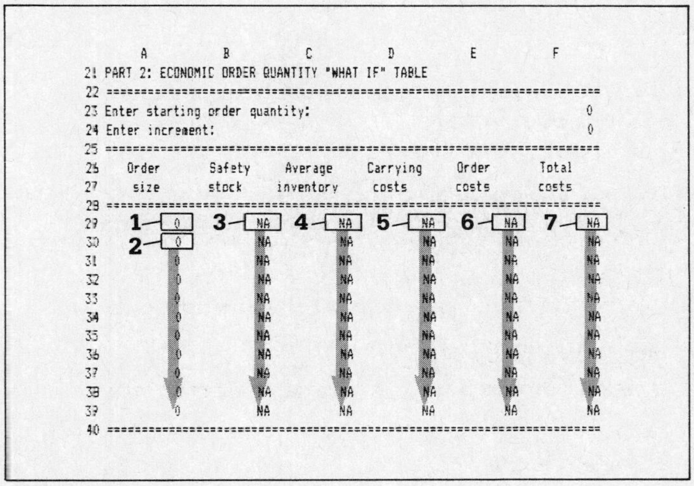


Enter zeros in F23 and F24 before you begin typing in formulas described below. Format rows 26 and 27 to display contents in the middle of the cells; format rows 29 through 39 to display contents aligned with the right edge of the cells.

### 1

**Enter a formula** that carries down the starting order quantity from cell F23.

**Highlight** A29 and type (EDIT) **F23** (↵)

### 2

**Enter and copy a formula** that adds the increment in cell F24 to the starting order quantity in cell A29.

**Highlight** A30 and type (EDIT) **A29+F$24** (↵)

**Copy to** A31 through A39

### 3

**Enter and copy a formula** that carries down the safety stock from cell F7.

**Highlight** B29 and type **@IF(A29>0,F$10,"NA")** (↵)

**Copy to** B30 through B39

### 4

**Enter and copy a formula** that calculates the average inventory on hand. This formula divides the order size (cell A29) by 2 and then adds the safety stock figure (cell B29).

**Highlight** C29 and type **@IF(A29>0,A29/2+B29,"NA")** (↵)

**Copy to** C30 through C39

### 5

**Enter and copy a formula** that calculates the annual carrying costs by multiplying the unit carrying costs (cell F11) by the average inventory (cell C29).

**Highlight** D29 and type **@IF(C29>0,C29*F$8,"NA")** (↵)

**Format** Currency

**Copy to** D30 through D39

### 6

**Enter and copy a formula** that calculates the annual order costs by multiplying the cost per order (cell F9) by the number of orders needed per year (the total number of units needed annually in cell F7 divided by the order size in cell A29).

**Highlight** E29 and type **@IF(A29>0,F$9*F$7/A29,"NA")** (↵)

**Format** Currency

**Copy to** E30 through E39

## 7

**Enter and copy a formula** that calculates total costs by adding carrying costs (cell D29) to ordering costs (cell E29).

**Highlight** F29 and type **@IF(D29>0,D29+E29,"NA")** (↵)

**Format** Currency

**Copy to** F30 through F39

## Check the Formulas

Now enter some sample numbers in rows 23 and 24.

After recalculation, your results should match those shown in the illustration.

| | A | B | C | D | E | F |
|---|---|---|---|---|---|---|
| 21 | PART 2: ECONOMIC ORDER QUANTITY "WHAT IF" TABLE | | | | | |
| 22 | ========================= | | | | | |
| 23 | Enter starting order quantity: | | | | | 0 |
| 24 | Enter increment: | | | | | 10 |
| 25 | ========================= | | | | | |
| 26 | Order | Safety | Average | Carrying | Order | Total |
| 27 | size | stock | inventory | costs | costs | costs |
| 28 | ========================= | | | | | |
| 29 | 0 | NA | NA | NA | NA | NA |
| 30 | 10 | 0 | 5 | $15 | $360 | $375 |
| 31 | 20 | 0 | 10 | $30 | $180 | $210 |
| 32 | 30 | 0 | 15 | $45 | $120 | $165 |
| 33 | 40 | 0 | 20 | $60 | $90 | $150 |
| 34 | 50 | 0 | 25 | $75 | $72 | $147 |
| 35 | 60 | 0 | 30 | $90 | $60 | $150 |
| 36 | 70 | 0 | 35 | $105 | $51 | $156 |
| 37 | 80 | 0 | 40 | $120 | $45 | $165 |
| 38 | 90 | 0 | 45 | $135 | $40 | $175 |
| 39 | 100 | 0 | 50 | $150 | $36 | $186 |
| 40 | ========================= | | | | | |

## Step 4 Save Your Work

Now that the EOQ spreadsheet is finished, save your work. Make sure that your data disk is in drive B, and don't forget to make a backup copy of the spreadsheet on another disk.

*To save the frame containing the spreadsheet to the disk:*

**Highlight** A1 or the frame border

**Press** **Ctrl-**(↵)

**Message** SAVING
Document saved

## Clear the Sample Data

Clear the spreadsheet for entry of your own data.

*To fill the cells containing sample numbers with zeros:*

**Highlight** F6 and type **0** (↵)
F7 and type **0** (↵)
F8 and type **0** (↵)
F9 and type **0** (↵)
F11 and type **0** (↵)
F24 and type **0** (↵)

**Result** All the numbers you entered on the spreadsheet will be replaced by zeros, and the formulas will recalculate to show zero or NA. Your blank spreadsheet should look like the illustration on page 165.

## Save Your Work

Now that you've cleared the spreadsheet of the sample data, be sure to save it again using the file name E EOQ.

*To name the frame containing the blank spreadsheet:*

**Highlight** the frame border

**Press** **Space Bar** to get the name EOQ on the edit line

**Type** **E** (SP)

**Press** (↵)

*To save the frame labeled E EOQ:*

**Press** **Ctrl-**(↵)

**Result** The new frame containing the blank spreadsheet will be saved to the disk along with the old frame.

# 8 More Cash from the Cash You've Got

Toward the beginning of this text, we promised that we would show you ways to make more money by using your existing cash better. We have talked about the foundation of these techniques already, since they all start with developing good control of the cash flows in your business. Specifically, we discussed such items as making better use of trade discounts (both incoming and outgoing) and using cash flow modifications to minimize your use of debt.

But there is more. Those techniques focus on the negative—how *not* to lose control of your cash unnecessarily, how *not* to spend more money than you need to spend to get something accomplished. There are also positive ways, based on these same underlying techniques, to maximize your cash. This chapter tells you about some of them and directs you to the appropriate sources for more detailed information.

Usually, the bigger your company, the better these techniques will work. But just because the rich get richer is no reason for the rest of us to pass up our tiny slices of the pie. Today, thanks to the competitive forces in the banking industry, even individuals can make use of some of the possibilities described. And, when you get right down to it, aren't a few extra dollars—which cost you nothing in money or risk—worth the trouble? There's nothing that feels as good as getting "free" money...especially from a bank!

## Investable Cash

The notion of investable cash is fairly clear; this means cash that you have control of, but do not need just now. Key to the notion is that you will not need the cash for a specified period of time. Although the length of time itself is of relatively little importance, you do need to determine what that period of time is for this specific chunk of cash in your business.

Determining *how much cash will be available for how long* is one of the functions of your cash budget. The net monthly cash and cumulative cash lines are designed to display this information each month. Although this is a good start, to do real "cash management" (as a banker would refer to these functions), you will need to get down to the weekly, or even the daily, cash levels of your business. To do this, you will have to modify the basic cash budget summary.

We can quickly see why a monthly summary is inadequate for cash management purposes. (This is a warning not to use the existing summary for cash management.) Consider a company in which the cash flows in steadily, while the outflows are bunched around the end of the month. Its monthly cash budget summary would show:

| | |
|---|---|
| Inflows: | $100,000 |
| Outflows: | 90,000 |
| Net monthly cash: | 10,000 |

Looked at by weeks, however, the amounts of investable cash look different:

| *Weeks:* | *1* | *2* | *3* | *4* | *5* | *6* |
|---|---|---|---|---|---|---|
| Inflows | 25,000 | 25,000 | 25,000 | 25,000 | 25,000 | 25,000 |
| Outflows | — | — | — | 90,000 | — | — |
| Net cash (period) | 25,000 | 25,000 | 25,000 | (65,000) | 25,000 | 25,000 |
| Cum. cash | 50,000 | 75,000 | 10,000 | 35,000 | 60,000 | |

Viewed this way, this particular company has $25,000 to invest for at least 21 days, $50,000 to invest for at least 14 days, etc. It's all in the point of view. Please note that things would appear still another way if we took the budgeting periods down to "daily by week." If this owner really wanted to do so, he might be able to shift all his payments to the last *day* of the month, thereby extending the potential investment periods by almost a full week.

As you can see, the notion of investable cash, though simple, is fairly flexible. It depends mainly on your ingenuity and on how well you are able to ensure that cash flows into and out of your company on schedule. This *is not a budgeting issue.* This is an implementation and execution-of-plan issue. Neat, orderly projections (like the one just shown) will not move your banker to pay you interest. What he wants is the money that the projections promise so that he can invest it in whatever he expects will make the interest he is paying you worth his trip.

The last point should carry its own warning, but we'll spell it out, just in case...*never* leave your company without enough of a cash cushion to get it through at least a minor crisis. Once you have committed to an investment, it is generally expensive to get out before the planned end. Often the alternative is to borrow short-term to cover those unanticipated requirements—a very costly way to do business. It also generally wipes out the benefit gained from the investment. Determine, based on your analyses of prior cash requirements and previous emergencies, what size cash cushion makes sense for your business (and your peace of mind) *before* you even begin to contemplate short-term investing. Then *never* violate your own rule.

## Who Can Play

As you have seen in other sections of this book, although all companies can benefit from using the methods of managing business cash that we describe, some types of companies seem to be "naturals" for one aspect or another. The same is true, in spades, for cash management techniques. The most obvious candidates for cash management techniques are those companies that have relatively large inflows at one or several points of the year and outflows that are spread more evenly through the year.

A new magazine, for example, or a new spa, would take annual subscriptions. The cash would come in early while the costs (other than set-up costs) would be spread throughout the subscription year. Some medical facilities collect premiums quarterly, while paying their expenses and other costs on a monthly basis. What better way to ensure that the funds are there when you need them (picking up extra money besides) than to invest some of the temporary surplus in interest-bearing ways?

Insurance companies are classics of this genre. In fact, they generally make their money on investing premiums until they are needed. During the recent period during which investment return rates were so high, it was no accident that insurance companies began to compete by reducing their costs to buyers.

While cash management programs will yield the greatest return for these kinds of companies, the returns for other companies are nothing to sneeze at either. Most banks have rules about *who* can invest *how* —usually restricting the amounts and time periods. If you meet their minimums, you can be in the game. In this age of competitive banking, if you do not meet the requirements of your regular bank, you might consider checking the limits of other banks in the area. You may still be able to get into the game.

Do keep in mind, that banks these days are also into maintaining "relationships" with customers. You may not want to shift all your banking relationships simply to get into this game. If that appears to be what is required, take time to weigh the intangibles against the potential investment gains before you make the switch.

## Potential Rewards

But why not simply put the funds in an interest-bearing checking account? Or into your business' savings account? The answer can be seen in percentage points. The various kinds of regular accounts pay 5% to 5.5% (sometimes compounded daily). Interest or yields on other kinds of short-term investments have run as high as 14% and have recently ranged around 9-10%. Typically, an institution pays you interest for each day they use your money.

Clearly, you must have to give up something to get that extra money. As we said earlier, that "something" is access to your funds. Whereas you generally have unlimited access to your money in a bank account, cash when you want it, cash-management-type investments usually limit access in some significant ways. Some institutions permit only a specified number of withdrawals from investment-based accounts. Others will use your money for a specified period of time—no longer, no shorter.

There is a range of options, but the clear tradeoff is money for access. Many institutions also charge fees for certain investment instrument-based transactions. Check with your bank(s) in advance. You might shop for the best deal, since banks are now attempting to differentiate themselves from their fellows by seeking specific kinds of customers. You need to know all these things before you ante up at the table.

## Some Potential Program Options

**Retail lockbox.** If you run the kind of business that is constantly deluged with numerous small checks, a lockbox service may be just what you need. Essentially, the lockbox provides a wonderful method of reducing the time it takes from the receipt of a customer check to the time it actually becomes usable cash to your business. Although the time decrease is measured in days, days count when you play the cash management game seriously.

Under your current system, a check comes in at your office. Your people handle it, log it in, and eventually send it off to the bank with the day's deposit. Under a lockbox system, the checks come in at your special box at the Post Office. Bank employees pick it up, open and log the payment, make the deposit, and send you the paperwork for review. They also separate out any strange checks or correspondence for your review. The time from receipt of check to actual cash inflow can be shortened significantly in this way. How much it is shortened depends on your volume, your business range, and your efficiency.

Needless to say, banks charge for this service. The issue for you, then, is whether the savings from (1)less internal paperhandling, and (2)longer investment periods justify the expense of the service. The price will generally depend on your volume and the complexity of the task you ask the bank to perform. Unless you have a computerized billing process, it is unlikely that a lockbox could work for you.

**Out-of-area banking.** You would be amazed at how many sizable firms write all their outflow checks on the Fifty-Third National Bank of Heaven-Only-Knows-Where, Midwest. There is method to their madness. It increases the time it takes for a check on their firm to clear. Thus, they add a day or so of control over their cash. If the sums are large enough, that day adds up to money. While we do not recommend that you consider going to that length, we do point out that these firms know that there is gold in them thar hills. This is one way to tap some of it.

**Cash management accounts (CMAs).** Many banks now offer some form of CMA to their customers. At its most advantageous to the customer (and, therefore, generally available only to large customers), the bank maintains at least two accounts for the customer. One is an investment account and the other is a checking account. The bank's cash management people will keep the checking account balance at zero, transferring funds from the other account(s) to cover required outflows and transferring all surpluses into the investment account(s). Again, if large sums are involved, a customer can make good money.

## Do-it-Yourself Cash Management Options

Although we do not expect that you will qualify (yet) for all the options banks now offer, we do hope that you will consider the underlying dynamics. In general, if you are failing to take advantage of *any* short-term investment opportunities that you qualify for, you are giving away substantial sums of money. And giving them away *to banks*! (While they probably could use these sums, these days, we believe that you could use them more. And, besides, the money is yours. You deserve the return.)

But any short-term investment has to start with your estimate of your cash flows for an upcoming time period(s)—your cash budget. Your objective then becomes to maintain control of the largest amount of cash for the longest period of time possible—prudent control, of course. If you pay bills when they appear, for example, consider holding them and paying later, but still within the allotted time. What kind of a return could you get by using that money in another way for the period of the delay?

If you are being offered a discount for early payment, evaluate that in the same way. Trade off the proposed discount against the return you could make by investing those funds for the interim period. But, to make the tradeoff real, you actually have to *invest* the money at that alternative rate. Otherwise you lose both the potential investment return and the discount.

If you routinely keep large balances in your checking account, consider approximating the zero-balance route. If you are worried about losing access to funds for more than a day or two, try a savings account as an interim measure. That way, you will gain at least something for your cash surpluses.

## Cautions

Two notes of caution. First, it is incredibly easy to get caught up in the game of maximizing cash. It develops a kind of beat-the-system momentum of its own. Do not let it obscure the real purpose of the business—to make money doing or selling or making whatever.

Second, remain aware that winning at the money management game is not generally worth destroying the business relationships that you have spent time building. Pushing a supplier to the limit to gain an extra day or two is probably not worth the long-term hassle. Besides, you may someday need a hand from just that supplier.

These are notes mainly about priorities. We believe in managing your business better through controlling your cash flows. But we believe that the main purpose of such activities lies in the proper planning and control of your business affairs. Making money on your money is nice for any business, but is a largely peripheral activity for most. Once it starts overwhelming good business judgment, it is time to either quit playing that game, change your basic business, or hire a professional to play with the money.

## Conclusion

This book has been about how to manage your business better by managing its inflows and outflows of cash. We believe that cash is an outstanding medium for management because it is so real. Businesses cannot run without cash—however profitable they may appear in their annual statements. Understanding cash is vital.

This book provides a method and tools for planning and controlling cash. While we cannot guarantee success and riches if you adopt our approach (sorry!), we do contend that the approach will help you to maximize the value and use of the resources you have or can obtain. To the extent that your expertise at cash budgeting makes bankers and investors feel more comfortable, our approach may help you to get funding. And, to the extent that among the major failings of many smaller businesses are lack of planning and feedback and inadequate controls, this approach to management through managing your business cash can help ensure success.

In short, we hope we've helped. We wish you well.

# The Blank Worksheets

## Cash Budget Summary

| | A | B | C | D | E | F | G | H | I | J | K | L | M | N |
|---|---|---|---|---|---|---|---|---|---|---|---|---|---|---|
| 1 | CASH BUDGET SUMMARY - FIRST YEAR | Sep 87 | Oct 87 | Nov 87 | Dec 87 | Jan 88 | Feb 88 | Mar 88 | Apr 88 | May 88 | Jun 88 | Jul 88 | Aug 88 | Total |
| 2 | [CASH INFLOWS] | | | | | | | | | | | | | |
| 3 | [............................] | | | | | | | | | | | | | $0 |
| 4 | [............................] | | | | | | | | | | | | | 0 |
| 5 | [............................] | | | | | | | | | | | | | 0 |
| 6 | [............................] | | | | | | | | | | | | | 0 |
| 7 | [............................] | | | | | | | | | | | | | 0 |
| 8 | [............................] | | | | | | | | | | | | | 0 |
| 9 | [............................] | | | | | | | | | | | | | 0 |
| 10 | [............................] | | | | | | | | | | | | | 0 |
| 11 | [............................] | | | | | | | | | | | | | 0 |
| 12 | ------------------------ | | | | | | | | | | | | | |
| 13 | Total cash inflows | 0 | 0 | 0 | 0 | 0 | 0 | 0 | 0 | 0 | 0 | 0 | 0 | 0 |
| 14 | ======================== | | | | | | | | | | | | | |
| 15 | [CASH OUTFLOWS] | | | | | | | | | | | | | |
| 16 | [............................] | | | | | | | | | | | | | 0 |
| 17 | [............................] | | | | | | | | | | | | | 0 |
| 18 | [............................] | | | | | | | | | | | | | 0 |
| 19 | [............................] | | | | | | | | | | | | | 0 |
| 20 | [............................] | | | | | | | | | | | | | 0 |
| 21 | [............................] | | | | | | | | | | | | | 0 |
| 22 | [............................] | | | | | | | | | | | | | 0 |
| 23 | [............................] | | | | | | | | | | | | | 0 |
| 24 | [............................] | | | | | | | | | | | | | 0 |
| 25 | ------------------------ | | | | | | | | | | | | | |
| 26 | Total cash outflows | 0 | 0 | 0 | 0 | 0 | 0 | 0 | 0 | 0 | 0 | 0 | 0 | 0 |
| 27 | ======================== | | | | | | | | | | | | | |
| 28 | Opening cash balance | 0 | | | | | | | | | | | | |
| 29 | Net monthly cash flow | 0 | 0 | 0 | 0 | 0 | 0 | 0 | 0 | 0 | 0 | 0 | 0 | 0 |
| 30 | Cumulative cash before loans | 0 | 0 | 0 | 0 | 0 | 0 | 0 | 0 | 0 | 0 | 0 | 0 | 0 |
| 31 | ======================== | | | | | | | | | | | | | |
| | | | | | | | | | | | | | | 0 |
| | | 0 | 0 | 0 | 0 | 0 | 0 | 0 | 0 | 0 | 0 | 0 | 0 | 0 |

## Cash Inflow Supplement

| | A | B | C | D | E | F | G | H | I | J | K | L | M | N | O |
|---|---|---|---|---|---|---|---|---|---|---|---|---|---|---|---|
| 1 | CASH INFLOWS SUPPLEMENT | Month: | Sep 87 | Oct 87 | Nov 87 | Dec 87 | Jan 88 | Feb 88 | Mar 88 | Apr 88 | May 88 | Jun 88 | Jul 88 | Aug 88 | Total |
| 2 | [NET SALES] | | | | | | | | | | | | | | |
| 3 | [........................] | | $0 | $0 | $0 | $0 | $0 | $0 | $0 | $0 | $0 | $0 | $0 | $0 | $0 |
| 4 | [........................] | | 0 | 0 | 0 | 0 | 0 | 0 | 0 | 0 | 0 | 0 | 0 | 0 | 0 |
| 5 | [........................] | | 0 | 0 | 0 | 0 | 0 | 0 | 0 | 0 | 0 | 0 | 0 | 0 | 0 |
| 6 | [........................] | | 0 | 0 | 0 | 0 | 0 | 0 | 0 | 0 | 0 | 0 | 0 | 0 | 0 |
| 7 | [........................] | | 0 | 0 | 0 | 0 | 0 | 0 | 0 | 0 | 0 | 0 | 0 | 0 | 0 |
| 8 | [........................] | | 0 | 0 | 0 | 0 | 0 | 0 | 0 | 0 | 0 | 0 | 0 | 0 | 0 |
| 9 | [........................] | | 0 | 0 | 0 | 0 | 0 | 0 | 0 | 0 | 0 | 0 | 0 | 0 | 0 |
| 10 | [........................] | | 0 | 0 | 0 | 0 | 0 | 0 | 0 | 0 | 0 | 0 | 0 | 0 | 0 |
| 11 | [........................] | | 0 | 0 | 0 | 0 | 0 | 0 | 0 | 0 | 0 | 0 | 0 | 0 | 0 |
| 12 | [........................] | | 0 | 0 | 0 | 0 | 0 | 0 | 0 | 0 | 0 | 0 | 0 | 0 | 0 |
| 13 | ------------------------ | | | | | | | | | | | | | | |
| 14 | Total sales | | 0 | 0 | 0 | 0 | 0 | 0 | 0 | 0 | 0 | 0 | 0 | 0 | 0 |
| 15 | ======================== | | | | | | | | | | | | | | |
| 16 | [CASH INFLOWS] | | | | | | | | | | | | | | |
| 17 | ======================== | | | | | | | | | | | | | | |
| 18 | Collection | Percent | | | | | | | | | | | | | |
| 19 | period | of total | **Sep 87** | **Oct 87** | **Nov 87** | **Dec 87** | **Jan 88** | **Feb 88** | **Mar 88** | **Apr 88** | **May 88** | **Jun 88** | **Jul 88** | **Aug 88** | **Total** |
| 20 | ======================== | | | | | | | | | | | | | | |
| 21 | Cash | 0% | 0 | 0 | 0 | 0 | 0 | 0 | 0 | 0 | 0 | 0 | 0 | 0 | 0 |
| 22 | 30 days | 0% | 0 | 0 | 0 | 0 | 0 | 0 | 0 | 0 | 0 | 0 | 0 | 0 | 0 |
| 23 | 60 days | 0% | | 0 | 0 | 0 | 0 | 0 | 0 | 0 | 0 | 0 | 0 | 0 | 0 |
| 24 | 90 days | 0% | | | 0 | 0 | 0 | 0 | 0 | 0 | 0 | 0 | 0 | 0 | 0 |
| 25 | 120 days | 0% | | | | 0 | 0 | 0 | 0 | 0 | 0 | 0 | 0 | 0 | 0 |
| 26 | 150 days | 0% | | | | | 0 | 0 | 0 | 0 | 0 | 0 | 0 | 0 | 0 |
| 27 | Over 150 days | 0% | | | | | | 0 | 0 | 0 | 0 | 0 | 0 | 0 | 0 |
| 28 | ------------------------ | | | | | | | | | | | | | | |
| 29 | Bad debts | 0% | 0 | 0 | 0 | 0 | 0 | 0 | 0 | 0 | 0 | 0 | 0 | 0 | 0 |
| 30 | ======================== | | | | | | | | | | | | | | |
| 31 | Total cash inflows | 0% | 0 | 0 | 0 | 0 | 0 | 0 | 0 | 0 | 0 | 0 | 0 | 0 | 0 |
| 32 | ======================== | | | | | | | | | | | | | | |
| 33 | Total uncollected sales | | | | | | | | | | | | | | 0 |
| 34 | ======================== | | | | | | | | | | | | | | |

## Cash Outflow Supplement (with Leads and Lags)

| | A | B | C | D | E | F | G | H | I | J | K | L | M | N | O | P | Q | R |
|---|---|---|---|---|---|---|---|---|---|---|---|---|---|---|---|---|---|---|
| 1 | CASH OUTFLOW SUPPLEMENT | Month | Year | | | | | | | | | | | | | | | |
| 2 | **WITH LEADS AND LAGS** | 9 | 87 | | | | | | | | | | | | | | | |
| 3 | ------------------------ | | | | | | | | | | | | | | | | | |
| 4 | | Supplier | Credit | Date | Total | | | | | | | | | | | | | Total du- |
| 5 | | billing | period | payment | amount | | | | | | | | | | | | | in the |
| 6 | Name of supplier: | date | (days) | is due | due | Sep 87 | Oct 87 | Nov 87 | Dec 87 | Jan 88 | Feb 88 | Mar 88 | Apr 88 | May 88 | Jun 88 | Jul 88 | Aug 88 | period |
| 7 | ------------------------ | | | | | | | | | | | | | | | | | |
| 8 | [......................] | September 1, 87 | 0 | Sep 1, 87 | $0 | $0 | $0 | $0 | $0 | $0 | $0 | $0 | $0 | $0 | $0 | $0 | $0 | $ |
| 9 | [......................] | September 1, 87 | 0 | Sep 1, 87 | 0 | 0 | 0 | 0 | 0 | 0 | 0 | 0 | 0 | 0 | 0 | 0 | 0 | 0 |
| 10 | [......................] | September 1, 87 | 0 | Sep 1, 87 | 0 | 0 | 0 | 0 | 0 | 0 | 0 | 0 | 0 | 0 | 0 | 0 | 0 | 0 |
| 11 | [......................] | September 1, 87 | 0 | Sep 1, 87 | 0 | 0 | 0 | 0 | 0 | 0 | 0 | 0 | 0 | 0 | 0 | 0 | 0 | 0 |
| 12 | [......................] | September 1, 87 | 0 | Sep 1, 87 | 0 | 0 | 0 | 0 | 0 | 0 | 0 | 0 | 0 | 0 | 0 | 0 | 0 | 0 |
| 13 | [......................] | September 1, 87 | 0 | Sep 1, 87 | 0 | 0 | 0 | 0 | 0 | 0 | 0 | 0 | 0 | 0 | 0 | 0 | 0 | 0 |
| 14 | [......................] | September 1, 87 | 0 | Sep 1, 87 | 0 | 0 | 0 | 0 | 0 | 0 | 0 | 0 | 0 | 0 | 0 | 0 | 0 | 0 |
| 15 | [......................] | September 1, 87 | 0 | Sep 1, 87 | 0 | 0 | 0 | 0 | 0 | 0 | 0 | 0 | 0 | 0 | 0 | 0 | 0 | 0 |
| 16 | [......................] | September 1, 87 | 0 | Sep 1, 87 | 0 | 0 | 0 | 0 | 0 | 0 | 0 | 0 | 0 | 0 | 0 | 0 | 0 | 0 |
| 17 | [......................] | September 1, 87 | 0 | Sep 1, 87 | 0 | 0 | 0 | 0 | 0 | 0 | 0 | 0 | 0 | 0 | 0 | 0 | 0 | 0 |
| 18 | [......................] | September 1, 87 | 0 | Sep 1, 87 | 0 | 0 | 0 | 0 | 0 | 0 | 0 | 0 | 0 | 0 | 0 | 0 | 0 | 0 |
| 19 | ------------------------ | | | | | | | | | | | | | | | | | |
| 20 | Total cash outflows | | | | 0 | 0 | 0 | 0 | 0 | 0 | 0 | 0 | 0 | 0 | 0 | 0 | 0 | 0 |
| 21 | ======================== | | | | | | | | | | | | | | | | | |

## Cash Budget vs. Actuals

```
                 A                B         C          D          E          F         G          H          I
 1 CASH BUDGET VS. ACTUALS    [---------This month: September, 1987---------][-----------Year-to-date: 1987-------------]
 2 Inflows & Outflows          Budget     Actual    $ variance % variance   Budget     Actual   $ variance % variance
 3 ==========================================================================================================
 4 [CASH INFLOWS]
 5 [.........................]     $0         $0         $0        .0%        $0         $0         $0        .0%
 6 [.........................]      0          0          0        .0%         0          0          0        .0%
 7 [.........................]      0          0          0        .0%         0          0          0        .0%
 8 [.. ......................]      0          0          0        .0%         0          0          0        .0%
 9 [.........................]      0          0          0        .0%         0          0          0        .0%
10 [.. ......................]      0          0          0        .0%         0          0          0        .0%
11 [.........................]      0          0          0        .0%         0          0          0        .0%
12 [.. ......................]      0          0          0        .0%         0          0          0        .0%
13 [.........................]      0          0          0        .0%         0          0          0        .0%
14 ----------------------------------------------------------------------------------------------------------
15 Total cash inflows               0          0          0        .0%         0          0          0        .0%
16 ==========================================================================================================
17 [CASH OUTFLOWS]
18 [.........................]      0          0          0        .0%         0          0          0        .0%
19 [.. ......................]      0          0          0        .0%         0          0          0        .0%
20 [.........................]      0          0          0        .0%         0          0          0        .0%
21 [.. ......................]      0          0          0        .0%         0          0          0        .0%
22 [.........................]      0          0          0        .0%         0          0          0        .0%
23 [.. ......................]      0          0          0        .0%         0          0          0        .0%
24 [.........................]      0          0          0        .0%         0          0          0        .0%
25 [.. ......................]      0          0          0        .0%         0          0          0        .0%
26 [.........................]      0          0          0        .0%         0          0          0        .0%
27 ----------------------------------------------------------------------------------------------------------
28 Total cash outflows              0          0          0        .0%         0          0          0        .0%
29 ==========================================================================================================
30 Net cash flow                    0          0          0        .0%         0          0          0        .0%
31 ==========================================================================================================
```

## Aging Accounts Receivable

```
          A          B        C          D          E          F          G          H
 1 AGING ACCOUNTS RECEIVABLE
 2 Account       Total    Current [--------- Days past due ----------] Average
 3 name/number    due        0        30         60         90        120        days
 4 ===========================================================================
 5 [..........]    $0        $0        $0         $0         $0         $0         NA
 6 [..........]     0         0         0          0          0          0         NA
 7 [..........]     0         0         0          0          0          0         NA
 8 [..........]     0         0         0          0          0          0         NA
 9 [..........]     0         0         0          0          0          0         NA
10 [..........]     0         0         0          0          0          0         NA
11 [..........]     0         0         0          0          0          0         NA
12 [..........]     0         0         0          0          0          0         NA
13 [..........]     0         0         0          0          0          0         NA
14 [..........]     0         0         0          0          0          0         NA
15 ===========================================================================
16 Total due        0         0         0          0          0          0         NA
17 ---------------------------------------------------------------------------
18 Percentage       NA        NA        NA         NA         NA         NA
19 ===========================================================================
```

## Trade Discounts

```
          A            B            C            D            E
 1 PART 1: TRADE DISCOUNTS SPREADSHEET
 2 ==================================================================
 3                [ENTER "WHAT IFS"]
 4
 5 Enter amount due:                                            $.00
 6 Enter the discount offered (in %):                           .00%
 7 Number of days in which bill must be paid for discount:         0
 8 Number of days in which bill must be paid:                      0
 9
10                [SAVINGS/COST OF DISCOUNT]
11
12 Savings with discount                                        $.00
13 Effective annual interest rate without discount                NA
14
15                [COST OF BORROWING TO TAKE DISCOUNT]
16
17 Enter interest rate at which you can borrow or invest:       .00%
18 Interest cost of loan                                          NA
19 Net savings from borrowing                                     NA
20 ==================================================================
21 PART 2: TRADE DISCOUNTS "WHAT IF" TABLE
22 ==================================================================
23 Enter starting amount due:                                      0
24 Enter increment                                                 0
25 ==================================================================
26    Total      [----- With discount ------][- Borrowing for discount -]
27  amount due     Savings    Amount paid      Cost      Net savings
28 ------------------------------------------------------------------
29       $.00        $.00         $.00         $.00         $.00
30        .00         .00          .00          .00          .00
31        .00         .00          .00          .00          .00
32        .00         .00          .00          .00          .00
33        .00         .00          .00          .00          .00
34        .00         .00          .00          .00          .00
35        .00         .00          .00          .00          .00
36        .00         .00          .00          .00          .00
37        .00         .00          .00          .00          .00
38        .00         .00          .00          .00          .00
39        .00         .00          .00          .00          .00
40 ==================================================================
```

## Economic Order Quantity

```
        A           B           C           D          E          F
 1 PART 1: ECONOMIC ORDER QUANTITY SPREADSHEET
 2 ====================================================================
 3
 4                          [ENTER "WHAT IFS"]
 5
 6 Enter the purchase price per unit:                              $.00
 7 Enter the number of units used annually:                           0
 8 Enter the carrying costs per unit:                              $.00
 9 Enter the cost per order:                                       $.00
10 Enter safety stock (on hand when reorder arrives):                 0
11 Enter lead time needed for reorders (in days):                     0
12
13
14                [ECONOMIC ORDER QUANTITY AND RELATED VALUES]
15
16 Economic order quantity                                           NA
17 Number of orders placed per year                                  NA
18 Lowest possible cost of ordering and carrying inventory           NA
19 Order point (inventory on hand when reorder is placed)             0
20 ====================================================================
21 PART 2: ECONOMIC ORDER QUANTITY "WHAT IF" TABLE
22 ====================================================================
23 Enter starting order quantity:                                     0
24 Enter increment:                                                   0
25 ====================================================================
26    Order        Safety    Average     Carrying     Order       Total
27     size        stock    inventory     costs       costs       costs
28 ====================================================================
29          0         NA         NA         NA         NA          NA
30          0         NA         NA         NA         NA          NA
31          0         NA         NA         NA         NA          NA
32          0         NA         NA         NA         NA          NA
33          0         NA         NA         NA         NA          NA
34          0         NA         NA         NA         NA          NA
35          0         NA         NA         NA         NA          NA
36          0         NA         NA         NA         NA          NA
37          0         NA         NA         NA         NA          NA
38          0         NA         NA         NA         NA          NA
39          0         NA         NA         NA         NA          NA
40 ====================================================================
```

## Cash Outflow Supplement (without Leads and Lags)

```
                A                      B      C      D      E      F      G      H      I      J      K      L      M      N
 1 CASH OUTFLOWS SUPPLEMENT         Sep 87 Oct 87 Nov 87 Dec 87 Jan 88 Feb 88 Mar 88 Apr 88 May 88 Jun 88 Jul 88 Aug 88  Total
 2 [CASH OUTFLOWS]
 3 [...............................]    $0     $0     $0     $0     $0     $0     $0     $0     $0     $0     $0     $0     $0
 4 [...............................]     0      0      0      0      0      0      0      0      0      0      0      0      0
 5 [...............................]     0      0      0      0      0      0      0      0      0      0      0      0      0
 6 [...............................]     0      0      0      0      0      0      0      0      0      0      0      0      0
 7 [...............................]     0      0      0      0      0      0      0      0      0      0      0      0      0
 8 [...............................]     0      0      0      0      0      0      0      0      0      0      0      0      0
 9 [...............................]     0      0      0      0      0      0      0      0      0      0      0      0      0
10 [...............................]     0      0      0      0      0      0      0      0      0      0      0      0      0
11 [...............................]     0      0      0      0      0      0      0      0      0      0      0      0      0
12 ------------------------------------------------------------------------------------------------------------------------
13 Total cash outflows                   0      0      0      0      0      0      0      0      0      0      0      0      0
14 ========================================================================================================================
```

# Index

Boldfaced page numbers, such as **103**, indicate that Tips on that subject appear on that page.

# Disk Order Form

TO:
**Curtin & London, Inc.**
Box 363
Marblehead, MA 01945

(617) 631-0762

☐ YES . . . I want to save time and energy. Rush me the disk to accompany **Cash Flow Management with Framework.**

My computer is a:
☐ IBM Personal Computer or PC XT
☐ Compaq Portable Computer
☐ Columbia MPC
☐ Other ____________________

Send to: (Please print. Note that we cannot ship via UPS to P.O. box numbers.)

Name ____________________

Company ____________________

Street ____________________

City __________ State ______ Zip ______

☐ I am paying **$41.70** ($39.95 + $1.75 shipping).

☐ I am paying **$43.95** ($39.95 + $4.00 shipping). Please ship via Second Day Air.

(Mass. residents add 5%)

☐ My check to **Curtin & London, Inc.** is enclosed

☐ Bill to my MasterCard # ____________________

☐ Bill to my VISA card # ____________________

The expiration date for my card is ____________________

Signature ____________________

☐ Please add me to your mailing list for announcements of other new business/computer books and disks

**Return policy:** No returns accepted unless disk is defective. If defective, return disk within 10 days of receipt and we will mail you a replacement disk immediately. Sorry, no refunds.

Prices subject to change without notice.

**SAVE TIME AND ENERGY** . . . A special disk is available that contains all of the spreadsheets used in this book. Although this disk isn't essential, it will save you time and energy because you won't have to enter the spreadsheets yourself and it eliminates the possibility of introducing errors. You can begin immediately to explore the principles and problems of your business. Since Curtin & London disks are not write-protected, you can adapt or customize the spreadsheets and make copies for use on other computers. However, please note that Curtin & London disks are protected by copyright, and may *not* be duplicated for resale.

**Other titles in the Curtin & London Business/Computer series:**

**Accounting with Symphony**

**Preparing Your Business Plan**
1-2-3 edition
Multiplan edition
Symphony edition

**Preparing Your Business Budget**
Symphony edition

**Cash Flow Management**
1-2-3 edition
Symphony edition

**Controlling Financial Performance**
1-2-3 edition
Multiplan edition
IBM/VisiCalc edition
Apple/VisiCalc edition

**Analyzing Your Financial Statements**
Symphony edition

**Planning and Budgeting**
Symphony edition
1-2-3 edition
Multiplan edition
IBM/VisiCalc edition
Apple/VisiCalc edition

**Business Decision Making**
1-2-3 edition
Multiplan edition
IBM/VisiCalc edition
Apple/VisiCalc edition

**Business Graphics**
Symphony edition
1-2-3 edition

**Business Problem Solving**
1-2-3 edition
Multiplan edition

**The WordStar Handbook**

**Contemporary Business Letters with WordStar**

**The Apple Writer II Handbook**

**Contemporary Business Letters with Apple Writer II**